TOBACCO LITIGATION

TOBACCO LITIGATION

AFCO v TIA

The Case Against Passive Smoking

Editors

Roland Everingham BA LLB
Stephen Woodward BSc (Hons)

LEGAL BOOKS
SYDNEY

Published by Legal Books
a division of International Business Communications Pty Ltd
The Hat Factory
14 Charles Street
Redfern NSW 2016
Australia

First published in Australia 1991
Published edition © 1991 International Business Communications Pty Ltd

National Library of Australia
Cataloguing—in—Publication entry

ISBN 1 86316 020 5

1. Australian Federation of Consumer Organizations – Trials, litigation, etc. 2. Tobacco Industry Association – Trials, litigation, etc. 3. Products liability – Tobacco – Australia. 4. Passive smoking – Australia. I. Everingham, Roland. II. Woodward, Stephen.

346.94038

Book Design	Trevor Hood
Cover Design	John Windus
Keyboarding	Rebecca McGregor
Desktop Publishing	Belinda Way
Proofreading	Robyn Joils
Editorial Advice	Jill Matthews
Publisher	Oliver Freeman
Printed by	Robert Burton Printers 63 Carlingford Road Sefton NSW 2162 Australia

Contents

Section Three Additional Source Material

Publisher's Acknowledgement

The publisher acknowledges the assistance provided by CCH Australia Limited in the provision of page bromides of the headnotes and judgments and other source material published in Sections Two and Three of this book.
While this material is drawn directly from CCH's *Australian Trade Practices Reporter* (ATPR), CCH has no responsibility for or involvement with any of the other material published in the book or any views expressed therein.

Dedication

This book is dedicated to the witnesses for AFCO who gave freely of their time, knowledge and experience and who made the conduct and success of the litigation possible:

Dr Bruce Armstrong, Commissioner of Health for the State of Western Australia;

Dr Antony Breslin, Senior Specialist in Charge (Chest Diseases) at the Repatriation General Hospital, Concord, Sydney;

Sir Richard Doll, formerly Regius Professor of Medicine at the University of Oxford;

Professor Dwight Janerich, Professor of Epidemiology and Director of the Cancer Epidemiology Program and Cancer Prevention Research Unit at Yale University School of Medicine;

Professor Louis Landau, Professor of Child Health at the University of Western Australia;

Dr Peter Le Souef, Director of the Department of Respiratory Medicine at Princess Margaret Hospital for Children, Perth;

Professor Anthony McMichael, Professor of Occupational and Environmental Health in the Department of Community Medicine at the University of Adelaide;

Dr Terry Nolan, Senior Lecturer in the Department of Paediatrics at the University of Melbourne;

Professor Peter Phelan, Professor and Chairman, Department of Paediatrics at the University of Melbourne;

Professor Bernard Stewart, Associate Professor in the School of Paediatrics at the University of New South Wales;

Professor Dimitrios Trichopoulos, Professor of Epidemiology at the Harvard School of Public Health;

Professor Nicholas Wald, Professor and Head of the Department of Environmental and Preventive Medicine at St Bartholomew's Hospital Medical College at the University of London.

Foreword

On 7 February 1991, His Honour Justice Morling of the Federal Court of Australia handed down an historic judgment in which he painstakingly evaluated the medical science on the adverse health effects of secondhand tobacco smoke. His Honour concluded there is scientific proof that cigarette smoke causes lung cancer, respiratory disease in children and attacks of asthma. He considered the evidence compelling and in some instances overwhelming. The decision excited considerable media and public interest both locally and internationally. This publication of the full decision, interlocutory decisions and commentary by Professor Harland of Sydney University is in response to that interest.

It is anticipated that the publication will be of considerable guidance to persons or organisations engaging in litigation with tobacco companies, to trade associations and others in related areas concerning advertising and sponsorship. It is planned to publish a second edition or supplementary material as more tobacco litigation is concluded. Persons interested in contributing to future editions of this publication are invited to contact the authors of this Foreword.

The action between the Australian Federation of Consumer Organisations Inc (AFCO) and the Tobacco Institute of Australia Limited (TIA) commenced with the potential for being an arid dissection of whether an advertisement published by the Tobacco Institute was false and misleading. The matter concluded, however, as a marathon public interest test case concerning the adverse health effects of passive smoking. The court transcript records some 6000 pages of evidence, 20 expert witnesses gave evidence both in Australia and overseas, and a 211-page judgment was handed down. The decision of Justice Morling is the first authority of a Superior Court dealing directly with the causative effects of passive smoking and lung cancer, and respiratory diseases.

Individuals and public health organisations had considerable successes in the 1980s in tobacco litigation. This decade, however, has already seen greater success and more sophistication in the use of the law as a mechanism to enhance the public health of the community. This trend will continue during the 1990s, no doubt accelerated by the success of the AFCO case against the TIA. At present a number of other legal proceedings or enquiries are underway in Australia. One in particular concerns whether the broadcast of the 1990 Australian Grand Prix was in breach of the Australian ban on the broadcast of cigarette advertisements on television.

AFCO has acknowledged the assistance and support of the Minister for Justice, Senator Tate, and his predecessors, and the Office of Legal Aid and Family Services in these proceedings. The Australian government has provided substantial financial support which assisted in the conduct of the proceedings. Similiarly the NSW Legal Aid Commission provided funding which facilitated the commencement of the procedings. The assistance of Action on Smoking and Health Limited, particularly Amanda Marlin, is acknowledged. Likewise, Cashman & Partners and especially Susan Smith.

AFCO, its then Director, Robin Brown, then Chairman Gary Mason and other Board members are to be commended for their conviction and commitment.

Particular tribute is paid to Peter Cashman, for his involvement and support throughout the proceedings, and Neil Francey, of counsel, who was the principal advocate for AFCO before Justice Morling.

Roland Everingham and Stephen Woodward

Section One
Commentary

The legal context of the decision

*David Harland**

Interest in the decision of Justice Morling of the Federal Court of Australia in *Australian Federation of Consumer Organisations Inc v Tobacco Institute of Australia Ltd* will centre on the judge's careful and detailed analysis of the scientific evidence relating to passive smoking and on his conclusions on the evidence as to the adverse effects of passive smoking on the health of non-smokers. The purpose of this comment is to explain briefly the way in which the issue came before the court and the legal implications of the decision.

The litigation concerned an advertisement published by the Tobacco Institute in July 1986. The advertisement (see p163 below) made several claims, but its essence was the claim that "there is little evidence and nothing which proves scientifically that cigarette smoke causes disease in non-smokers". The Australian Federation of Consumer Organisations (AFCO) claimed that the advertisement contravened s52 of the Trade Practices Act and sought an injunction under s80 of that Act forbidding the repetition of the advertisement and some of the claims made in it.

The Trade Practices Act 1974 is federal legislation which contains both provisions dealing with restrictive trade practices ("anti-trust" or competition law) and with consumer protection. Included in the consumer protection provisions of the Act is a division containing a series of sections prohibiting various misleading or unfair trade practices. They constitute what in some other legal systems (for example, in the Nordic countries) would perhaps most commonly be referred to as "marketing law". Although designed primarily to protect consumers, these sections are for the most part not restricted to conduct directed specifically at consumers.

Misleading or deceptive conduct

The case concerns s52, the most general of these marketing law provisions. Section 52 provides:

> "A corporation shall not, in trade or commerce, engage in conduct that is misleading or deceptive or is likely to mislead or deceive."

Most of the other sections in this part of the Act deal with more specifically defined conduct (eg misleading representations concerning the price of goods or services or the country of origin of goods, bait advertising, pyramid selling etc) and a contravention of them gives rise to criminal liability. Because of its very broad nature a contravention of s52 does not entail criminal liability, but an injunction may be granted under s80 to forbid a repetition of conduct that offends the section. Where a person has suffered loss as a result of offending conduct (eg by being induced to make a contract of purchase as a result of misleading conduct by the seller) other remedies such as damages or the setting aside of the contract may be available, but the present litigation did not involve such remedies.

Section 52 has in the main been interpreted broadly by the courts. To "mislead" simply means to "lead into error". The section imposes a strict liability, irrespective of any questions of fault or moral blameworthiness. It is therefore not necessary to prove that the company whose conduct is complained of had any intention to mislead or deceive. Nor is it necessary to prove that anybody was actually misled or deceived, so long as the conduct has a capacity or tendency (though not merely a remote possibility) to do so. Proof that individuals have actually been deceived may be helpful, but it is not essential or even conclusive, the question of whether particular conduct is misleading or deceptive being ultimately one for the court itself to determine in an objective manner.[1]

Standing and injunctions

Section 80 of the Trade Practices Act provides that an injunction against a contravention of the Act (including, of course, s52) may be granted by the court "on the application of the Minister, the Commission or any other person". The Commission referred to here is the Trade Practices Commission, an independent statutory agency having the main responsibility for enforcing the Act.

AFCO had complained to the Commission about the Tobacco Institute's advertisement. The Institute eventually agreed to publish a further advertisement which the Commission accepted as a sufficient correction, and the Commission agreed with the Institute not to take further action against it as a result of the original advertisement. AFCO was dissatisfied with the "follow-up" advertisement and accordingly instituted proceedings against the Tobacco Institute seeking an injunction.

Systems of civil procedure have traditionally been based on individualistic assumptions relating to the enforcement of private rights by those with a personal stake in the subject matter in controversy and there has been a widespread recognition that there is a need to modify these assumptions so as to enhance access to the courts in cases where public interest issues are involved.[2]

The rules as to standing (ie those defining the proper plaintiff to bring particular proceedings) assume importance principally where, as in this case, a plaintiff is seeking to obtain a remedy such as an injunction to assert a public right or interest (rather than where a plaintiff is seeking to vindicate a private or personal right in an action such as one for damages for breach of contract).

In common law countries private citizens seeking such a remedy traditionally had to establish that the conduct complained of infringed some private right of theirs or caused damage to them over and above that suffered by the general public. (An exception arose in those cases where the plaintiff obtained the *fiat* or permission of the Attorney-General to sue in the name of the Attorney-General to represent the public interest.)

There has been a clear trend in judicial decisions in Australia towards widening the scope of the standing test, though it is not clear how far this process will be taken by the courts, and it seems probable that AFCO's action would have failed on this initial point if it had had to rely on the general law. However, some statutes have widened or even removed standing requirements for actions relating to the subject matter dealt with by the statute in question.

The Trade Practices Act is such a statute and the reference in s80 to "any other person" removes any requirements as to standing when an injunction is sought to restrain a contravention of the Act. The courts have resisted attempts to read restrictions into this phrase. Consequently, for example, a trader may, even though motivated essentially by its own commercial interests rather than those of consumers, rely on s80 to obtain an injunction to restrain misleading advertising of a competitor.[3]

The insistence that the phrase "any other person" must be interpreted literally was confirmed both by a single judge of the Federal Court (see p132) and by an appeal bench of the Court (see p140) when the Tobacco Institute at an early stage of the litigation sought to have AFCO's claim struck out (a procedural move which, if successful, would have put an end to the litigation without the merits of AFCO's claim being examined). It was held that the fact that the Commission settled its concerns with the Tobacco Institute and agreed not to institute proceedings against it in no way prevented AFCO (as "any other person") instituting its own proceedings against the Institute based on the advertisement. This was so even though AFCO had in the first instance complained to the Commission about the advertisement and urged it to take action.

While in some such cases the bringing of subsequent proceedings by a third party might be an "abuse of process" which would justify the court in concluding that in fairness to the defendant the action should not be allowed to continue, it was held that there was no basis for any such approach in the present case. Despite its important role in enforcing the Trade Practices Act, the Commission's agreement not to sue cannot render lawful conduct which contravenes the Act.

The approaches towards standing so far described have focused on the interest of the plaintiff in the subject matter of the action (or in some cases, including the present, the absence of need for any such interest). It should perhaps be mentioned that another approach is to look to the formal legal status of the plaintiff.[4] Thus in some European countries (most notably Germany) the primary means of enforcing laws concerning unfair marketing practices is the institution of proceedings by competitors or trade associations and, more recently, by consumer associations.

In other countries primary enforcement responsibility may lie with public officials or agencies (such as the Consumer Ombudsman in the Nordic countries), but consumer and some other associations may also sue. A consumer organisation will normally have to satisfy certain formal requirements designed to ensure that only bona fide organisations which truly represent the interests of consumers are able to initiate such actions.

It will be apparent from what has been said above that this approach has not been adopted in Australia, the view having been taken that the rules as to legal costs and the power of the courts to dismiss frivolous or vexatious actions provide sufficient safeguard against abuse. AFCO would presumably satisfy any reasonable test as to ability to represent the consumer interest, it being the peak consumer organisation in Australia and taking the form, as its name implies, of a federation of consumer groups from all over the country. (Some discussion of AFCO's role will be found in the judgment reprinted at pp147-62) However, it was not legally necessary for AFCO to satisfy any such test in order to be able to rely on s80 of the Trade Practices Act.

The case illustrates the importance of legal systems providing some means whereby at least consumer and other organisations (and arguably also individuals) should be able to bring actions in appropriate cases to enforce marketing practices law. In many countries at least, the high cost of legal proceedings may make such actions rare (such has certainly been the Australian experience). However, the existence of such means of action enables proceedings to be brought if enforcement agencies refuse to act in particular cases which may be seen as raising important issues or where, as AFCO thought was the situation in the present case, the action taken by such an agency is unsatisfactory.

"In trade or commerce"

Conduct will only contravene s52 if it occurs "in trade or commerce". This phrase was intended to limit the scope of the section by making it clear that the new standards of behaviour imposed by the Trade Practices Act were to be imposed only on those who in some sense could be said to be acting in a business capacity rather than in a purely private capacity. In other words s52 is directed at marketplace activity. The phrase "in trade or commerce" has in general been interpreted in a broad sense, though in a recent decision the High Court of Australia placed some limitations on the phrase.[5]

The exact effect of this decision is not yet clear and the details of the issue need not detain us here. However, we should note that Justice Morling held that the Tobacco Institute's advertisement was conduct "in trade or commerce". Accepting that participation by a trading corporation in a debate on a matter of public or social controversy may often not be conduct in trade or commerce, he nonetheless concluded that the publication of this advertisement, being calculated to protect the market for cigarette products by refuting criticism of them, was an activity within "the central conception" of trade or commerce.

In an earlier decision[6] Justice Morling had been concerned with a situation where a timber industry trade association was involved with a government department in the production of a film as a public relations exercise, the object being in part to answer criticism of the industry and thereby to protect indirectly the interests of members of the association. It was held that the exhibition of the film constituted conduct "in trade or commerce". It would therefore appear that while purely political debates will not be subject to the Trade Practices Act[7], what might be called advocacy advertising by an industry association designed to advance, even if indirectly, the commercial interests of its members will be conduct in trade or commerce and therefore subject to s52.

The meaning of the advertisement

It is well established in cases on s52 that in ascertaining the meaning of a representation one looks to the audience addressed.[8] Thus, in the case of an advertisement in the mass media, one looks to the meaning likely to be placed on it by the general public rather than by specialists or experts. Consistently with this approach Justice Morling held that the reference in the advertisement to "evidence" of the effect of passive smoking included reference to the published opinions of scientists, whether or not such material would normally be admissible in a court of law under the technical rules of evidence (eg the rule against so-called "hearsay" evidence). Likewise, most readers would take the reference to scientific proof to mean compelling or convincing evidence, even though scientists themselves do not commonly use the term "scientific proof".

Fact or opinion?

The Tobacco Institute argued that the advertisement would be understood by readers as being no more than an expression of opinion and that s52 does not operate to restrict publication of opinions on scientific issues. It has often been held that for conduct to be misleading or deceptive in contravention of s52 it must involve, at least by implication, a representation as to some present or past fact. Thus the mere fact that an opinion proves to be incorrect does not involve the speaker in a contravention of s52. However, the distinction drawn is by no means as limiting on the scope of s52 as might at first sight appear, because it has been held that a person expressing an opinion is impliedly representing at least that he or she does in fact hold that opinion and very often (especially when the speaker has special knowledge or expertise) that there are reasonable grounds to justify the opinion.[9]

At the same time, courts have shown themselves sensitive to the danger of s52 being applied in such a way as unreasonably to inhibit free discussion and debate. In the context of statements made by way of argumentative opinion in a debate on some matter of controversy, they will not be quick to find that an opinion honestly held was misleading because not qualified in light of contrary opinions which might be held by others. Thus, for example, in a case involving a statement to shareholders forecasting the profitability of a company which was the subject of a contested take-over bid, it was said that it must be remembered that "what was being communicated to shareholders was the company's opinion not a treatise".[10]

In response to the argument that the advertisement was an expression of opinion, Justice Morling held that the statement in the advertisement was not expressed to be an opinion, but was an assertion as to the state of the evidence on the question of whether cigarette smoke causes disease in non-smokers. In any event, even if the advertisement did assert an opinion rather than a statement of fact, the evidence was such that there was no rational basis for the use of the phrase "little evidence". On either basis, given the judge's findings on the strength of the scientific evidence on the casual connection between passive smoking and disease, the advertisement was in contravention of s52.

Corrective advertising

The courts have power, where an advertisement is found to contravene s52, to order corrective advertising to be published.[11] This power has, however, been exercised very cautiously. In the present case Justice Morling thought that an injunction alone would be a sufficient remedy. So much time had elapsed since the advertisement was published that members of the public reading a corrective advertisement would not have any clear recollection of what was said in the original advertisement. In the event, the very widespread publicity which followed the release of Justice Morling's judgment resulted in a far more effective conveying to the general public of his findings as to the misleading nature of the Tobacco Institute's claims than would have been likely to have been achieved by any corrective advertising.

The impact of legal costs

The high cost of legal proceedings will often prove to be the ultimate barrier to access to the courts when some form of public interest litigation is being considered. The costs of litigation will in many cases be quite beyond the means of most individuals or community organisations (and, even though there have been some important changes in this respect in Australia in recent years, legal aid schemes will often not be designed so as to take adequate account of the special features of public interest litigation). This problem is compounded in those legal systems, of which Australia is one, which normally apply the rule that "costs follow the event".

Under this approach a plaintiff who loses must, in addition to paying his or her own costs, also pay the costs (both for lawyers and other expenses such as court fees and those of expert witnesses) of the successful defendant.

A recent report showed that despite the liberal remedies available to private litigants consumers are making very little use in the courts of the Trade Practices Act.[12] The most serious inhibiting factor was that of legal costs and affected not just individual consumers but also consumer organisations, which are normally unable to give an open-ended commitment to one particular case because of the effect this could have on overall resources and their activities in other areas.

The decision of Justice Morling is important in respect of one aspect of the cost barriers to public interest litigation. As Justice Morling held that AFCO succeeded in its claim, there was little doubt that AFCO should obtain an order that the Tobacco Institute pay its costs of the litigation. However, the costs paid under such an order are normally calculated on a basis (technically called "party and party" costs) which usually falls considerably short of the expenses actually incurred by the successful litigant. On this basis the unsuccessful party will normally be liable for around one-half to two-thirds of the costs actually incurred by the successful party.[13]

Justice Morling commented that AFCO's costs must have run into several hundred thousand dollars and that the costs which it could not recover if an order for costs were made on the usual basis were likely to be considerable. This result was avoided by the judge making an order that the Tobacco Institute pay AFCO's costs on the basis that AFCO recover its costs in full, subject only to the exclusion of any unreasonably large amounts or any amounts unreasonably incurred.

Justice Morling's reasons for making this order are set out at pp124-29. His principal reason was that it was very much in the public interest that the Tobacco Institute be restrained from making statements which might mislead members of the public on matters affecting their health and that a litigant in AFCO's position should not be heavily out-of-pocket as a result of taking such action to serve the public interest. While Justice Morling commented that there may be cases which are successfully brought in the public interest but in which it would not be appropriate to make a costs order on the basis adopted in this case, this aspect of the decision is an important precedent which, if applied in later cases, will be a significant step towards lowering the barriers which so frequently impede public interest litigation.[14]

Smokeless tobacco

It is appropriate to make brief reference to a matter related to the passive smoking litigation, namely the ban placed in Australia on the sale of smokeless tobacco products. The two matters are related in the sense that both relate to the control of tobacco products and that in both AFCO was involved in litigation.

The Trade Practices Act contains provisions relating to mandatory safety standards for consumer goods and banning orders in respect of unsafe goods.[15] Section 65C provides that where it appears to the Minister for Consumer Affairs that goods of a particular kind will or may cause injury to any person, the Minister may, by a notice published in the *Commonwealth Gazette*, declare the goods to be unsafe goods. Subject to certain conditions which need not be noted here, the sale of goods which are the subject of such a banning notice is a criminal offence.

Unless previously revoked a notice remains in force for 18 months. If at the end of the 18-month period a mandatory safety standard has not been proclaimed under the Act, the Minister may by notice in the *Gazette* impose a permanent ban. Where the Minister proposes to make a banning order, the Trade Practices Act enables a supplier of goods which would be affected to require a conference to be held before the Trade Practices Commission. After the conference the Commission must report to the Minister recommending either that the proposed order be made (with or without amendment) or that it not be made. The Minister must have regard to the Commission's recommendation before making a final decision, and if the Minister decides not to act in accordance with the recommendation the reasons for so deciding must be published.

These provisions are designed to allow suppliers likely to be affected by a banning order to make representations and produce any relevant evidence and to have these considered by an independent authority before any final decision is made.

In January 1988 the Minister published a notice that he proposed to ban the supply of smokeless tobacco products intended for oral use and snuffs intended for oral use on the grounds that they cause oral cancers, throat tumours and other medical or pathological consequences. A supplier required a conference to be held.

The Commission recommended that the proposed action be limited to oral snuffs as it was not persuaded that the evidence concerning the health effects of chewing tobacco was of sufficient weight to justify a ban. (The Commission did, however, consider there was sufficient evidence of health risk associated with chewing tobacco to justify other less drastic action in respect of such tobacco.) The Minister disagreed with this recommendation and in October 1989 imposed an 18-month banning order on both chewing tobacco and oral snuffs. At the time of writing the Minister was proposing to impose a permanent ban on these products.

The supplier which required the conference subsequently challenged the Minister's action on administrative law and constitutional grounds. An application for an order preventing the conference proceeding until this challenge had been decided was refused by the Federal Court.[16]

One ground for the challenge was that goods may only be declared unsafe under s65c where they will or may cause "injury". The argument that the proposed order would be invalid because "injury" means physical injury and not was held to be one which had only a slight chance of success (the matter did not have to be finally determined in these preliminary proceedings).

Subsequently AFCO sought to join in these proceedings as an interested party. It was held that AFCO was entitled to do so. This depended on the standing provisions of the federal Administrative Decisions (Judicial Review) Act 1977 which, while not as broad as those under s80 of the Trade Practices Act, were nonetheless sufficient for AFCO's purpose. Because of its importance for public interest litigation, the decision of the appeal bench of the Federal Court on this issue is reprinted at pp147-62.

Conclusion

The passive smoking litigation illustrates the important role that consumer and other public interest organisations can play in enforcement of the law. For this to happen it is of course necessary for any remaining problems concerning standing to be overcome and some approaches towards this are illustrated in the material re-printed in this book. We have also noted the problem of legal costs in this context and the fact that Justice Morling's judgment is important in showing one way in which these problems can be lessened.

As has already been indicated, most interest in Justice Morling's judgment will focus on his discussion of the scientific evidence and his conclusions on the evidence as to the causal link between passive smoking and disease in non-smokers. In finding that there was strong evidence of such a link Justice Morling rejected the suggestion that while cigarette smoke may be annoying to some non-smokers, passive smoking is not a health problem. His judgment brings together citation and analysis of major published studies and of the oral evidence given before him. This will be of great value to those concerned with smoking and health issues no matter what might be the ultimate result of appeal against the decision.

Justice Morling's factual conclusions appear already to have had a significant impact in Australia on the public debate on smoking issues. His judgment will clearly be used extensively by those urging governments and others (such as employers and those in control of enclosed public places) to institute further control measures and may very well prompt an increase in litigation on smoking issues.[17] One note of caution should, however, be issued. Where, for example, an employee sues his or her employer for damages in respect of illness claimed to have been caused by exposure to tobacco smoke in the workplace, Justice Morling's judgment will not be directly applicable in that the plaintiff will have to establish independently that passive smoking can cause illness in non-smokers (and, of course, that this particular plaintiff's illness was so caused). This is because a case such as this may be applied in subsequent cases between different parties as a precedent on questions of law, but this is not so in regard to purely factual issues.

Nonetheless, Justice Morling's judgment will be an invaluable starting point of reference for the scientific evidence relating to passive smoking and disease. In a broader sense the litigation was, as Justice Morling himself noted, "in the nature of a test case on the issue whether passive smoking is a hazard to the health of non-smokers" and in the long run his judgment is likely to be significant mainly for its impact on attitudes towards the health and public policy implications of passive smoking.

References

1. On the scope of s52 see generally Harland D. Misleading or deceptive conduct: the breadth and limitations of the prohibition. *Journal of Contract Law* 1991; 4(2). Healey D, Terry A. *Misleading or Deceptive Conduct*. Sydney: CCH Australia Ltd, 1991.
2. See further Harland D. *Group actions – A discussion of the Australian proposals, with some other perspectives from Asia and the Pacific*. Paper presented at 7th European Workshop on Consumer Law, October 1990. (The proceedings of the Workshop are in course of publication by the Centre for Consumer Law, Catholic University of Louvain, Louvain-la Neuve, Belgium.)
3. See eg *Colgate Palmolive Pty Ltd v Rexona Pty Ltd* (1981) 37 ALR 391; *Hospital Contribution Fund of Australia Ltd v Switzerland Australia Health Fund Pty Ltd* (1988) 78 ALR 483.
4. See Harland, *supra* n2.
5. *Concrete Constructions (NSW) Pty Ltd v Nelson* (1990) 169 CLR 594.
6. *Glorie v WA Chip & Pulp Co Pty Ltd* (1981) 39 ALR 67.
7. See *Durant v Greiner* (1990) ASC 56-000 (unsuccessful action under similar State law against Premier and Minister for Education concerning statements about school closures).
8. See in particular *Taco Co of Australia Inc v Taco Bell Pty Ltd* (1982) 42 ALR 177 at p202.
9. See in particular *Global Sportsman Pty Ltd v Mirror Newspapers Ltd* (1984) 55 ALR 25.
10. *Bell Resources Ltd v Broken Hill Proprietary Co Ltd* (1986) ATPR 40-702. See also *Glorie v WA Chip & Pulp Co Pty Ltd* (1981) 39 ALR 67; *Industrial Equity Ltd v North Broken Hill Holdings Ltd* (1986) 64 ALR 292.
11. For a good example of the extensive action which may be required in an appropriate case see *Janssen Pharmaceutical Pty Ltd v Pfizer Pty Ltd* (1986) ATPR 40-654.
12. National Consumer Affairs Advisory Council. *Consumer Redress and Part V of the Trade Practices Act*. Canberra: Australian Government Publishing Service, 1988.
13. Australian Law Reform Commission. *Grouped Proceedings in the Federal Court* (Report No 46). Canberra: Australian Government Publishing Service, 1988: 107.
14. See further Francey N. Public-interest litigation can pay. *Australian Law News*, 1991; 26(4): 22.
15. For a discussion of these provisions see Harland D. Post market control of technical consumer goods in Australia. Micklitz H-W (ed). *Post Market Control of Consumer Goods*. Baden-Baden: Nomos Verlagsgesellschaft, 1990: 1-83.

16. *US Tobacco Co v Minister for Consumer Affairs* (1988) 79 ALR 430.
17. See Everingham R. Tobacco tussle ends with landmark Federal Court judgment. *Law Society Journal* 1991; 29(5): 61.

Note: It should be noted that references to page numbers of judgments mentioned in this article relate specifically to pages in this book, and not to the original judgments.

---

* *David Harland is Challis Professor of Law at the University of Sydney, Sydney, Australia.*

Passive smoking causes lung cancer, asthma attacks, and respiratory disease

*Simon Chapman and Stephen Woodward**

On 7 February 1991 Justice Trevor Morling of the Federal Court of Australia handed down a ruling on involuntary passive smoking.[1] If upheld on appeal the Morling judgment will enter the history of modern public health as one of the major turning points in the worldwide efforts to reduce smoking related diseases.

The judgment concerned a case brought by the Australian Federation of Consumer Organisations against the Tobacco Institute of Australia over an advertisement lodged in 14 major Australian newspapers on 1 July 1986. The advertisement, headed "A message from those who do ... to those who don't", advanced the argument that "there is little evidence and nothing which proves scientifically that cigarette smoke causes disease in non-smokers". It argued that environmental tobacco smoke was basically an issue of "annoyance" and did not constitute a "health hazard" or "health risk". It cited three health agencies – the Institute of Cancer Research in the United Kingdom; the American Cancer Society; and the World Health Organisation – in ways that implied that these agencies also disputed the view that passive smoking was dangerous.

The publication of the advertisement seemed to be timed to mitigate the influence of two forthcoming events: the public release of the Australian National Health and Medical Research Council's report *Effects of Passive Smoking on Health*, which had been adopted in June 1986[2], and a resolution to ban smoking on all public transport, including airlines, due to be debated at the Australian Labor Party's biennial national conference, 7-11 July 1986. This resolution would have been seen as critical to the tobacco industry because the party's rules require it, when in government, to implement its platform. The Labor Party was in power in 1986, so if this resolution was passed there was a strong likelihood that it would become government policy and pass into law. The government banned smoking on all passenger flights in Australia in 1987.

Institute hounded for three years

The Federal Court judgment brought to a head a concentrated three-year campaign of hounding the Tobacco Institute over the advertisement. This campaign saw the Institute humiliated on four occasions, with the final court ruling likely to set in motion what media commentators predict could be an avalanche of civil litigation. Immediately after the publication of the advertisement Dr Paul Magnus of the National Heart Foundation and Stephen Woodward of Action on Smoking and Health (ASH) contacted officials of the three agencies cited in the advertisement to determine whether the advertisement accurately reflected their research or policies. Officials from each agency duly replied in letters to the press, each strongly objecting to the distortions and misrepresentations in the advertisement.

Then the Australian Council on Smoking and Health, a Western Australian based lobby group, complained about the advertisement to the advertising and media industries' self regulatory body, the Advertising Standards Council. The Council, which has a long history of being attacked by public health interests as a less than impartial, industry stacked body[3-4], none the less upheld the Council's complaint, with details being reported in the press on 20 October 1986. These little castigations were but nothing to what was to follow. Unbeknown to the main Australian smoking control lobby groups, the Australian Federation of Consumer Organisations had undertaken a different plan of action. The Federation is the peak policy body of the consumer movement in Australia and several of its officials had attended the International Organisation of Consumers' Unions world congress in Bangkok the previous year. The congress marked the formal entry of the consumer movement into the tobacco control field, with delegates being urged to return home and apply the consumer movement's lobbying muscle and particular skills with business regulatory matters to a hitherto largely neglected foe for the consumer movement: the tobacco industry.

The decision of the Australian Federation of Consumer Organisations about an appropriate avenue for action over the advertisement was to prove astute. It took its complaint to the Federal Government's Trade Practices Commission, a body concerned with the administration of the Trade Practices Act, which prohibits, among other matters, misleading and deceptive advertising. After receiving the complaint the Commission carried out an investigation but resolved the matter on the basis of an undertaking that the Tobacco Institute of Australia would not republish the advertisement and would publish a corrective advertisement in the same 14 newspapers, providing additional information "so the readers may judge the matter for themselves". Dissatisfied with this outcome, the Federation sought an undertaking from the Tobacco Institute that it would never again use the words "there is little evidence and nothing which proves scientifically that cigarette smoke causes disease in non-smokers" or make any similar statement in any advertising or in any promotional material. The Federation also required that the Tobacco Institute should not cite a study referred to in the advertisement as being "based on a wealth of statistical detail from a study involving 12,000 people".[5] The relevant subjects in the study had numbered about 700.

The Tobacco Institute refused to give such an undertaking and so on 11 June 1987 the Federation instituted proceedings in the Federal Court of Australia for an injunction to restrain the Institute from making such statements. The Institute challenged the Federation's rights to bring these proceedings but failed in a ruling in 1988. The interlocutory skirmishes were over and a battle royal was about to start. Witnesses began to be called from 20 November 1988, with the court sitting for 90 days, including for a period in the United Kingdom. The consumers' federation called such expert witnesses as Professor Tony McMichael (Adelaide), Professor Lou Landau (Western Australia), Professor Peter Phelan (Melbourne), Sir Richard Doll (Oxford), Professor Nick Wald (St Bartholomew's Hospital), Professor Dimitros Trichopoulos (Harvard), and Professor Dwight Janerich (Yale). The Tobacco Institute called statistical consultants, physicians, and toxicologists from Australia, the United States, Britain, and Sweden. By the end of proceedings on 25 September 1990 the Institute had spent an estimated $A5 million in legal fees and witness expenses. The consumers' federation received some legal aid from the Federal Minister for Justice and Consumer Affairs but the bulk of its expenses were borne by its counsel, solicitors, and witnesses, who deferred payment of fees and expenses as the litigation became increasingly protracted. Agencies which support research on heart disease and cancer also made important contributions.

Justice Morling had presided over the Royal Commission into the death of baby Azaria Chamberlain at Ayer's Rock in central Australia. The Commission resulted in the acquittal of the baby's mother and involved the evaluation of some of the most intricate and protracted scientific evidence ever to come before a court. The judge was thus experienced in evaluating complex scientific matters against legal considerations. Justice Morling's 211-page judgment reviews numerous epidemiological studies and five major reviews on passive smoking and assesses the evidence of 20 expert witnesses called by the Federation and the Tobacco Institute of Australia.

"Overwhelming evidence"

Morling's conclusions included that "there is compelling scientific evidence that cigarette smoke causes lung cancer in non-smokers" (p87). He found that "there is overwhelming evidence ... that passive smoking causes some people to experience attacks of asthma" (p118) and said that he could not "accept that the draftsman of the advertisement held an opinion to the contrary. No rational basis exists for the holding of an opinion that there is little evidence and nothing which proves scientifically that cigarette smoke causes attacks of asthma" (p119).

Of respiratory disease in young children he concluded:

> "In my opinion the only conclusion open on the evidence is that the statement that there was little evidence and nothing which proves scientifically that cigarette smoke causes disease in non-smokers was demonstrably false in 1986 in so far as it applied to respiratory disease in children in the first year of life. The statement remains false to this day. In my view the falsity of the statement is demonstrated whatever meaning one gives to the terms 'little evidence' and 'scientific proof'. I share the opinion expressed by Professor Phelan that the evidence establishing a casual relationship between passive smoking and respiratory disease in very young children is overwhelming. The evidence is of such strength that it constitutes scientific proof. The evidence is of two kinds, epidemiological and clinical. I cannot help observing that none of the witnesses called by the respondent were specialist paediatricians or epidemiologists. On the other hand, the applicant's witnesses included specialists in both these fields. I think that the respondent would have called specialists in these fields, of whom there must be many in this country and overseas, had they been able to give evidence favourable to the respondent's case" (p112).

Justice Morling noted that despite the resources of the international tobacco industry, the Tobacco Institute was unable to find even one epidemiologist who would testify in a manner contrary to the epidemiologists called by the Federation:

> "The respondent failed to call one witness whose special expertise is in epidemiology and of whom it could be said that he 'properly' held views contrary to those expressed by the distinguished epidemiologists called by the applicant. It is a fair assumption, I think, that such a witness would have been called by the respondent had he been available. In these circumstances, the concession [concerning the possibility of contrary assessments of the evidence] made [by epidemiological witnesses for the applicant] was little more than an admission of the theoretical possibility that another epidemiologist may hold contrary views, rather than a concession that any competent epidemiologist does in fact hold contrary views" (p63).

Justice Morling was almost uniformly critical of the Tobacco Institute's witnesses as being concerned to criticise only particular studies, whereas the Federation's witnesses

> "... tended to regard the separate items of scientific material – for example, epidemiological studies, the 'no threshold' for carcinogens theory, the presence of carcinogens in environmental tobacco smoke, and cotinine levels in non-smokers – as constituent parts of a mosaic, each piece itself representing some evidence that environmental tobacco smoke causes cancer in non-smokers" (p70).

Witnesses criticised

He described Professor Gary Huber (a professor of medicine in Texas) as "evasive", some of his answers "unsatisfactory", and said that he "did not find Professor Huber a satisfactory witness in all respects". He added that, "Of all the witnesses called by the respondent, I found him the least impressive" (p80). Of Dr Sven Malmfors, a consultant toxicologist called by the Tobacco Institute, Justice Morling said, "It seems to me that Dr Malmfors' requirements for the establishment of scientific truth are almost unobtainable" (p81). Similarly, of emeritus Professor John Clayton (Arizona) he noted, "Professor Clayton is of the opinion that toxicology has not provided any proof that mainstream smoke causes lung cancer in active smokers" (p82), and that Clayton was not prepared to concede that the International Agency for Research on Cancer's conclusions about the evidence of the carcinogenicity of various components to tobacco smoke were soundly based.

Justice Morling's most caustic remarks were perhaps reserved for a Californian consulting statistician, Dr Maxwell Layard, of whom he wrote:

> "Plainly he has a very close association with the tobacco industry and depends on it for most of his income. ... I do not think that Dr Layard expressed opinions which he does not hold, but I do think his hypercritical approach to the epidemiological studies may not be disassociated with his close connection with the tobacco industry" (p74).

The implications of the Morling judgment are likely to be profound. Directors of State cancer councils around Australia report that they have been inundated with inquiries concerning potential civil actions against employers who have so far refused to implement smoke free workplaces. Since 1985 there have been eight workers' compensation cases involving monetary payouts to workers claiming severe discomfort or disease arising from involuntary, passive smoking.[6] In the most publicised of these an out of court settlement of $A65,000 was made by a transport employer to a bus driver employee, Sean Carroll, with lung cancer after legal argument that his years of exposure to environmental tobacco smoke had caused the lung cancer.[7] The decision was reported widely in the Australian press as a likely precedent that would precipitate the introduction of smoking bans in workplaces by employers anxious to avoid illness compensation litigation. Mr Carroll died on 25 January, 14 days before the Morling judgment.

A recent survey by the National Heart Foundation in New South Wales of that State's top 232 private and public sector companies found that 56 per cent have introduced smoke free workplaces, 47 per cent in the past year (unpublished data). This trend has almost certainly been motivated by management concerns about possible litigation. In 1986 the Australian Attorney General said in the Australian parliament, "injury from passive smoking is reasonably foreseeable and ... consequently such an injury could give rise to an action for damages at common law".[8]

In 1978 the Roper report to the United States Tobacco Institute declared of the passive smoking issue, "This we see as the most dangerous development to the viability of the tobacco industry that has yet occurred"[9], and suggested that, "The strategic and long run antidote to the passive smoking issue is ... developing and widely publicising clear-cut, credible, medical evidence that passive smoking is not harmful to the non-smoker's health". The advertisement by the Tobacco Institute of Australia was surely a product of such thinking and the Morling judgment has probably dealt a death blow to any industry's hopes of further applications of the Roper "antidote".

Trojan horse effect

Why did the tobacco industry decide to fight this expensive case till the end? We believe the most obvious, but strangely underanalysed answer lies in the Trojan horse effect of passive smoking restrictions on sales resulting from reduced smoking opportunities when smoking is restricted.[10] For example, a study of the impact of the 1988 introduction of a total ban on smoking in Australian public service buildings found that, six months after the ban, the average smoker reduced his or her smoking over a 24-hour period by 5.18 cigarettes.[11] Heavy smokers reduced by 7.9 cigarettes, a 26.6 per cent decrease. It was calculated that if half of the office workplaces introduced such policies in the next five years, 654,880,000 cigarettes would be foregone in one year. At $A0.10 a cigarette, this would represent an annual amount of $A6,548,800 at 1988 prices lost in retail cigarette sales. The rate of adoption of smoking bans at work was found to be much higher than that in the National Heart Foundation study referred to above. Extrapolated world wide, the advance of restrictions on smoking in enclosed spaces will cost the industry hundreds of millions of dollars.

In 1978, the same year as the Roper report warnings to the American tobacco industry, William Hobbs, a president of the tobacco multinational RJ Reynolds said about anti-smoking measures "If they caused every smoker to smoke just one less cigarette a day, our company would stand to lose $92 million in sales annually. I assure you that we don't intend to let that happen without a fight". After the Morling judgment the odds on public health winning such a fight have improved mightily.

Copies of the Morling judgment are available from Action on Smoking and Health, 5th Floor, 64 Kippax Street, Surry Hills, 2010, Australia.

References

1. *Australian Federation of Consumer Organisations Incorporated v Tobacco Institute of Australia*, Federal Court of Australia, No NG 253 (1987). Judgment by Justice Trevor Morling, 7 February 1991.
2. National Health and Medical Research Council. *Effects of Passive Smoking on Health*. Canberra: Australian Government Publishing Service, 1987.
3. Chapman S, A David and Goliath story: tobacco advertising in Australia. *British Medical Journal* 1980; 281: 1187-90.
4. Chapman S, Mackay B. Good for the goose, good for the gander: Complaints and judgments about smoking and anti-smoking advertisements under advertising self regulation. *Media Information Australia* 1984; 31: 47-54.
5. Lee PN, Chamberlain J, Alderson MR. Relationship of passive smoking to risk of lung cancer and other smoking-associated diseases. *British Journal of Cancer* 1986; 54: 97-105.
6. Winstanley M. *Tobacco in Australia. Facts and Issues*. Surry Hills: Action on Smoking and Health (Australia), 1989.
7. Woodward SD, Winstanley MH. Lung cancer and passive smoking at work: the Carroll case. *Medical Journal of Australia* 1990; 153: 682-84.
8. *House of Representatives. Hansard* 1986, November 13. Advice from the Attorney General. (p2979.)
9. Roper Organization Incorporated. *A Study of Public Attitudes Toward Cigarette Smoking and the Tobacco Industry*. Vol 1. United States: Roper Organization Incorporated, 1978.
10. Chapman S, Borland R, Hill D, Owen N, Woodward S. Why the tobacco industry fears the passive smoking issue. *International Journal of Health Services* 1990; 20(3): 417-27.
11. Borland R, Chapman S, Owen N, Hill D. Effects of workplace bans on cigarette consumption. *American Journal of Public Health* 1990; 80(2): 178-80.

(Accepted 27 February 1991)

Note: Reproduced with permission from the *British Medical Journal*. This article was previously published as: Chapman S, Woodward S. Australian court rules that passive smoking causes lung cancer, asthma attacks, and respiratory disease. *British Medical Journal* 1991; 302: 943-45.

It should be noted that references to page numbers of the Morling judgment in this reproduction relate specifically to pages in this book, and not to the original judgment.

* *Dr Simon Chapman is Senior Lecturer in the Department of Community Medicine, University of Sydney, Westmead Hospital, Sydney, Australia.*

Stephen Woodward is Executive Director of Action on Smoking and Health Limited (ASH), Sydney, Australia.

Why the tobacco industry fears the passive smoking issue

Simon Chapman, Ron Borland, David Hill
*Neville Owen and Stephen Woodward**

The tobacco industry has identified the passive smoking issue as the single most important problem confronting its economic future. During the 1980s, the industry has been engaged in an elaborate and expensive international campaign seeking to refute the evidence against passive smoking's effects on health and to position the issue as one essentially concerned with civil liberties and smokers' "rights". There are three main reasons for the industry's concern: first, the passive smoking issue allows a widening of the definition of smoking beyond its discussion as a *personal* habit, legitimising it as a *social* problem; second, successful cases of litigation against employers by workers with histories of chronic exposure to environmental tobacco smoke have created an industrial climate of concern leading to workplace smoking restrictions and bans; and third, the proliferation of smoking restrictions reduces smoking opportunities and thus reduces total cigarette consumption and hence financial returns to the industry. Based on the results of a large Australian study of a workplace smoking ban, an estimated 654.88 million cigarettes with a retail value of $A6,549 thousand would be foregone annually in Australia alone if 50 per cent of white-collar worksites were to ban smoking. Finally, the passive smoking issue can be considered a Trojan horse to its less discussed effects: the reduced morbidity and mortality likely to result *in smokers* from the significant reductions in smoking frequency that occur with the proliferation of smoking restrictions introduced in the name of concern for the health of *non-smokers*.

In May 1978, in its sixth biennial national opinion survey report to the US Tobacco Institute, the Roper Organization, Inc, wrote of the growing public concern about involuntary "passive" smoking: "This we see as the most dangerous development to the viability of the tobacco industry that has yet occurred".[1] The Roper report suggested a six-point set of tactics to its tobacco industry clients, arguing that "The strategic and long run antidote to the passive smoking issue is ... developing and widely publicising clear-cut, credible, medical evidence that passive smoking is not harmful to the non-smoker's health". The suggested tactics included proposing segregated public facilities "as the lesser of two evils", promoting the "where will it all end" argument about government intrusions on liberty, and portraying those active in arguing for smoking control as "fumaphobes" and "zealots... with an unreasonable fear of cigarette smoking".

In the years that have followed the Roper report, the international tobacco industry has shown many signs of having heeded the advice it received. Its tactics have included:

- Sponsoring scientific conferences (Vienna, 1985; Tokyo, 1987) in the apparent attempt to display commitment to the principles of scientific impartiality, but to also perpetuate the definition of the involuntary smoking issue as a "debate" demanding the postponement of policy decisions, which the tobacco industry argues are unwisely predicted on the belief that sufficient evidence has already been amassed.
- Giving widespread publicity to the unofficial comments of individual delegates to one of these conferences in a manner that seemed designed to suggest that the comments were the official conclusions of the conference.
- Suggesting that the World Health Organisation officially supported the Vienna conference, and so by inference, the unofficial summary that emanated from it [2].
- Publishing and widely distributing quasi-scientific booklets[3-4], workplace smoking policy kits[5], pamphlets and "advertorials"[6-8], on themes consistent with the Roper recommendations.
- Distorting comments by (for example) the Vice President of the American Cancer Society[9-10] and the British Institute of Cancer Research[11] so as to imply that those agencies believed passive smoking was not a health issue.
- Supporting the establishment and activities of "smokers' rights groups" such as the British "FOREST" (Freedom Organisation for the Right to Enjoy Smoking Tobacco) and the Australian "Fair Go".

In 1989, the British tobacco industry's trade association, The Tobacco Advisory Council, published two information booklets on the subject[3-4]. Reviewing the booklets in the *British Medical Journal*, Professor Nicholas Wald concluded somewhat rhetorically:

> "Although the arguments in these booklets are weak, it is interesting that the Council has gone to such lengths to defend environmental tobacco smoke. Why has it chosen this hazard, rather than active smoking?"[12]

In this article we offer several suggestions in response to Professor Wald's question. We analyse the likely reasons for the tobacco industry's concern, and outline some of the implications for the changing face of smoking control in countries where concern about passive smoking has received wide publicity. We argue that the likely main public health impact of restrictions or bans on smoking in enclosed environments – substantial reductions in smoking frequency among smokers – should receive much more attention from researchers and commentators. These reductions should lead to corresponding reductions in tobacco-caused disease in *smokers*, to a far greater degree than any health benefits flowing to *non-smokers*. To date, the focus of the overwhelming majority of research and commentary on the health implications of passive smoking has examined the health of non-smokers.

Smoking: No longer a personal issue

The primary reason why the passive smoking issue must concern the tobacco industry is the way in which this issue had radically redefined the terms within which smoking can be discussed. Unlike quitting smoking and preventing its onset, passive smoking is potentially an issue for everyone, smokers and non-smokers alike. Cessation and prevention are potential issues for smokers, future smokers, and those such as parents who are concerned for them. Yet as subjects of public awareness efforts, these issues suffer a major disadvantage in that the view is widespread that smoking is one's own business, a matter of personal choice. The focus on passive smoking allows transcendence of the view of smoking as personal because it redefines smoking as a *public* health issue, moving it nearer to positions analogous to infectious disease, drunken driving, and other health issues on which metaphors of blame, public nuisance, and therefore control are conferred with legitimacy from the dominant culture. For non-smokers, the increasing evidence showing passive smoking to be dangerous positions smoking as an affront to one's own health and to a perfectly reasonable preference for smoke-free air. For smokers, it shatters any comfortable illusions that their smoking is purely their *own* affair.

In appropriating the unassailable issue of the right to avoid noxious and irritating fumes,

Table 1

Support for smoking bans in various public places

Area	Percentage support				
	Total	Men	Women	Blue Collar	White Collar
Public transport	70	66	73	64	76
Restaurants	59	57	61	56	60
Hospital waiting rooms	76	75	77	76	77
Enclosed work areas	61	55	68	55	68
Aircraft	57	55	60	53	62
Hotel bars	31	30	31	30	33
Enclosed entertainment areas	58	54	61	53	61

passive smoking legitimises the desire (previously often suspected as quasi-authoritarian or meddling) of many non-smokers to control the smoking of others. This is because it allows non-smokers to argue that the focus of the issue is no longer *your* smoking but *my forced, unwilling* smoking. In this way, the passive smoking issue has the propensity to create what might be termed a "reserve army" of smoking control advocates. Proselytising against smoking has hitherto been an activity of two main groups: those motivated by public health concerns (generally health and medical workers) and those who have an essentially puritanical, paternalistic, or ageist agenda of smoking being somehow *wrong* either for anyone, or for specified gender (invariably women) or age groups (children). The passive smoking issue has drawn into this arena a large number of people motivated by concerns for their personal comfort and health. As such, it represents a revolution in the social definition of smoking and consequently in the ways in which it can be discussed and its control legitimised.

Public support for restrictions

This analysis would appear to have considerable empirical support from at least two sources. First, there is impressive and mounting evidence that substantial majorities of both smokers and non-smokers agree that passive smoking can damage the health of non-smokers[13], and approve of restrictions on smoking in enclosed places, including workplaces. In a study of smoking bans in workplaces in Australia, 95 per cent of never-smokers, 90 per cent of ex-smokers, and 57 per cent of smokers agreed or strongly agreed that "overall, the ban was a good thing" six months after mandated bans were implemented. There was an overall increase in approval from before the ban's implementation[14], with smokers increasing their approval of bans after implementation more than non-smokers. A March 1986 survey of 2000 adults in the Australian States of New South Wales and Victoria found majority support for total prohibition of smoking in six of seven locations nominated (Table 1).[15] Ninety per cent of Australians also believed that cafes and restaurants should provide separate areas for smokers and non-smokers, and 63 per cent would prefer to sit in such areas.[16]

Second, if the editorial content of newspapers is a barometer of cultural preoccupations and public opinion, the recent coverage given to passive smoking in Australian newspapers is salutary. A study of all coverage of tobacco-related topics in all capital city newspapers for a 12-month period in 1987-88 found that the passive smoking issue ranked a clear first across all forms of article.[17] Of 1601 news items and letters coded for content, news and commentary on the December 1987 ban on smoking on all domestic airline flights ranked first (187 items), with articles on smoking in the workplace ranking third (78 items) and smoking on other forms of public transport sixth (63 items). Aggregated, articles on any aspect of passive smoking appeared at 125 per cent greater frequency than the next most common principal category.

Industrial litigation implications of exposure to environmental tobacco smoke

In Australia since 1985 there have been eight workers' compensation cases involving monetary payouts to workers claiming severe discomfort or disease arising from involuntary, passive smoking.[18] In the most publicised of these, an out-of-court settlement of $A65,000 was made by a transport employer to a bus driver employee with lung cancer, following legal argument that his years of exposure to passengers' environmental tobacco smoke had caused the lung cancer. The decision was discussed widely in the Australian press as a likely precedent case that would precipitate the introduction of smoking bans in workplaces by employers anxious to avoid illness compensation litigation.

While there has not been any formal study of the reasons for introducing workplace smoking bans and restrictions in Australian industry, the proliferation of such restrictions in recent years seems certain to be largely motivated by management concerns about possible litigation. In 1986, the Australian Attorney General said in the Australian parliament that "injury from passive smoking is reasonably foreseeable and that consequently such an injury could give rise to an action for damages at common law".[19]

Effects of smoking restrictions on smoking opportunities and total cigarette consumption

Increased public antipathy toward exposure to sidestream tobacco smoke, coupled with fear of litigation in employers and civic authorities, is leading to increased restrictions on smoking, through voluntary agreements and regulations. As the places in which smoking is allowed are reduced it is likely that smokers' tobacco consumption will decline – an obvious concern to the tobacco industry. In this section, we review what is known about the effects on cigarette consumption of workplace smoking bans, and develop a likely scenario regarding cigarette consumption as the adoption of restrictions on smoking becomes more widespread. We will argue that the likely scenario has net benefits in public health terms, as well as providing smokers with a means of regulating their habit. When legislation, regulation, or social antipathy acts to prevent or inhibit smoking in enclosed public places, it seems likely that cigarette consumption will be reduced, commensurate with the duration of the times when smoking would otherwise occur.

Reduced consumption associated with workplace smoking restrictions

Of all the occasions or times when smoking is not permitted, the longest durations for most people occur during work hours in those workplaces with restrictions and bans on smoking. Four studies have now been published describing the effects on cigarette consumption in smokers who are not permitted to smoke at work.[20-23] All four found evidence of reductions in smoking. The most recent of these, and the only study of the four with a prospective design, examined the impact of the 1988 introduction of a total ban on smoking in Australian Public Service buildings, the worksites of Australia's largest employer group (over 170,000 workers).[23] Smokers in 44 different work locations were surveyed prior to the introduction of workplace smoking bans. A survey six months later found that the average smoker reduced his or her smoking over a 24-hour period by 5.18 cigarettes a day. Light smokers did not change consumption significantly, while moderate smokers reduced by an average of 5.8 cigarettes per day (or 29.1 per cent of usual consumption) and heavy smokers by 7.9 cigarettes (a 26.6 per cent decrease).

Compensatory smoking?

A common response to suggestions that restrictions on opportunities for smoking will lead to an overall reduction in smoking frequency during a 24-hour period is the claim that, because of the addictive nature of tobacco smoking, many smokers will compensate for those cigarettes foregone by smoking more than they would otherwise in the periods adjacent to times when they cannot smoke. The study reported above examined possible compensatory smoking behaviour by requiring respondents to record the number of cigarettes smoked during seven separate periods of the day. In this way the study was able to compare (for example) smoking frequency during lunch breaks and before and after work, prior to and following the ban. There was an overall reduction in consumption of about seven cigarettes per day during the hours spent inside buildings, and a compensation of only 1.8 cigarettes in the time periods before and after work and during time spent outside buildings. The study did not measure "puff" topography, so it remains possible that cigarettes smoked in times adjacent to worktimes were smoked "harder." The lack of any compensatory smoking at coffee breaks and lunch times suggest that smokers were generally not making extraordinary efforts to maintain consumption. Further, the lack of compensation in the evening (excluding the hour immediately after work) suggests that any compensation was restricted to the periods immediately surrounding the periods of enforced abstinence.

The spread of workplace smoking restrictions

On the assumption that smoking bans will be progressively introduced beyond the Australian Public Service into private sector office-type occupational settings, we have estimated the impact on reduced consumption using the results of the study described above as a benchmark of expected reductions.

In Australia in August 1988, approximately 4,450,800 persons worked in occupations that usually are located within offices, shops, or other enclosed settings.[24] If we assume smoking rates in such settings are approximately the same (24.7 per cent) as those in the white-collar sections of the Australian Public Service sampled in the study described above, the corresponding extrapolation of annual cigarettes foregone by such workers would be calculated thus:

4,450,800 workers x 0.247 = 1,099,348 smokers

1,099,348 smokers x 5.18 cigarettes x 230 working days/years = 1,309,760,000 cigarettes foregone

On an assumption that 50 per cent of such workplaces introduce such policies in the next five years, then 654,880,000 cigarettes would be foregone in one year. At $A0.10 per cigarette, this would represent an annual loss of $A6,548,800 (at 1988 prices) in retail cigarette sales.

Might smoke-free workplaces promote quitting?

Although research has not yet shown that smoke-free workplaces are responsible for increasing smoking cessation among smokers, it is reasonable to suppose that they may play important roles in this regard, although it will require the power of large longitudinal studies to demonstrate such effects. Smokers in the contemplation stage of the smoking cessation process[25] at the time smoking bans are introduced, or those who take up a new job where smoking is not allowed, might well be "triggered" to stop smoking. Moreover, work is a common setting for relapse during quitting attempts[26], so workplace bans could be expected to assist quitting smokers to survive situations that might otherwise result in relapse. Also likely in the long term is that persons entering the workforce as non-smokers will be "protected", not only from passive exposure to cigarette smoke, but also social influence that may lead them to commence smoking. An Australian population survey showed that among young adult smokers, 21 per cent commenced smoking regularly for the first time at work.[27] Furthermore, 7 per cent specifically acknowledged that they had been influenced by workmates to take up the habit. These data show that workplace bans have the potential to make a significant contribution to reducing the uptake of smoking.

Smoking bans outside the workplace: Aircraft

The workplace is not the only context in which smoking has been restricted. Considerable time is spent by the smoking public in commuting and travelling on non-smoking surburban, inter- and intra-state buses and trains; patronising cinemas, theatre, and concert halls; visiting museums, exhibitions, hospitals, and other enclosed public places; and attending church. In nearly all of these places in Australia, and in an increasing number of other countries, smoking is totally prohibited. The erosion of time available for smoking in the manner described above for workplaces could also be calculated for these other restricted zones, albeit involving great complexity. As an index of smoking foregone in just one of these contexts, consider the following case of the smoking ban on aircraft.

Smoking has been banned on all domestic flights in Australia since December 1987. The number of domestic passenger flying hours in Australia during the year ending 30 June 1988 was 23,606,842.* Official figures on the provision of seats for smokers prior to the introduction of the ban are not available for the seven major Australian domestic airlines, but let us assume that before the ban an average of 20 per cent of seats were allocated to smokers – a figure that applied in Canada in 1988[29], a country with a comparable prevalence of smoking and a similar socioeconomic population profile. If it is assumed that the average smoking passenger was a 25-cigarettes-a-day smoker who smoked an average of 1.56 cigarettes during each hour of a 16-hour day, then a qualified estimate of the number of cigarettes likely to be foregone by the 20 per cent of smoking passengers travelling on Australian domestic airlines in 1987/88 may be obtained in the following manner: 20 per cent of 23,606,842 total passenger hours equals 4,721,369 smoker passenger hours; 4,721,369 hours at 1.56 cigarettes per hour equals 7,365,335 cigarettes foregone. With the average retail price of a cigarette in 1988 being $A0.10, then cigarettes costing a total of $A736,534 in retail sales would not be purchased, assuming that compensatory pre- and post-flight increases in smoking did not take place. On the basis of evidence in the workplace discussed above, we believe that only insignificant compensatory smoking would be likely.

There can be little doubt that the tobacco industry has made calculations similar to those above. In 1978 – the same year as the Roper report warnings to the American tobacco industry – William Hobbs, a president of the tobacco multinational RJ Reynolds, said about anti-smoking measures, "If they caused every smoker to smoke just one less cigarette a day, our company would stand to lose $92 million in sales annually. I assure you that we don't intend to let that happen without a fight".[30] Since 1978, the proliferation of laws and regulations concerning environmental tobacco smoke, together with the rising tide of public opinion supportive of such restrictions, had almost certainly caused the customers of companies such as RJ Reynolds to reduce smoking by considerably more than one cigarette per day. The international industry's opposition to regulations designed to control passive smoking should be seen first and foremost in the light of this concern for the erosion of smoking opportunities and thus the industry's market.

Reduced risk among smokers who reduce consumption: A "Trojan horse" effect

By "Trojan horse" we mean that the current preoccupation within the passive smoking issue with the potential harm being caused to non-smokers acts to mask what in public health terms ought clearly to be a subject of more extensive and detailed study: the impact of passive smoking control policies on the incidence of smoking-caused diseases in smokers whose consumption falls as a result of these restrictions. As Peto and Doll have commented, "The risks of passive smoking are certainly trivial compared with the risks to smokers themselves".[31]

Almost all of the argument to restrict or ban smoking in enclosed public places has proceeded from a concern to protect non-smokers from involuntarily breathing environmental tobacco smoke. The 1986 US Surgeon General's report reflected this concern in its title, *The Health Consequences of Involuntary Smoking*[32], and in all but four postscript-like pages of its 359-page length, where the little available evidence on the "indirect effects" of workplace bans such as those on cessation rates and on smoking frequencies in continuing smokers were reviewed. Yet in terms of public health impact, restrictions on smoking introduced in the interests of preventing involuntary smoking may well prove to be a Trojan horse to what has to date been a barely investigated yet potentially profound effect: the impact on smoking prevalence and smoking frequency, and therefore on smokers' own health, of restrictions on smoking in public.

* Passenger hours are calculated from Commonwealth Department of Transport data[28] thus:

$$\frac{\text{Total passenger kilometres travelled}}{\text{Average aircraft speed}} = \frac{13{,}267{,}045{,}000\text{ km}}{562\text{ km/hr}}$$

$$= 23{,}606{,}842 \text{ passenger hours}$$

Cigarette smoking has a dose-response relationship with each of the major diseases in which it plays a causative role.[33] In the Australian study described above, reduction in consumption due to workplace bans was greatest among medium and heavy smokers. The dose-response relationship between cigarettes consumed and overall and disease-specific mortality suggests that the mean reduced daily consumption found in the Australian study may eventually be associated with a corresponding reduction in tobacco-caused diseases in those who might otherwise be smoking more. Doll's and Peto's[34] review of lung cancer mortality in several countries concluded that international differences in mortality rates and temporal trends observed were generally consistent with different tar yields and intakes across both time and countries. The cigarettes being smoked in Australia in 1989 have considerably lower tar yields than those smoked during past decades[18], making extrapolation of likely reductions in mortality based on past dose-response relationships largely speculative. Nonetheless, a reduction in consumption of the order of 25 per cent would be expected over time to significantly reduce tobacco-caused disease.

The decline and fall of the notion of "smokers' rights"

The progressive introduction of restrictions and prohibitions on smoking in enclosed spaces has been motivated by concern about personal comfort and health, and precipitated by the recommendations of major reports, which in turn were commissioned in response to the accumulating research evidence implicating passive smoking in acute and chronic disease. The theme uniting the various objections to these restrictions has been that of "smokers' rights" – a generally unspecified allusion to an inalienable assumption of rights said to apply to smokers. These alleged rights bear some reflection against the history of arguably comparable "rights" that have long since eroded.

In Elizabethan England, the free exercise of flatulence even among company was considered normal and not proscribed by considerations of politeness or offensiveness. Similarly, public expectoration was commonplace across all social classes in Victorian and Edwardian England, and the practice remains widespread in many countries today without drawing any social or legal approbation.[35] There are some pertinent similarities between flatulence, spitting, and smoking. Each behaviour is essentially personal but being not involuntary, is each capable of being exercised in both private and in public settings. As well, the performance of each behaviour is usually motivated by a desire to make oneself more comfortable, and so its execution is accompanied by a feeling of relief and pleasure. While those performing any of these three behaviours derive some pleasure from them, all three have also emerged as the focus of social ostracism, and in the case of spitting and smoking, legal sanctions. The control of spitting is thought to have played an important part in the control of tuberculosis. The personal pleasure these behaviours allow to their perpetrators also causes unpleasant, and in the case of spitting and smoking, potentially harmful results to those exposed to the products of these behaviours.

In view of these parallels, it is salutary to speculate on the likely reception that would be given to earnest talk about "farters' rights" or "spitters' rights". Clearly, such terms would be greeted with derision, while "smokers' rights" continues to maintain some currency as a serious concept. The derision accorded to the former terms would partly reflect their strangeness, but derive mostly from the bombastic apposition of essentially private and discreet behaviours with the legalistic tone intrinsic to the word "rights". Perhaps the principal difference between the three behaviours is that it is only smoking that involves a purchased commodity (cigarettes), and hence only for smoking have powerful groups of financially vested interests taken any role in attempting to define the behaviour as one appropriate to as many public situations as possible. There is no financial gain to be made in promoting the social acceptability of flatulence or spitting.

The evolution of social norms against public spitting and flatulence has relegated these practices to private and generally solitary occasions in most Western countries. It is interesting to speculate whether the rapidly changing social climate about smoking will eventually cause talk of "smokers' rights" to be considered the utterances of a bygone era, and smoking itself largely reduced to the status of a private, solitary behaviour or one exercised among consenting adults in private. Just as the spittoon is now a relic of the past in most cultures, perhaps the ashtray may soon also grace the shelves of antique and curio shops.

References

1. Roper Organization Incorporated. *A Study of Public Attitudes Toward Cigarette Smoking and the Tobacco Industry*. Vol 1. United States: Roper Organization Incorporated, 1978.
2. Masironi R. Tobacco lobby misrepresented WHO [letter]. *Australian Financial Review*, 6 August 1986: 15.
3. Tobacco Advisory Council (UK). *Smoke and the Non-smoker*. London, 1989.
4. Tobacco Advisory Council (UK). *Scientific Aspects of Environmental Tobacco Smoke*. London, 1989.
5. Tobacco Institute of Australia Ltd. *Smoking in the Work-place*. Sydney, undated.
6. Tobacco Institute of Australia. Do you mind if I smoke? [advertisement]. *The Australian Women's Weekly,* March 1985: 84-89.
7. Tobacco Institute of Australia. A message from those who do ... to those who don't [advertisement]. *The Age,* 4 July 1986: 6.
8. Tobacco Institute of Australia. Our contribution to the debate [advertisement]. *The Australian*, 8 July 1986: 2.
9. Garfinkel L. Cancer's aides words with tobacco concern's twist [letter]. *New York Times*, 5 June 1984.
10. Garfinkel L. Passive smoking [letter]. *The Advertiser* (Australia), 4 October 1986.
11. Weiss R, Peto J. Passive smokers mislead by ads [letter]. *Australian Financial Review*, 25 July 1986.
12. Wald N. Tobacco industry denies risk of passive smoking. *British Medical Journal* 1989; 299: 331.
13. Hill D. Public opinion in Victoria about the dangers of passive smoking. *Medical Journal of Australia* 1986; 144: 615.
14. Borland R, et al. *Changes in Acceptance of Workplace Smoking Bans Following Their Implementation: A Prospective Study*. Melbourne: Centre for Behavioural Research in Cancer, Anti-Cancer Council of Victoria, 1989.
15. Mills S. Most want more bans on smoking in public: Poll. *The Age* (Melbourne), 12 April 1986: 13.
16. Borland R, Hill D. Public attitudes to smoke-free zones in restaurants. *Medical Journal of Australia* 1989; 150: 407.
17. Chapman S. The news on smoking: Editorial coverage of tobacco and health issues in Australian newspapers, 1987-88. *American Journal of Public Health* 1989; 70(10): 1419-21.
18. Winstanley M. *Tobacco in Australia. Facts and Issues*. Surry Hills: Action on Smoking and Health (Australia), 1989.
19. *House of Representatives. Hansard* 1986, November 13. Advice from the Attorney General. (p2979.)
20. Rosenstock IM, Stergachis A, Heaney C. Evaluation of smoking prohibition policy in a health maintenance organisation. *American Journal of Public Health* 1986; 76: 1014-15.
21. Petersen LR, et al. Employee smoking behaviour changes and attitudes following a restrictive policy on worksite smoking in a large company. *Public Health Rep* 1988; 103: 115-20.
22. Beiner L, et al. A comparative evaluation of a restrictive smoking policy in a general hospital. *American Journal of Public Health* 1989; 79: 192-95.
23. Borland R, et al. Effects of workplace bans on cigarette consumption. *American Journal of Public Health* 1990; 80(2): 178-80.
24. Australian Bureau of Statistics. *The Labour Force*. Catalogue No 6203.0. Canberra: Australian Bureau of Statistics, August 1988.
25. Prochaska JO, et al. Measuring processes of change: Applications to the cessation of

smoking. *Journal Consult Clinical Psychology* 1988; 56: 520-28.

26. Borland R. Slip-ups and relapse in attempts to quit smoking. *Addictive Behaviours* 1990; in press.
27. Hill D, Borland R. *Adults' Accounts of Where They Began Regular Smoking and Who Influenced Them to Start.* Melbourne: Centre for Behavioural Research in Cancer, Anti-Cancer Council of Victoria, 1989.
28. Commonwealth Department of Transport. *Personal Communication*, 4 October 1989.
29. Makabenta LP. Smoking or non-smoking? *Business Traveller* April 1988: 16-19.
30. *Financial Times* (UK), 27 September 1978.
31. Peto J, Doll R. Passive smoking. *British Journal of Cancer* 1986; 54: 381-83.
32. United States Surgeon General. *The Health Consequences of Involuntary Smoking – A Report of the Surgeon General.* Rockville, Md: US Department of Health and Human Services, Public Health Service, Centers for Disease Control, Center for Health Promotion and Education, Office on Smoking and Health, 1986.
33. International Agency for Research on Cancer. *Tobacco Smoking – IARC Monographs on the Evaluation of the Carcinogenic Risk of Chemicals to Humans.* Vol 38. Lyon: International Agency for Research on Cancer, 1986.
34. Doll R, Peto R. The causes of cancer: Quantitative estimates of avoidable risks of cancer in the United States today. *Journal of the National Cancer Institute* 1981; 66(6): 1191-1308.
35. Elias N. The civilizing process. Vol 1. *The History of Manners.* New York: Pantheon, 1980.

Note: This article was previously published in *The International Journal of Health Services* 1990; 20(3): 417-27. Reproduced with permission.

---

* *Dr Simon Chapman is Senior Lecturer in the Department of Community Medicine, University of Sydney, Westmead Hospital, Sydney, Australia.*

Dr Ron Borland is Deputy Director and Dr David Hill is Director of the Centre for Behavioural Research in Cancer at the Anti-Cancer Council of Victoria.

Dr Neville Owen is Senior Lecturer in the Department of Community Medicine, University of Adelaide.

Stephen Woodward is Executive Director of Action on Smoking and Health Limited (ASH), Sydney, Australia.

Section Two
The Judgment

[¶41-079] AUSTRALIAN FEDERATION OF CONSUMER ORGANISATIONS INC v THE TOBACCO INSTITUTE OF AUSTRALIA LIMITED
Federal Court of Australia
Judgment delivered 7 February 1991

Trade practices — Misleading or deceptive conduct — Cigarettes — Advertisement in newspaper — Statement that "there is little evidence and nothing which proves scientifically that cigarette smoke causes disease in non-smokers" — Whether the statement made in trade or commerce — Whether statement misleading or deceptive — Evidence — Meaning of evidence — Admissibility of scientific journals — Whether passive smoking causes cancer — Whether passive smoking causes respiratory disease — Whether passive smoking causes asthma — Meaning of asthma — Meaning of scientific proof — Epidemiological studies — Whether capable of proving causal relationship — Delay in bringing proceedings — Discretion — Injunction restraining further publication of advertisement — Trade Practices Act 1974, sec 52.

The applicant ("AFCO") alleged that the respondent ("Tobacco Institute") engaged in misleading or deceptive conduct in breach of sec 52 of the Trade Practices Act ("the Act") by causing an advertisement to be published on 1 July 1986 in several newspapers distributed in Australia. Two paragraphs in the advertisement were specifically alleged to be misleading or deceptive:

- **para 3 stating that "... there is little evidence and nothing which proves scientifically that cigarette smoking causes disease in non-smokers" ("the statement"); and**
- **para 5 stating that "the Institute's conclusions are based on a wealth of statistical detail from a study involving 12,000 people".**

The Tobacco Institute conceded that the words of para 5 did not give an accurate description of the number of people involved in the study undertaken by the Institute of Cancer Research and consented to an order restraining the repetition of those words. It resisted the claims that the words of para 3 were misleading or deceptive or likely to mislead or deceive.

AFCO complained to the Trade Practices Commission ("the TPC") of the Tobacco Institute's conduct in publishing the advertisement. The Tobacco Institute undertook to run a follow-up advertisement in a form which had been agreed upon by the TPC and that follow-up advertisement was published in January 1987. AFCO was dissatisfied with the terms of the follow-up advertisement and asserted it did not correct what it claimed to be the misleading or deceptive words of the original advertisement. AFCO sought undertakings from the Tobacco Institute as to the content of future advertisements but these were refused and these proceedings commenced.

By its defence the Tobacco Institute denied that it engaged in conduct proscribed by sec 52 of the Act. Further, it relied upon the publication of the follow-up advertisement and an undertaking it had given to the TPC not to re-publish the original advertisement as justification for the Court refusing the relief claimed. It also claimed that AFCO had been guilty of laches, acquiescence and delay in bringing these proceedings.

The Tobacco Institute unsuccessfully applied to have the statement of claim struck out upon grounds which were no longer material ((1988) ATPR ¶40-874). An appeal against that decision was dismissed ((1988) ATPR ¶40-916).

As to the nature of passive smoking, the Court found the following:

- sidestream smoke is smoke that is emitted directly from a burning cigarette, pipe or cigar ("SS");
- mainstream smoke is cigarette smoke which is drawn through the tobacco into the smoker's mouth ("MS");
- environmental tobacco smoke is the combination of sidestream smoke and the fraction of exhaled mainstream smoke not retained by the smoker ("ETS");
- in contrast with mainstream smoke, environmental tobacco smoke is diluted into a larger volume of air, and it ages prior to inhalation.

Held: respondent engaged in misleading or deceptive conduct.

Whether advertisement published "in trade or commerce"?

The advertisement had the potential, and was no doubt intended, to protect the commercial interests of cigarette manufacturers and distributors.

Accepting that conduct "in trade and commerce" is confined to conduct which is itself an aspect of activities which, of their nature, bear a commercial character the proper conclusion was that the publication of the advertisement was conduct "in trade or commerce".

Meaning of advertisement

1. The advertisement was directed at the general public.

2. Many readers of the advertisement would think that the reference to "evidence" was a reference to, inter alia, opinions of competent scientists whether based on their own research or on the published results of the research of others.

Readers of the advertisement would conclude that there was little in the form of published opinions of scientists or groups of scientists to support the proposition that cigarette smoking caused disease in non-smokers. Accordingly, the major reviews were admissible to show whether readers would be misled if they reached that conclusion.

3. In the context of the advertisement, the words "nothing which proves scientifically that cigarette smoke causes disease in non-smokers" meant "nothing which affords compelling or convincing evidence that cigarette smoke causes disease in non-smokers". This was the meaning which most readers would give to the words.

Admissibility of evidence to show that statements in advertisement continued to be misleading after date of publication

The Tobacco Institute's submission that 1 July 1986 was the only relevant date for examining the correctness of the statement in the advertisement should be rejected.

Cancer

Was there more than a little evidence that cigarette smoke caused cancer in non-smokers?

1. AFCO established that, in relation to the disease of cancer, it was misleading and deceptive to state on 1 July 1986 that there was then little evidence that cigarette smoke caused disease in non-smokers.

So far from there then being little evidence that cigarette smoke caused lung cancer in non-smokers, there was much evidence to that effect.

2. The evidence of a link between passive smoking and lung cancer came from epidemiological studies supported by strong biological plausibility.

3. The opinions of the experts called by AFCO were to be preferred to the opinions expressed by the experts called by the Tobacco Institute.

4. The experts were entitled to explain the contents of the primary articles and to depose as to the strengths and weaknesses of the studies referred to in them.

5. In substance, what the reader of the advertisement was told was that inhalation of cigarette smoke by non-smokers might be annoying to them but it was not a health problem.

Having regard to the totality of the advertisement, the reference to "little evidence" seemed to be a reference to evidence which was so inconsequential as not to support a reasonable apprehension that passive smoking might give rise to a medical or health problem.

6. The Court was unable to accept that evidence of an association between passive smoking and lung cancer could not be regarded as some evidence of a causal relationship between the two.

7. Nor did the Court accept the Tobacco Institute's related submission that epidemiological evidence alone could not establish a cause and effect relationship.

Was there scientific proof that cigarette smoke caused cancer in non-smokers?

1. In the context of the advertisement the words "nothing which proves scientifically that cigarette smoke causes disease in non-smokers" meant "nothing which affords compelling or convincing evidence that cigarette smoke causes disease in non-smokers". Reading the statement in this way it was erroneous when it was first made on 1 July 1986 and remained so.

2. The conclusion that cigarette smoke caused lung cancer in non-smokers could not be drawn from any one epidemiological study or piece of evidence. But it could be drawn from the totality of the available data and by valid reasoning from it.

3. Once it was accepted:

- **that passive smoking involved inhalation of environmental tobacco smoke which contained carcinogens;**
- **that there was no safe threshold level of exposure to carcinogens;**

- **that some of the studies referred to in the primary articles showed a statistically significant association between spousal smoking and lung cancer; and**
- **the meta-analysis of the results in such studies disclosed a statistically significant (adjusted) risk ratio of about 1.53 or 1.42 for non-smokers compared with non-smokers not exposed to environmental tobacco smoke;**

then there was compelling scientific evidence that cigarette smoke caused lung cancer in non-smokers.

Although not based upon findings made by the authors of the major reviews, the Court's conclusion was consistent with those findings.

Respiratory disease in young children (under 12 months)

1. The only conclusion open on the evidence was that the statement that there was little evidence and nothing which proved scientifically that cigarette smoke caused disease in non-smokers was demonstrably false in 1986 in so far as it applied to respiratory disease in children in the first year of life.

2. The statement remained false and its falsity was demonstrated whatever meaning given to the terms "little evidence" and "scientific proof".

3. The evidence, epidemiological and clinical, establishing a causal relationship between passive smoking and respiratory disease in very young children was overwhelming. The evidence was of such strength that it constituted scientific proof.

Asthma

1. There was overwhelming evidence, which was not really disputed by the Tobacco Institute, that passive smoking caused some people to experience attacks of asthma.

It was unnecessary to have regard to any of the epidemiological studies to prove that this was the case.

However, the majority of the studies supported the opinions expressed by AFCO's witnesses.

2. On the other hand, AFCO had not shown that cigarette smoke of itself caused what might be described as the underlying condition of asthma.

3. An attack of asthma fitted easily within the dictionary definitions of "disease".

Many lay persons would not distinguish between asthma and an attack of asthma. Those who did would regard the underlying condition of asthma referred to in some of the evidence as a latent disease and an attack of asthma as an acute manifestation of the disease.

4. People who were prone to asthma attacks could reasonably have gained the impression from the statement that they were not at risk of suffering attacks of asthma by reason of being exposed to cigarette smoke.

5. The evidence that cigarette smoke caused attacks of asthma was so overwhelming that it could not be accepted that the draftsman of the advertisement held an opinion to the contrary.

It was not suggested, nor could it have been, that any scientist could properly have held such a contrary opinion.

6. AFCO established that the statement made in the advertisement was misleading and deceptive in so far as it applied to the disease of asthma. This was so whether the relevant date be regarded as 1 July 1986 or at any date thereafter.

Otitis media (middle ear infection)

The Court was not satisfied there was scientific proof of a causal association between passive smoking and otitis media (middle ear effusion and "glue ear") but was persuaded on the strength of the oral evidence and the primary articles that there was, in 1986, more than a little evidence that passive smoking caused recurrent otitis media in children.

Did the advertisement state fact or opinion?

1. The statement made in the advertisement was not expressed to be an opinion. It was an assertion of the state of the evidence on the question whether cigarette smoke caused disease in non-smokers.

2. The statement must be read in the context of the whole of the advertisement.

What the reader was told in the statement was not that some innominate person or body held an opinion as to the relationship between cigarette smoke and disease in non-smokers. Rather the reader was told what the state of the evidence was on the subject.

3. In any event, it was impossible to believe that a person who, on 1 July 1986 or at any time subsequently, acquainted himself with the available evidence as to the relationship between cigarette smoke and disease in non-smokers could have concluded that it was "little".

Laches, acquiescence and delay

In the circumstances, there was no substance in the defence based on laches, acquiescence and delay. The delay in commencing the proceedings was not great, nor was the Tobacco Institute prejudiced by such delay as occurred.

Discretion

There was a strong public interest in the Tobacco Institute being prevented from making the statement that there was little evidence and nothing which proved that cigarette smoke caused disease in non-smokers.

Relief

AFCO was entitled to injunctive relief in appropriate terms, but not to an order for the Tobacco Institute to publish an advertisement correcting what was said in the advertisements published on 1 July 1986 and in January 1987.

[*Headnote by the CCH TRADE PRACTICES EDITORS*]

DMJ Bennett QC with NF Francey (instructed by Cashman and Partners) for the applicant.
BSJ O'Keefe QC with BW Walker (instructed by Clayton Utz) for the respondent.

Before: Morling J.

Morling J.:

1. *Introduction — the advertisement*

In a letter written in 1606 by a Doctor of Physic to a Gentleman it was asserted that tobacco was:

"1. Not safe for youth

2. It shorteneth life

3. It breedeth many diseases

4. It breedeth melancholy

5. It hurteth the mind

6. It is ill for the smokers issue."

(*British Journal of Preventive and Social Medicine* (1973), 27, 150).

Nearly four centuries after the Doctor of Physic wrote his letter the debate about the alleged harmful effects of tobacco continues. The applicant claims that the respondent has engaged in conduct that is misleading or deceptive or is likely to mislead or deceive in contravention of s. 52 of the *Trade Practices Act* 1974 ("the Act"). The alleged contravention is claimed to have occurred by reason of the publication of an advertisement on 1 July 1986 in several newspapers distributed in Australia. It is not in issue that the respondent caused the advertisement to be published. The advertisement was in the following terms:

> **"A message from those who do ... to those who don't**
>
> Some non-smokers are annoyed by cigarette smoke. This is a reality that's been with us for a long time.
>
> Lately, however, many non-smokers have been led to believe that cigarette smoke in the air can actually cause disease.
>
> And yet there is little evidence and nothing which proves scientifically that cigarette smoke causes disease in non-smokers.
>
> The London Times reported findings from the Institute of Cancer Research in Surrey, England, published in this month's edition of the 'British Journal of Cancer,' that 'passive smoking' for life-long non-smokers carries no significant increase in the risk of lung cancer, bronchitis or heart disease (all allegedly associated with smoking).
>
> The Institute's conclusions are based on a wealth of statistical detail from a study involving 12,000 people.
>
> In a study by a Vice-President of the American Cancer Society in 1981 which involved 175,000 people, it was reported that 'passive smoking' had 'very little, if any' effect on lung cancer rates among non-smokers.
>
> In the follow-up study published in 1985, no statistically significant increase in risk was reported.
>
> Researchers at the Harvard School of Public Health found that a non-smoker would have to spend 100 hours straight in the smokiest bar to 'absorb' the equivalent of a single filter tip cigarette.
>
> Major reviews on 'passive smoking' over the last few years have concluded that 'passive smoking' cannot be shown to be a health risk. The weight of evidence is summed up in the remarks at the conclusion of the 1984 Vienna Health Conference which was held in co-operation with the World Health Organisation: 'should law makers wish to take legislative measures with regard to passive smoking, they will, for the present, not be able to base their efforts on a demonstrated health hazard from passive smoking.'
>
> Often our own concerns about health can take an unproved claim and magnify it out of all proportion; so what begins as a misconception turns into a frightening myth.
>
> Alright, cigarette smoke may be annoying to some non-smokers, but how shall we deal with these problems? Confrontation? Segregation? Legislation?
>
> No.
>
> We think annoyance is neither a government nor a medical problem. It's a people problem. Smokers can help by being more considerate and responsible. Non-smokers can help by being more tolerant. And both groups can help by showing more respect for each others rights and feelings.
>
> Don't let intolerant minority pressure groups use you to create divisions between Australians.
>
> Authorised by John Dollisson, Tobacco Institute, Gold Fields House, Sydney."

It is the words of the third and fifth paragraphs which the applicant submits are misleading or deceptive or likely to mislead or deceive. The respondent concedes that the words of the fifth paragraph do not give an accurate description of the number of people involved in the study undertaken by the Institute of Cancer Research, and consents to an order restraining the repetition of those words. It resists the claims that the words of the third paragraph are misleading or deceptive or likely to mislead or deceive.

For ease of reference, I shall hereafter refer to the contents of para. 3 of the advertisement as "the statement".

2. *The history of the litigation*

On 25 July 1986 the applicant complained to the Trade Practices Commission of the respondent's conduct in publishing the advertisement. On 7 January 1987 the Commission informed the applicant that the respondent had undertaken to run a follow-up advertisement in a form which had been agreed with the Commission and which was accepted by it as a sufficient correction of the original advertisement and that, as a consequence, it considered the matter closed.

The follow-up advertisement was published in January 1987. It did not refer to what was said in the third paragraph of the original advertisement. After referring to other parts of the original advertisement it concluded with the following quotation from remarks made by two scientists at the conclusion of the 1984 Vienna Health Conference:

> "A drawback in all epidemiological studies up to now consists in the fact that they have been conducted without sufficient quantification of the contamination from passive smoking. Further epidemiological investigations, in which the problem of registering the amount of passive contamination will have to be dealt with more, are urgently needed. New attempts at doing so have been indicated. Since, due to the annoyance connected with passive smoking and the possible hazard to high-risk groups, it also further constitutes a controversial social problem, international co-operation among the various scientific disciplines is the order of the day. Should lawmakers wish to take legislative measures with regard to passive smoking, they will, for the present, not be able to base their efforts on a demonstrated health hazard from passive smoking."

The applicant was dissatisfied with the terms of the follow-up advertisement and asserted that it did not correct what it claimed to be the misleading and deceptive words of the original advertisement. The applicant sought from the respondent undertakings as to the content of future advertisements but the respondent refused to give them.

Thereupon the present proceedings were commenced. By its defence the respondent denies that it has engaged in conduct proscribed by s. 52. Further, it relies upon the publication of the follow-up advertisement and an undertaking it has given to the Commission not to re-publish the original advertisement as justification for the Court refusing the relief claimed by the applicant. It also claims that the applicant has been guilty of laches, acquiescence and delay in bringing the proceedings.

The respondent applied to have the statement of claim struck out upon grounds which are no longer material. The application was refused. Leave to appeal against the decision was granted, but the appeal was dismissed: (1988) 19 FCR 469.

3. *Was the advertisement published "in trade or commerce"?*

It was submitted on behalf of the respondent that in publishing the advertisement it did not engage in conduct in trade or commerce. It was argued that the advertisement should be read as a contribution to the public health debate as to the alleged effect of environmental tobacco smoke on the health of non-smokers and that it has only a tenuous connection with dealings between cigarette manufacturers and distributors on the one hand and smokers on the other. It was argued that conduct is not proscribed by s. 52 if it is merely conduct in relation to trade or commerce, that s. 52 applies only to conduct *in* trade or commerce, and that the most that can be said of the respondent's conduct in publishing the advertisement is that it was conduct of the former kind.

It was further submitted that there is a great range of plausible circumstances in which people may make statements calculated to affect the lives and pecuniary interests of others. Counsel postulated the example of a campaign in support of higher indirect taxation which, if heeded by government, might affect the price of goods and thus their market appeal. The legislature cannot have intended, so it was submitted, that such political or intellectual activities would constitute conduct in trade or commerce within the meaning of those words in s. 52. Such conduct, so it was said, would plainly be conduct which may affect trade or commerce and thus, in one sense, be conduct in relation to trade or commerce but it would not be conduct within the purview of s. 52 because it would not be conduct *in* trade or commerce.

As was pointed out in *Concrete Constructions (NSW) Pty Ltd v. Nelson* (1990) ATPR ¶41-022 at pp 51,363-51,364; (1990) 64 ALJR 293 at 295 by *Mason* CJ, *Deane, Dawson* and *Gaudron* JJ. the words "trade or commerce" when used in the context of s. 52 of the *Trade Practices Act* are not terms of art but are terms of common knowledge of the widest import. As their Honours there said, the real problem involved in the construction of s. 52 arises from the requirement that the conduct to which the section refers be "in" trade or commerce. Their Honours said:

> "The phrase 'in trade or commerce' in sec. 52 has a restrictive operation. It qualifies the prohibition against engaging in conduct of the specified kind. As a matter of language, a prohibition against engaging in conduct 'in trade or commerce' can be construed as encompassing conduct in the course of the myriad of activities which are not, of their nature, of a trading or commercial character but which are undertaken in the course of, or as incidental to, the carrying on of an overall trading or commercial business. If the words 'in trade or commerce' in sec. 52 are construed in that sense, the provisions of the section would extend, for example, to a case where the misleading or deceptive conduct was a failure by a driver to give the correct hand signal when driving a truck in the course of a corporation's haulage business. It would also extend to a case, such as the present, where the alleged misleading or deceptive conduct consisted of the giving of inaccurate information by one employee to another in the course of carrying on the building activities of a commercial builder. Alternatively, the reference to conduct 'in trade or commerce' in sec. 52 can be construed as referring only to conduct which is itself an aspect or element of activities or transactions which, of their nature, bear a trading or commercial character. So construed, to borrow and adapt words used by *Dixon* J. in a different context in *Bank of N.S.W. v. The Commonwealth* (1948) 76 C.L.R. 1 at p. 381, the words 'in trade or commerce' refer to 'the central conception' of trade or commerce and not to the 'immense field of activities' in which corporations may engage in the course of, or for the purposes of, carrying on some overall trading or commercial business.
>
> As a matter of mere language, the arguments favouring and militating against these alternative constructions of sec. 52 are fairly evenly balanced. The scope of the prohibition imposed by sec. 52 is, however, governed not only by 'the terms in which it is created' but by 'the context in which it is found': see *Yorke v. Lucas* (1985) ATPR ¶40-622 at p. 47,055; (1985) 158 C.L.R. 661 at p. 668; and, generally, *Bank of N.S.W. v. The Commonwealth*, at p. 285. In that regard, it is of particular significance that the words 'trade' and 'commerce' have 'about them a chameleon-like hue, readily adapting themselves to their surroundings': *O'Brien v. Smolonogov* (1983) ATPR ¶40-418 at p. 44,851; (1983) 53 A.L.R. 107 at p. 113, quoting *F.C of T. v. Whitfords Beach Pty. Ltd.* (1981-1982) 150 C.L.R. 355 at pp. 378-379. Section 52(2) precludes limiting the scope of sec. 52(1) by implication drawn from the contents of other provisions of Pt V. Nonetheless, when the section is read in the context provided by other features of the Act, which is 'An Act relating to certain Trade Practices', the narrower (i.e. the second) of the alternative constructions of the requirement 'in trade or commerce' is the preferable one. Indeed, in the context of Pt V of the Act with its heading 'Consumer Protection', it is plain that sec. 52 was not intended to extend to all conduct, regardless of its nature, in which a corporation might engage in the course of, or for the purposes of, its overall trading or commercial business. Put differently, the section was not intended to impose, by a side-wind, an overlay of Commonwealth law upon every field of legislative control into which a corporation might stray for the purposes of, or in connection with, carrying on its trading or commercial activities. What the section is concerned with is the conduct of a corporation towards persons, be they consumers or not, with whom it (or those whose interest it represents or is seeking to promote) has or may have dealings in the course of those activities or transactions which, of their nature, bear a trading or commercial character. Such conduct includes, of course, promotional activities in relation to, or for the purposes of, the supply of goods or services to actual or potential consumers, be they identified persons or merely an unidentifiable section of the public."

Cigarettes are articles of commerce and restrictions on their use by consumers may render them less attractive as such, resulting in adverse economic consequences for their manufacturers and distributors. No doubt the participation by a trading corporation in a debate on a matter of public or social controversy will often not be conduct in trade or commerce. But the publication of the advertisement in the present case should not be viewed in isolation. It was published by a trading corporation which, so it may be safely inferred, was concerned to ensure that the sale of cigarettes would not be adversely affected by a belief on the part of the public as to a possible causal link between cigarette smoke and disease in non-smokers. The existence of such a link, or of evidence suggesting it, could affect the sale of cigarettes in various ways, e.g. public pressure to restrict the smoking of cigarettes in places where non-smokers are present.

The advertisement had the potential, and was no doubt intended, to protect the commercial interests of cigarette manufacturers and distributors. Accepting that conduct "in trade or commerce" is confined to conduct which is itself an aspect of activities which, of their nature, bear a commercial character I think the proper conclusion is that the publication of the advertisement was conduct "in trade or commerce". Advertising products for sale is an aspect or element of the selling of those products. The selling of the products is indisputably a trading or commercial activity. Advertising may serve a number of purposes. One purpose may be to refute criticism of the seller's products thus protecting the market for them. The advertisement published by the respondent was calculated to achieve such a purpose.

To borrow the words used by *Dixon* J. in *Bank of New South Wales v. The Commonwealth* (1948) 76 CLR 1 at 381 quoted in *Concrete Constructions* at 295, the publication of the advertisement was an activity within "the central conception" of trade or commerce. In my opinion the publication of the advertisement was conduct "in trade or commerce".

4. *The meaning of the advertisement*

(i) *Context and class of readers*

The meaning that the words of the third paragraph of the advertisement convey to a reader is of central importance to the case. Much argument was directed to the meaning of the words "evidence", "proves scientifically" and "disease". In my opinion it would be wrong to ascribe a meaning to any of those words, or to the whole paragraph, in isolation from the context in which they are set. As *Gibbs* C.J. observed in *Parkdale Custom Built Furniture Pty Ltd v. Puxu Pty Ltd* (1982) 149 CLR 191 at 199, where the conduct complained of consists of words it would not be right to select some words only and to ignore others which provide the context which gives meaning to the particular words.

When considering whether readers would be misled or deceived by the words complained of, regard must be had to the class of persons likely to read the advertisement. The advertisement is directed at the general reading public.

(ii) *Meaning of "evidence"*

It is plain that the reference to "evidence" is not a reference only to material that would be admissible in a court of law. Even in the argot of lawyers, "evidence" includes, in some context, hearsay material. The first meaning given for the word in the *Macquarie Dictionary* is "ground for belief". In para. 3 of the advertisement the word is used in the collocation of words "evidence ... that cigarette smoke causes disease ..." In my opinion many readers would understand the word as referring to data or material which affords grounds for believing that cigarette smoke causes disease in non-smokers. Such material would, in my opinion, include the published results of studies and research work, including collection of data, undertaken by scientists of repute. Many such published results, in the form of articles which have appeared in learned scientific journals, were tendered as part of the applicant's case and I admitted them into evidence.

Articles of this kind were referred to during the course of the case as "primary articles" and it will be convenient to so describe them in these reasons. Some of the primary articles contained comments by the authors on the research work and opinions of others and objection was taken to the admissibility of such comments.

The applicant also tendered a number of reports issued by scientific organisations and professional bodies which have considered the question whether cigarette smoke adversely affects the health of non-smokers. These reports were referred to during the course of the trial as "major reviews" and I shall so describe them in these reasons. They included the following: a monograph on the evaluation of the carcinogenic risk of chemicals to humans issued by the International Agency for Research on Cancer, which is part of the World Health Organisation ("the IARC report"); a report of a working party on the effects of passive smoking on health adopted by the Australian National Health and Medical Research Council ("the NH & MRC report"); a report on environmental tobacco smoke by the National Research Council, which is the principal operating agency of the National Academy of Sciences of the United States of America ("the N.R.C. report"); a report made in 1986 by the Surgeon General of the United States of America on the health consequences of involuntary smoking ("the Surgeon General's report"); and the fourth report of the Independent Scientific Committee on Smoking and Health, being a committee appointed by the British Government and chaired by Sir Peter Froggatt ("the Froggatt report").

Mr O'Keefe Q.C., senior counsel for the respondent, submitted that the major reviews were not admissible as opinion evidence to show the state of science nor admissible as evidence of the existence, extent or quality of "evidence ... that cigarette smoke causes disease in non-smokers". He submitted that the passages in the major reviews upon which the applicant relies are based upon nothing more than the work and opinions of other scientists. He contended that the reviews were no more than hearsay out-of-court statements which could not be identified with any particular member or members of the committees responsible for their authorship. In his submission, the reference to "evidence" in the advertisement cannot reasonably be understood as referring to opinions expressed by scientists or a group of scientists on the original work of other scientists.

It was also argued that although the primary articles might be admissible to show what had appeared in the scientific literature, they were not admissible to prove the proposition that cigarette smoke causes disease in non-smokers.

I appreciate the force of these arguments, but it is necessary to keep firmly in mind that the question in the present case is whether the statement made in para. 3 of the advertisement is misleading or deceptive or likely to mislead or deceive. In my opinion, many readers of the advertisement would think that the reference to "evidence" is a reference to, inter alia, opinions of competent scientists whether based on their own research or on the published results of the research of others.

First, I think the opinions of competent experts on a matter falling within their field of expertise may afford grounds for belief as to that matter. Many readers (amongst whom would be included the educated as well as the uneducated and the adolescent as well as the mature) would understand such opinions to be evidence relevant to the question whether cigarette smoke causes disease in non-smokers. This understanding would be reinforced by a reading of the entire advertisement. Paragraph 3 is immediately followed by a number of paragraphs in which references are made to published findings and conclusions of scientists and groups of scientists. These references include a statement, in heavy type, that: "Major reviews on 'passive smoking' over the last few years have concluded that passive smoking cannot be shown to be a health risk". This statement is in turn followed by a reference to the "weight of evidence" which is said to be ascertained from the summation of views of persons who had attended a Health Conference in Vienna. In my opinion readers of the advertisement would conclude that there is little in the form of published opinions of scientists or groups of scientists to support the proposition that cigarette smoke causes disease in non-smokers. Accordingly, I think the major reviews are admissible to show whether readers would be misled if they reached that conclusion.

My decision in this case would have been the same had I formed a different view as to the admissibility of the major reviews. This is not surprising, since the contents of the primary articles which I admitted into evidence constitute the great bulk of the material upon which the authors of the major reviews base their opinions.

It was submitted that a reader who held the belief that the opinion of a scientist or a group of scientists was "evidence" would not hold that belief as a result of anything said in the advertisement, but rather as a result of his own misconception: cf. *Puxu* at p. 225. There would be something to be said for this argument if the advertisement did not contain references to findings and conclusions of scientists. But the inclusion of those references in the advertisement makes the argument unsustainable.

(iii) *Meaning of "scientific proof"*

It is necessary to consider what the phrase "nothing which proves scientifically" conveys to the reader of the advertisement. There was substantial consensus between witnesses that scientists themselves do not commonly use the term "scientific proof". Dr Leslie, a witness called by the respondent, said: "I do not think one ever talks about scientific proof".

Dr Armstrong, a witness called by the applicant, said that every scientist recognises that, at any particular point in time, his knowledge is imperfect and that with the advance of knowledge something which he presently thinks is proven may subsequently be proven to be wrong. He said that scientists accordingly resile from any belief in absolute proof and recognise that proof is relative to the existing state of knowledge. As another witness, Dr Le Souef, said: "The philosophical approach of science is that you cannot absolutely prove anything just as there is no absolute truth."

Nevertheless several witnesses gave what might be called working definitions of scientific proof. Dr Armstrong said: "The only real meaning of scientific proof that I can contribute is that one has a sufficient conviction about the certainty as to take certain consequential actions. The difficulty about this approach is that it gives a variable meaning to scientific proof according to the consequential action that may be called for. Dr Armstrong himself recognised this. As he said (T.1478):

> "... I do not believe that there exists any objective or identifiable standard which equals scientific proof. It is very much dependent upon the circumstances for which it is used. In the case of public health measures I would say that the necessary level of proof had been attained when it was considered to be more likely than not that the proposition was true. ... That is good enough when you are dealing with matters pertaining to public health and particularly, and again one would have to qualify this, where the measure that you propose is one which involves the removal of a hazard."

I think an observation made by Dr Witorsch, who was called by the respondent, affords the best guide to a definition of scientific proof. He said, in effect, that scientifically a proposition is proved when the data in support of it is compelling. I do not think Dr Witorsch's approach differs much from that taken by one of the applicant's witnesses, Sir Richard Doll, who thought that scientific proof was proof beyond reasonable doubt or "convincing" scientific proof.

I think that in the context of the advertisement, the words "nothing which proves scientifically that cigarette smoke causes disease in non-smokers" mean "nothing which affords compelling or convincing evidence that cigarette smoke causes disease in non-smokers". This is the meaning which I think most readers would give to the words.

5. *Admissibility of evidence to show that statements in advertisement continued to be misleading after date of publication*

The advertisement appeared in newspapers on 1 July 1986. Proceedings were not commenced in this Court until 11 June 1987. On that date an application was filed in which a claim was made for, inter alia, an order in the following terms:

> "1. An injunction restraining the Respondent its servants and agents from, in trade or commerce, engaging in conduct that is misleading or deceptive or is likely to mislead in the following respects:
>
> > a. stating that there is little evidence and nothing which proves scientifically that cigarette smoke causes disease in non-smokers;"

In the statement of claim, which was also filed on 11 June 1987, after references to the publication of the advertisement and other preliminary matters the allegation is made in para. 6 that, contrary to the statements contained in the advertisement, it is not the case that there is little evidence and nothing which proves scientifically that cigarette smoke causes disease in non-smokers. There follows an allegation that "in the premises" in or about July 1986 the respondent engaged in conduct proscribed by s. 52. Further allegations are then made that the applicant complained of the respondent's conduct to the Trade Practices Commission, that the Commission thereupon took certain action, and that consequent upon that action the respondent published a further advertisement in which it did nothing to correct the misleading conduct referred to earlier in the statement of claim. Thereafter allegations are made that the applicant sought an undertaking from the respondent "that it would not, in any future advertisement or promotional material, represent that there is little evidence and nothing which proves scientifically that cigarette smoke causes disease in non-smokers or any similar assertion". Allegations are then made that the respondent declined to provide the undertaking and in the final paragraph (para. 18) it is alleged that: "In the premises, the respondent has continued in trade or commerce to engage in conduct that is misleading, deceptive or is likely to mislead or deceive in contravention of Section 52 of the *Trade Practices Act*".

By its defence the respondent admitted that the undertaking had been sought from it and that it had declined to give it.

At the commencement of the hearing senior counsel for the applicant submitted to the Court a document which, according to him, identified the issues which fell to be determined in the case. One of the issues was said to be whether the statement in para. 3 of the advertisement "... is and would be true as from the date these proceedings are determined ...". Another issue was said to be whether the statement "was true when these proceedings were commenced in June 1987". In a similar document submitted to the Court by senior counsel for the respondent, one of the issues was said in effect to be whether the respondent was proposing to republish the advertisement.

Relevantly for present purposes, s. 80(1) of the Act provides that where the Court is satisfied that a person has engaged or is proposing to engage, in conduct that constitutes or would constitute a contravention of a provision of Part V of the Act (in which s. 52 appears) it may grant an injunction in such terms as it determines to be appropriate.

Since no claim for damages was made in the application, I take the essential allegations to be that the respondent on 1 July 1986 engaged in conduct proscribed by s. 52, that it had declined to undertake not to engage in similar conduct in the future, and that, accordingly, an injunction was sought pursuant to s. 80(1) of the Act to restrain the respondent from engaging in similar conduct.

As I have observed, it is alleged in para. 6 that "... it *is* not the case that there is little evidence ..." (emphasis added). Having regard to the use of the present tense, this is an allegation as to the state of the evidence at the date of the statement of claim, i.e. 11 June 1987.

However, it was argued on behalf of the respondent that the allegation in para. 8 that "In the premises, the Respondent did in or about July 1986, in trade or commerce, engage in conduct that was misleading ..." confines the allegation in para. 6 to the state of affairs that existed on 1 July 1986. It was submitted that because the Court has power under s. 80(4)(a) of the Act to grant an injunction restraining a person from engaging in conduct proscribed by s. 52, whether or not it appears to the Court that the person intends to engage again in conduct of that kind, the statement of claim should be construed as if there is no allegation that the respondent is proposing to engage in a repetition of past conduct.

I do not think the respondent's construction of the statement of claim is correct. Having regard particularly to the relief claimed in the application I think it is reasonably plain that what the applicant alleges is that by publishing the advertisement on 1 July 1986 the respondent engaged in conduct proscribed by s. 52, that it subsequently did nothing to correct that conduct, that it had refused to give an undertaking not to engage in similar conduct in the future and that accordingly it had continued in trade or commerce to engage in the conduct complained of. It is true that it would have been preferable for para. 18 of the statement of claim to have been framed so as to allege that the respondent "has continued and threatens to continue" rather than "has continued". But I think that on a fair reading of para. 18 it contains an allegation that the conduct complained of has continued up to the date of the statement of claim.

I should add that since the grant of the relief sought in the application requires the exercise of the Court's discretion the applicant was entitled to call evidence to prove that the statement remained misleading and deceptive as at the date of trial to persuade the Court to exercise the discretion in its favour.

There was much pre-trial correspondence between the parties in which particulars were sought and given of the allegations in the statement of claim. The respondent argues that this correspondence shows that the applicant particularised its claim in a manner different from the way I interpret the allegations in the statement of claim. There is some imprecision in the particulars given by the applicants but, in my opinion they do not limit the issues as the respondent contends. Accordingly, the respondent's submission that 1 July 1986 is the only relevant date for examining the correctness of the statement in the advertisement should be rejected.

6. *Nature of passive smoking*

Passive smoking involves inhalation of tobacco smoke from two sources: sidestream smoke and exhaled mainstream smoke. Sidestream smoke is smoke that is emitted directly from a burning cigarette, pipe or cigar. Mainstream smoke is cigarette smoke which is drawn through the tobacco into the smoker's mouth. The term "environmental tobacco smoke" refers to the combination of sidestream smoke and the fraction of exhaled mainstream smoke not retained by the smoker. In contrast with mainstream smoke, environmental tobacco smoke is diluted into a larger volume of air, and it ages prior to inhalation. Mainstream smoke, sidestream smoke and environmental tobacco smoke are sometimes referred to as "MS", "SS" and "ETS" respectively.

7. *Cancer* (i) *Explanation of some epidemiological and other terms*

In support of its case that the statement in para. 3 of the advertisement is misleading or deceptive or likely to mislead or deceive in so far as it relates to the disease of cancer, the applicant relied upon the evidence of a number of witnesses and the primary articles and major reviews to which I have referred. Before referring to the oral evidence it is convenient to set out some of the more important findings referred to in some of the primary articles. An understanding of the articles will be enhanced by a brief explanation of some of the terms used in the literature.

Epidemiology relies on statistical analysis of populations to estimate the incidence of disease amongst those exposed to particular agents. Results are usually reported in terms of odds ratios or relative risk ratios. These reflect the ratio between the frequency of, say, a disease in an exposed group and that in an unexposed group. A risk ratio of 1.0 means that the disease is no more frequent in the exposed group than in the unexposed group. In crude terms, a relative risk above 1.0 is said to be positive and one below 1.0 is said to be negative.

These results can be characterised as being statistically significant or not. Statistical significance is an expression of the relative confidence that a particular result is a true effect and not due merely to chance. The level of statistical significance conventionally used in the scientific literature is the 95% confidence level. If a result, or range of results, is statistically significant at the 95% confidence level then it means that the probability that those results are due merely to chance or random variation is 1 in 20 or less. The reader can be 95% sure that the true effect is the result as reported.

Often that result is reported as a range of values clustered around a single value called a point estimate. The point estimate is the best estimate of the relative risk, based on the available data. The two figures on either side of the point estimate (the upper and lower confidence limits) define the range of values which are also well supported by the data, at the chosen confidence level. This range is known as the confidence interval.

To take an example, an investigation of the association between exposure (to an agent) and outcome (disease), having opted for a confidence level of 95%, may produce a point estimate of 2.5, with upper and lower confidence limits of 3.5 and 1.5. This means that based on the raw data, the best estimate is that those exposed have a 2½ times greater chance of experiencing the disease than those not exposed. Further, one can be 95% sure that the true relative risk is somewhere between 1.5 and 3.5.

If the interval between the upper and lower confidence limits is wide, then the point estimate is less reliable than if it is narrow. Wide confidence intervals usually indicate a small number of observations.

The final point to note is the relationship between confidence intervals and statistical significance. The relative risk of disease normally associated with pure chance is 1.0: no increased risk, no decreased risk. So, using say the 95% confidence level, if the value 1.0 lies between the reported upper and lower confidence levels, then the probability that the result is due to chance has not been satisfactorily excluded, at the 95% level. Whenever the confidence interval straddles 1.0 then the result is not statistically significant. Two further illustrations may assist. Assume a 95% confidence level. Study A reports a point estimate of 2.5, with a confidence interval of 1.5 to 3.5. Study B reports a point estimate of 2.5 with a confidence interval of 0.8 to 4.0. The results in study A are statistically significant, those in study B are not.

I set out hereunder brief descriptions of some of the technical terms commonly found in the literature.

Case control study — a group who have a disease (the cases) are selected, and matched to a group who do not (the controls). Researchers then investigate whether or not individuals in each group were exposed to the agent of interest, and those results are then compared. A disease appears first and the investigation of exposure occurs retrospectively.

Cohort study — a group (cohort) of individuals is identified and then divided into those exposed and those who are not. The cohort is followed for a number of years, and the individuals who contract the disease are identified to determine if there is any difference in incidence between the groups. Accordingly, cohort studies are generally prospective.

Dose response relationship — a dose response relationship occurs when the observed incidence of the disease increases as the dose (or exposure to the relevant agent) increases. Such a relationship increases the likelihood that a statistical association in fact represents a true association.

Trend test — a test of statistical significance applied across a set of results to ascertain the probability that such a sequence of results could have been obtained by chance.

Publication bias — due to social, academic and other pressures, it may be that positive research results are written up and/or accepted for publication more frequently than are negative results. This can yield spurious results in meta-analysis.

Misclassification — if subjects are incorrectly classified then it may produce spurious results. The most commonly cited example in this case is the possibility of smokers claiming for a variety of social, medical and other reasons that they are non-smokers. Because of the strong association between active smoking and lung cancer, such misclassification artificially inflates the risk of lung cancer amongst non-smokers.

Confounding — this occurs when sources other than the exposure of interest (e.g. environmental tobacco smoke) operate to affect the outcome, and are not controlled for by researchers. Examples may include work-place pollution, diet, lifestyle, etc.

Data dredging — if within the one study, a number of hypothesised associations are tested, then a high or low result in one particular category might be expected to occur by pure chance. If 20 hypotheses are tested, for example, it would not be surprising to find that one of them is statistically significant at the 95% confidence level. To seize upon such isolated results is said to be data dredging.

Meta-analysis — this is a statistical technique used to combine the results of individual epidemiological studies, in order to derive a quantitative summarisation of data relating to a particular area of investigation.

Mutagenic — a mutagenic substance is a chemical that can induce change in the genetic material in a manner that is thought to be fundamental to the initiation of cancer.

Histological diagnosis of cancer — this biological technique involves obtaining a tissue sample from the patient and examining it under a microscope. It is considered the most reliable form of cancer diagnosis, particularly for distinguishing between primary and secondary cancers.

Cytological diagnosis of cancer — in the case of lung cancer, cytology involves obtaining cells from the lungs either by having the patient cough up cells in the sputum, or washing cells from the lung by use of bronchoalveolar lavage, or extraction with a specialised hollow needle under X-ray control. For a variety of reasons cytological diagnosis of cancer is not considered to be as comprehensive or reliable as histological diagnosis.

(ii) *The primary articles*

(a) *Trichopoulos et al.* — Lung Cancer and Passive Smoking

This study was published in the *International Journal of Cancer* in 1981. The abstract of the article, as published, reads as follows:

> "Fifty-one women with lung cancer and 163 other hospital patients were interviewed regarding the smoking habits of themselves and their husbands. Forty of the lung cancer cases and 149 of the other patients were non-smokers. Among the non-smoking women there was a statistically significant difference between the cancer cases and the other patients with respect to their husbands' smoking habits. Estimates of the relative risk of lung cancer associated with having a husband who smokes were 2.4 for a smoker of less than one pack and 3.4 for women whose husbands smoked more than one pack of cigarettes per day. The limitations of the data are examined; it is evident that further investigation of this issue is warranted."

This was a case-control study, the cases being all of the female, caucasian patients registered as residents of Athens who were admitted to any of three large hospitals in Athens between September 1978 and June 1980 with a final diagnosis of lung cancer other than adenocarcinoma or alveolar carcinoma. Of the 51 cases identified, 14 were histologically and 19 cytologically confirmed. In 18 cases the diagnosis was based on clinical and radiological evidence. A table published as part of the study shows the distribution of non-smoking women with lung cancer and of non-smoking control women according to current smoking habits of their husbands. The published data showed a statistically significant association between the husband's smoking and the woman's lung cancer risk. A non-smoking woman whose husband was a regular smoker had a risk of developing lung cancer which was twice as high as that of a non-smoking woman married to a non-smoker.

The authors of the study stated that it had obvious limitations, most seriously that the number of cases was small but that nevertheless the association between passive smoking and lung cancer was unlikely to be due to chance. They drew attention to the fact that, according to their study, the relative risk associated with passive smoking, i.e. 2.4 for all categories of smokers combined, was only slightly lower than the figure of 2.9 associated with active smoking by the women themselves. The authors offer a possible explanation for this circumstance in the text of their study.

The study reported in the *International Journal of Cancer* in 1981 was continued and further results of it were published in *The Lancet* in September 1983. The authors reported that there were then twice as may cases and 50% more controls in the study, but that the results remained substantially the same. The 1983 study, as published, wrongly calculated the relative risks. The correct relative risks of lung cancer associated with having a husband who smoked were 1.9 for a smoker of less than one pack and 2.5 for women whose husbands smoked more than one pack of cigarettes per day. Professor Trichopoulos explained in oral evidence that the equivalent figures which appeared in the 1983 publication, i.e. 2.4 and 3.4, were typographical errors. The 1983 figures (1.9 and 2.5) relate to the total data collected in the whole of the study, not merely to the data collected since the publication of the first study.

The authors concluded their 1983 study with a reference to a table including the abovementioned risk ratios of 1.9 and 2.5 and stated:

> "The table increases the credibility of the hypothesis implicating passive smoking as a factor in lung cancer. Given the small size in the relative risk and the many potential sources of bias, no single study will be able to provide convincing evidence for or against this hypothesis; only the convergence of results from different studies in different populations will permit a reasonably sound conclusion. We consider the Athens study a step in this direction."

(b) *Hirayama* — Nonsmoking wives of heavy smokers have a higher risk of lung cancer: a study from Japan

In the *British Medical Journal* of January 1981 Professor Hirayama, Chief of the Epidemiology Division of the National Cancer Centre Research Institute, Tokyo, published findings of a study undertaken in Japan. The abstract of the findings as published in the article is as follows:

"In a study in 29 health centre districts in Japan 91,540 non-smoking wives aged 40 and above were followed up for 14 years (1966-79), and standardised mortality rates for lung cancer were assessed according to the smoking habits of their husbands. Wives of heavy smokers were found to have a higher risk of developing lung cancer and a dose-response relation was observed. The relation between the husband's smoking and the wife's risk of developing lung cancer showed a similar pattern when analysed by age and occupation of the husband. The risk was particularly great in agricultural families when the husbands were aged 40-59 at enrolment. The husbands' smoking habit did not affect their wives' risk of dying from other disease such as stomach cancer, cervical cancer, and ischaemic heart disease. The risk of developing emphysema and asthma seemed to be higher in non-smoking wives of heavy smokers but the effect was not statistically significant.

The husband's drinking habit seemed to have no effect on any causes of death in their wives, including lung cancer.

These results indicate the possible importance of passive or indirect smoking as one of the causal factors of lung cancer. They also appear to explain the long-standing riddle of why many women develop lung cancer although they themselves are non-smokers. These results also cast doubt on the practice of assessing the relative risk of developing lung cancer in smokers by comparing them with non-smokers."

(c) *Hirayama* — Cancer Mortality in Nonsmoking Women with Smoking Husbands Based on a Large-Scale Cohort Study in Japan

This article (which appeared in *Preventive Medicine* in 1984) reported further conclusions reached by Professor Hirayama as a result of further data derived from his study referred to in the preceding article. The abstract of this further study reads as follows:

"Mortality of 91,540 non-smoking wives was studied in relation to the smoking habits of their husbands by means of a cohort study in Japan. During 16 years of follow-up, 200 deaths from lung cancer took place. The relative risks of lung cancer in these non-smoking wives were 1.00, 1.36, 1.42, 1.58 and 1.91 when husbands were nonsmokers, ex-smokers, or daily smokers of 1-14, 15-19, or 20 or more cigarettes daily, respectively. Corresponding relative risks for stomach cancer were 1.00, 1.16, 1.00, 1.00, and 1.01 respectively. Specificity of association and internal consistencies were observed. Among cancers of each site, a similar tendency toward risk elevation in non-smoking wives with smoking husbands was observed for nasal sinus cancer, brain tumors, and cancer of all sites besides lung cancer. In interpreting these results, the significance of proximity in exposure to sidestream smoke in Japanese homes was stressed."

Professor Hirayama made the following observation:

"This study confirms the correlation between lung cancer and spousal smoking reported previously. The correlation is quite specific in terms of diseases. For instance, no risk elevation at all was observed for stomach cancer. A striking internal consistency of association was also observed. The results were essentially similar when observed in terms of age of husbands, age of wives, occupation of husbands, and differing periods of observation. The results are in line with a Greek study by Trichopoulos and others and a U.S. study by Correa and others (external consistency), although they are slightly at variance with an American Cancer Society study in the United States and a case-control study conducted by Kabat and Wynder."

The reference to the American Cancer Society study is a reference to Garfinkel's study (infra).

Professor Hirayama also observed:

"When the effects of passive smoking due to husbands' smoking were compared with the effects of direct smoking in women, the results clearly indicated that the effect of passive smoking is less than one-fifth that of direct smoking. ... In terms of attributable risk, however, the effect of passive smoking on lung cancer in women is nearly as important as that of direct smoking because the population of intrahousehold passive smokers at risk is four times greater ... than the population of active smokers ... Therefore, although the relative risk of indirect smoking is much smaller than that of direct smoking the absolute excess deaths from lung cancer due to passive smoking may be quite important because of the large size of the exposed group — especially in countries such as Japan where the majority (nearly 70%) of adult men smoke but only a minority (15% or less) of adult women smoke.''

(d) *Garfinkel* — Time Trends in Lung Cancer Mortality Among Nonsmokers and a Note on Passive Smoking

This article appeared in the *Journal of the National Cancer Institute* in June 1981.

The author concluded that compared to non-smoking women married to non-smoking husbands, non-smokers married to smoking husbands showed very little, if any, increased risk of lung cancer. The study revealed a small increased risk of lung cancer for non-smokers married to smokers. The increased risk was not statistically significant. The mortality ratios for lung cancer in non-smoking women were 1.27 when the husbands were daily smokers of less than 20 cigarettes, and 1.10 when they smoked more than 20 cigarettes per day. The data examined by Garfinkel led him to conclude that ''it seems doubtful that those non-smokers who had been heavily exposed to cigarette smoke from others in their lives could have had many more precursor lesions for the development of lung cancer than non-smokers not so exposed. Therefore, there is evidence from these studies that passive smoking cannot play more than a very small role in the development of lung cancer''.

(e) *Chan and Fung* — Lung Cancer in Non-smokers in Hong Kong

This study was carried out in Hong Kong and was published in 1982. The relevant finding in the study is at variance with that found in the Hirayama 1981 study. Whereas Hirayama found that the mortality from lung cancer of non-smoking women exposed to cigarette smoke of their husband's was increased twofold, that was not confirmed by this study. The authors acknowledge that the group studied by them was very small in comparison to the group studied by Hirayama.

(f) *Correa et al.* — Passive Smoking and Lung Cancer

This study appeared in *The Lancet* in September 1983. Correa et al. undertook a case-control study involving 1338 lung cancer patients and 1393 comparison subjects in Louisiana, USA. They found that non-smokers marrried to heavy smokers had an increased risk of lung cancer, as did subjects whose mothers smoked. No association was found between lung cancer risk and paternal smoking. The authors said, inter alia,

''Spouse-smoking Effect

Our data strengthen the contention that heavy smoking by one member of the spouse pair increases the lung cancer risk of the non-smoking partner. Heavy smoking by wives may increase the risk of the light smoking husband but this finding requires further analysis and confirmation in larger series. Smoking by husbands did not affect the risk of lung cancer in women who smoked (relative risk 1.03), a finding that suggests that active smoking is so powerful that it overshadows any possible additional effect from concomitant passive exposure.

...

The effect of the smoking habits of the spouse on lung cancer risk was first reported by Hirayama in a Japanese cohort study. A cohort study in the United States reported a positive but not significant increase in risk for non-smoking women married to smoking husbands. A case-control study of non-smoking women diagnosed as having lung cancer in Greece reported relative risks of approximately 2.5 for those married to moderate smokers and 3 for those married to heavy smokers, with a significant linear trend. Our numbers are small but we think that the similarity between our findings and those of Trichopoulos et al. strengthens the suspicion that passive smoking may contribute to lung cancer risk.

Parental Smoking Effect

As far as we know, ours is the first case-control study of lung cancer reporting on parental smoking history. Parents' smoking behaviour influences the smoking habits of their offspring, but we found that the smoking behaviour of the father does not influence the lung cancer risk of his offspring whereas the behaviour of the mother does. This difference may reflect the closer and more prolonged contact that infants and young children have with their mothers than with their fathers.''

The authors expressed their conclusion as follows:

> ''The differences between the effects of passive exposure to spouse and maternal smoking are puzzling. Passive exposure to spouse smoking is mostly detected in non-smokers and light smoking males; maternal passive smoking effects are seen mostly in smokers. Passive smoking from spouses is introduced in adult life and in smokers is concurrent with their own active smoking. The magnitude of such an effect may be low when compared with active concomitant smoking and it may not be detectable when both types of smoking are present.
>
> Maternal smoking on the other hand, exerts its influences early in life and in the absence of active smoking is probably insufficient to produce carcinogenic effects. Our findings indicate that maternal smoking results in a slight increase in lung cancer risk but do not indicate whether the effect is due to enhanced active smoking of the offspring or to enhanced susceptibility to lung cancer induction after the challenge of active smoking later in life.''

(g) *Koo et al.* — Active and passive smoking among female lung cancer patients and controls in Hong Kong

This was a case control study carried out in Hong Kong and published in 1983. The study, in which the number of cases and controls were fairly small, did not reveal a positive association between lung cancer and passive smoking. The authors observed:

> ''Thus, if passive smoking had contributed to the risk for never smokers, it could only have acted as a co-factor in a multi-factorial aetiology. The controversial findings of various researchers ... on the role of passive smoking in lung cancer could well be due to a failure in identifying other co-factors in the carcinogenesis.''

(The reference to the ''various researchers'' is a reference to the findings of Garfinkel, Hirayama and Trichopoulos.)

(h) *Buffler et al.* — The Causes of Lung Cancer in Texas

This study was published in 1984 in *Lung Cancer: Causes and Prevention.* Amongst other results, the authors reported the following:

> ''The role of 'passive smoking' in contributing to risk of lung cancer was examined ... In this analysis the crude (or unadjusted) odds ratio are increased and significant for both males and females, 1.4 and 2.1, respectively. However, when the confounding effect of individual subject smoking was controlled by stratifying the male and female study groups into smokers (ever) and non-smokers (never) and examining the adjusted odds ratios, there was no significant increase in risk associated with passive smoking. In fact, the odds ratio for non-smokers living with a regular smoker were not increased for either males or females, 0.52 and 0.78, respectively. However, odds ratios for smokers living with a regular smoker were increased, although not significantly, 1.28 and 1.80 for males and females. The overall odds ratios (adjusted) associated with passive smoking were only slightly increased and not significant for eitheted7Xas [*sic*] females, 1.2 and 1.3, respectively. When the possibility of a 'passive smoking' effect was examined among non-smokers by the number of years lived with a regular smoker, there was very little difference in risk for females who lived with a regular smoker for 0-32 years. The odds ratios for males suggest an increase by [*sic*] are based on smaller numbers than the analysis in females.''

The authors noted that the ''lack of a 'passive smoking' effect when the confounding effect of smoking of individual study subjects is considered, is not consistent with early reports. Although subsequent reports are also not consistent with regard to this association, it may be that the study population available was not sufficiently large to detect a fairly low-level effect and that this association needs to be assessed in a considerably larger study population''.

(j) *Garfinkel et al.* — Involuntary smoking and lung cancer: A case-control study

This article appeared in the *Journal of the National Cancer Institute* in September 1985. The authors state, inter alia:

> "In a previous paper, we pointed out that in any study of involuntary smoking and lung cancer, categorizing nonsmokers by the smoking habit of the spouse may lead to error in classification of exposure. In the United States particularly, there may be many women, married to nonsmokers, who are exposed to the smoke of others at work or in other areas. Conversely, some individuals married to smokers may suffer acute effects from inhaling smoke and consciously avoid such exposure. A survey of 38,000 subjects by Friedman et al. confirmed this hypothesis. About 40% of women nonsmokers and 50% of men nonsmokers who were married to nonsmokers were exposed to the smoke of others for some periods of time during a week and 47% of nonsmoking women married to smokers reported that they were not exposed to tobacco smoke at home. In the study reported here, we record the smoking habit of husbands (total No. of cigarettes smoked and No. smoked at home), as well as the number of hours a day the subjects were exposed to the smoke of others at home, at work and in other areas.
>
> Other causes for concern are establishment of the microscopic diagnosis of primary lung cancer and verification of the smoking history. In a study of the histologic type of lung cancer in relation to asbestos exposure, 49 of 774 men and women with a discharge diagnosis of microscopically proved lung cancer were recorded as nonsmokers in the hospital chart. After review of hospital records, histologic sections, and interviews, only 10 cases remained who had died of primary lung cancer and who had never smoked. One-half of the others had smoked at some time and one-half the confirmed nonsmokers had a primary cancer other than that of the lung.
>
> It is apparent, therefore, that more studies on involuntary smoking are needed, with particular attention given to obtaining microscopic proof of primary lung cancer and more detailed information about exposures to cigarette smoke."

The authors undertook a case-control study in four hospitals from 1971 to 1981. All cases and controls were confirmed by histologic review of slides, and non-smoking status and exposures were verified by interviews. It was found that odds ratios increased with increasing numbers of cigarettes smoked by the husband, particularly if the cigarettes were smoked at home. The odds ratio for women whose husband smoked 20 or more cigarettes at home was 2.11. The authors' conclusions included the following:

> "We found an elevated risk of lung cancer, ranging from 13 to 31%, in women exposed to the smoke of others, although the increase was not statistically significant. The women who were married to smokers of 40 or more cigarettes a day or who were exposed to the smoke of at least 20 cigarettes a day at home showed a risk twice as high as that of women not exposed at all. This result is consistent with the dose-response risk of exposure to the husband's smoke shown in some case-control studies (2, 3)."

(The references at the end of the above quotation are references to Trichopoulos et al. (supra) and Correa et al. (supra).)

(k) *Akiba et al.* — Passive Smoking and Lung Cancer among Japanese Women

This article was published in the September 1986 issue of *Cancer Research,* but appears to have been first published prior to 1 July 1986 since it is referred to in the NH & MRC report which was adopted in June 1986.

The abstract of the article, as published, reads as follows:

> "A case-control study conducted in Hiroshima and Nagasaki, Japan, revealed a 50% increased risk of lung cancer among nonsmoking women whose husbands smoked. The risks tended to increase with amount smoked by the husband, being highest among women who worked outside the home and whose husbands were heavy smokers, and to decrease with cessation of exposure. The findings provide incentive for further evaluation of the relationship between passive smoking and cancer among nonsmokers."

The study was made as part of a case-control investigation of lung cancer among atomic bomb survivors conducted primarily to evaluate the interactive roles of cigarette smoking and ionizing radiation. Data were collected on the smoking habits of the subjects' spouses and parents. The article reports the effect of exposure to such passive smoking, particularly on married women who had never smoked themselves.

The study showed that there was an increase in lung cancer risk with increasing amounts smoked per day by the husband, with the odds ratio slightly exceeding 2 for women whose husbands were heavy smokers. The odds ratio of lung cancer among non-smoking women according to recency of exposure to their husbands' smoking were lower among women who had not been exposed within the last ten years than among women exposed within the last ten years.

All the results in this study were reported using 90% confidence intervals. The odds ratio for non-smoking females married to smoking husbands was 1.5, statistically significant at that level. For non-smoking husbands married to smoking wives the odds ratio was 1.8, not statically significant at the 90% level.

The authors said:

> "The results from this case-control study suggest that there may be a moderate excess in lung cancer risk associated with passive smoking. The odds ratios for lung cancer among non-smoking women tended to increase with amount smoked by their husbands, a trend seen among housewives as well as women who worked outside the home. The highest odds ratios among nonsmokers were for women who work in blue collar jobs whose husbands were heavy smokers, women presumably with the highest exposure to environmental tobacco smoke. There was little association with parental smoking or with ex-passive smoking, suggesting that cessation of exposure may lower risk.
>
> The findings are generally consistent with results of a national cohort study of mortality among Japanese women and of several epidemiological investigations conducted elsewhere in the world."

The Japanese study referred to by the authors is the Hirayama 1981 study, and the other studies to which they refer are the Trichopoulos et al. 1981 study, the Correa et al. 1983 study and the Garfinkel et al. 1985 study.

The authors admit to concerns about adequacy of data provided by surrogate respondents and reliability of diagnoses of lung cancer but also note some reassuring factors.

The authors summarise the views they formed as a result of their study as follows:

> "In summary, the results of this investigation suggest that exposure to environmental tobacco smoke may increase the risk of lung cancer among nonsmokers. The findings, from one of the two areas of the world where the possibility of a passive smoking hazard was first postulated, add to an accumulating body of evidence on the issue. While the total evidence is not definitive and not all studies show significantly positive associations, the results are suggestive enough to warrant further evaluation in larger studies where passive smoking exposures can be more fully quantified."

(1) *Lee et al.* — Relationship of passive smoking to risk of lung cancer and other smoking-associated diseases

This study was published in the *British Journal of Cancer* in 1986. The authors reported results based on 143 patients. They made the following observations:

> "Overall the results showed no evidence of an effect of passive smoking on lung cancer incidence among lifelong non-smokers. In male patients, relative risks were increased for some of the indices but numbers of cases were small and none of the differences approached statistical significance. In females, where numbers of cases were larger, such trends as existed tended to be negative ... The relative risk in relation to the spouse smoking during the whole of the marriage was estimated to be 0.80 for the sexes combined, with 95% confidence limits of 0.43 to 1.50."
>
> "In the present study no significant relationship of passive smoking to lung cancer incidence in lifelong non-smokers was seen, either in the analyses based on the information collected in hospital or in

subsequent inquiry of the spouses or both. It must be pointed out, however, that the number of lung cancer patients who had never smoked was rather small so that, though our findings are consistent with passive smoking having no effect on lung cancer risk at all, they do not exclude the possibility of a small increase in risk, ...''

(m) *Humble et al.* — Marriage to a Smoker and Lung Cancer Risk

This study appeared in the *American Journal of Public Health* in May 1987. In the introduction to their study, the authors make the following statement:

> ''In 1980 we began collecting data in a population-based case-control study designed to explain differing lung cancer occurrence in Hispanic and non-Hispanic Whites in New Mexico. The original study questionnaire included questions on tobacco smoke exposure from spouse smoking and on indirect exposure to asbestos through a spouse's job. This report describes the risks associated with these exposures in smokers and nonsmokers in New Mexico.''

The authors analysed the data according to two models. On the first model, among never smokers, cigarette smoking by a spouse, regardless of pipe or cigar use, was associated with a three-fold increased risk of lung cancer. (OR 3.2, 90% CI 1.5-7.2). For females only the odds ratio was 2.3 with CI 90% 0.9-6.6. For exposure to cigarettes only, the odds ratios were slightly lower (for all subjects 2.9 90% CI 1.3-6.7; for females only 1.8 90% CI 0.6-5.4.

Odds ratios from use of the second model tended to be lower.

No effect was detected for marriage to a smoker by a current or former cigarette smoker, according to either model.

Under the heading ''Discussion'' the authors made the following observations:

> ''In the context of a population-based case-control study in New Mexico, we have examined the risk of lung cancer associated with marriage to a cigarette smoker. The results indicated increased risk from this exposure in never smokers, but not in active smokers.
>
> Methodologic limitations of the case-control approach for studying the relation between involuntary exposure to tobacco smoke and lung cancer must be considered. Misclassification of both active and passive exposure to cigarette smoke is of particular concern.''

In conclusion, the authors made the following comments:

> ''The results of the present case-control study complement those from other case-control studies and from cohort studies, which showed increased lung cancer risks in never smokers married to smokers. The magnitude of the effect of marriage to a smoker in the present study, about a two-fold increase in risk ... is comparable to findings by Hirayama and by Akiba, et al., in Japan, by Trichopoulos, et al., in Greece, and by Correa et al., and by Dalager, et al., in the United States. A weak exposure-response relation was present with duration of passive exposure, but not with average number of cigarettes smoked daily by the spouse ...
>
> In active smokers, we found that residence with a smoker did not elevate lung cancer risk ... The lack of association in active smokers is consistent with the quantitative differences in the exposures of active and passive smoking.''

(n) *Pershagen et al.* — Passive Smoking and Lung Cancer in Swedish Women

Although this article was received for publication in January 1986 it was not published until 1987, when it appeared in the *American Journal of Epidemiology*. The abstract reads as follows:

> ''The relation between passive smoking and lung cancer was examined by means of a case-control study in a cohort of 27,409 nonsmoking Swedish women identified from questionnaires mailed in 1961 and 1963. A total of 77 cases of primary carcinoma of the bronchus or lung were found in a follow-up of the cohort through 1980. A new questionnaire in 1984 provided information on smoking by study subjects and their spouses as well as on potential confounding factors. The study revealed a relative risk of 3.3, constituting a statistically significant increase ($p < 0.05$) for squamous cell and small cell carcinomas in women married to smokers and a positive

dose-response relation. No consistent effect could be seen for other histologic types, indicating that passive smoking is related primarily to those forms of lung cancer which show the highest relative risks in smokers.''

The authors reported at p. 20 that:

''Pooling the control groups produces a relative risk of 3.3 for squamous cell and small cell carcinomas (95 per cent confidence interval (CI) = 1.1-11.4) associated with marriage to a smoker. Within this group, the relative risks were increased for both histologic types. The relative risks for the other histologic types and for the entire group are 0.8 (95 per cent CI = 0.4-1.5) and 1.2 (95 per cent CI = 0.7-2.1) respectively.''

Under the heading ''Discussion'' the authors stated the following:

''The results of our study indicate that exposure to environmental tobacco smoke is related to an increased risk of those histologic types of lung cancer which show the highest relative risks in smokers. This is in general agreement with the findings of Trichopoulos et al., Garfinkel et al., and Koo et al., although these authors looked at somewhat different carcinoma types and/or used other definitions of exposure.'' (p. 22)

(iii) *The major reviews*

I shall now refer to some of the more significant passages in the major reviews.

(a) *The Monograph on Tobacco Smoking issued by the International Agency for Research on Cancer*

The International Agency for Research on Cancer (''IARC'') is part of the World Health Organisation. This monograph (''the IARC report'') represents the views and opinions of an IARC working group on the evaluation of the carcinogenic risk of chemicals to humans. The group met in Lyons from 12-20 February 1985. The report was published in June 1986. The report is part of a monograph programme the objective of which is to elaborate and publish in the form of monographs, critical reviews of data on, inter alia, carcinogenicity for chemicals to which humans are known to be exposed, to evaluate the data in terms of human risk with the help of international working groups of experts, and to indicate where additional research efforts are needed.

In the report the term ''carcinogenic risk'' is taken to mean the probability that exposure to the chemical will lead to cancer in humans. Inclusion of a chemical in the report does not imply that it is a carcinogen, only that the published data have been examined. The 28 members of the IARC working group were drawn from a variety of academic, medical research and other institutions in Europe, Asia the Americas and Australia.

The manner in which IARC monographs are prepared is described in the report as follows. In advance of a meeting of a working group all relevant biological data concerning the substance under examination are collected by IARC. Six months before the meeting, articles containing relevant biological data are sent to experts, or are used by IARC staff, to prepare first drafts of the sections on biological effects. The complete drafts are then compiled by IARC staff and sent, prior to the meeting, to all participants in the working group for their comments. The working group meets to discuss and finalise the text of the monographs and to formulate the evaluations.

According to the report, the evidence for carcinogenicity from studies in humans is assessed by the working group and judged to fall into one of four groups, defined as follows:

''(i) Sufficient evidence of carcinogenicity indicates that there is a causal relationship between the exposure and human cancer.

(ii) Limited evidence of carcinogenicity indicates that a causal interpretation is credible, but that alternative explanations, such as chance, bias or confounding, could not adequately be excluded.

(iii) Inadequate evidence of carcinogenicity, which applies to both positive and negative evidence, indicates that one of two conditions prevailed:

(a) there are few pertinent data; or

(b) the available studies, whilst showing evidence of association, do not exclude chance, bias or confounding.

(iv) No evidence of carcinogenicity applies when several adequate studies are available which do not show evidence of carcinogenicity.'' (p. 24)

The final evaluations of the IARC working group appear at the end of the report and include the following:

> "There is sufficient evidence that tobacco smoke is carcinogenic to humans." (p. 314)

Whilst the reference to tobacco smoke in this evaluation is not entirely free from ambiguity, in my opinion it is a reference to tobacco smoke from three sources, viz., mainstream smoke, sidestream smoke and smoke exhaled to the general atmosphere by smokers.

The bulk of the report is concerned with the effects of tobacco smoke on active smokers. In relation to passive smoking it contains the following observation:

> "Several epidemiological studies have reported an increased risk of lung cancer in nonsmoking spouses of smokers, although some others have not. In some studies, the risk of lung cancer in nonsmokers increased in relation to the extent of spouses' smoking. Each of the studies had to contend with substantial difficulties in determination of passive exposure to tobacco smoke and to other possible risk factors for the various cancers studied. The resulting errors could arguably have artefactually depressed or raised estimated risks, and, as a consequence, each is compatible either with an increase or with an absence of risk. As the estimated relative risks are low, the acquisition of further evidence bearing on the issue may require large-scale observational studies involving reliable measures of exposure both in childhood and in adult life." (p. 308)

In a section headed "Conclusions and Evaluations", the following appears:

> "Tobacco smoke affects not only people who smoke but also people who are exposed to the combustion products of other people's tobacco. The effects produced are not necessarily the same, as the constituents of smoke vary according to its source. Three main sources exist: (i) mainstream smoke, (ii) sidestream smoke, and (iii) smoke exhaled to the general atmosphere by smokers. Smokers are exposed to all three to a greater extent than are nonsmokers. It follows that it is unlikely that any effects will be produced in passive smokers that are not produced to a greater extent in smokers and that types of effects that are not seen in smokers will not be seen in passive smokers. Examination of smoke from the different sources shows that all three types contain chemicals that are both carcinogenic and mutagenic. The amounts absorbed by passive smokers are, however, small, and effects are unlikely to be detectable unless exposure is substantial and very large numbers of people are observed. The observations on nonsmokers that have been made so far are compatible with either an increased risk from 'passive' smoking or an absence of risk. Knowledge of the nature of sidestream and mainstream smoke, of the materials absorbed during 'passive' smoking and of the quantitative relationships between dose and effect that are commonly observed from exposure to carcinogens, however, leads to the conclusion that passive smoking gives rise to some risk of cancer." (p. 314)

(b) *The National Health and Medical Research Council report on Effect of Passive Smoking on Health*

Some time prior to June 1986 the Australian National Health and Medical Research Council set up a working party on the effects of passive smoking on health. The Chairman was Dr A.J. McMichael who, at the time, was Senior Principal Research Scientist, CSIRO Division of Human Nutrition. The other members of the working party were:

> Dr R. Antic, Director of Thoracic Medicine, Royal Adelaide Hospital,
>
> Dr C. Baker, Acting Executive Director of the Public Health Service of South Australian Health Commission,
>
> Professor L. Landau, of the Department of Child Health at Princess Margaret Hospital for Children, Perth,
>
> Professor S.R. Leeder, Head of the Department of Community Medicine, Westmead Hospital, Westmead,
>
> Dr J.D. Potter, Senior Research Scientist at the CSIRO Division of Human Nutrition,
>
> Dr A. Woodward, Lecturer in the Department of Community Medicine, Royal Adelaide Hospital, and
>
> Dr A.F. Dick, of the Health Care Committee of the Commonwealth Department of Health.

The report of the working party was adopted by the National Health and Medical Research Council in June 1986.

Chapter 7 of the report deals with passive smoking and cancer. The following quotations from the report do not include a number of footnotes in which reference is made to the published work of other scientists:

> "*7.1 Introduction*
>
> Tobacco smoke contains approximately sixty known or suspected carcinogenic chemicals, of which at least fifty occur in the phase that contains particulate matter. The carcinogenic activity of tobacco smoke appears to require this particulate phase. Animal bioassays indicate that sidestream tobacco tar is more carcinogenic per unit weight than mainstream tar. For public health purposes, therefore, it would be prudent to assume, at this stage of research activity, that mainstream and sidestream smoke have similar human carcinogenic potency.
>
> There is no disagreement about the biological plausibility of an association between passive smoking and lung cancer. Active smoking is the major known cause of lung cancer, and there is a well-established monotonic increase in risk with increasing dose-rate. Further, no 'safe level' threshold dose appears to exist. Thus, although the dose rate for passive smokers is, overall, substantially lower than for active smokers, it is a reasonable inference from the studies of active smokers that passive smokers experience a real, albeit smaller, increase in lung cancer risk. Nevertheless, it remains unknown how active and passive smoking might differ in terms of actual carcinogens delivered to the respiratory tract. Sidestream smoke is qualitatively richer in many smoke constituents than is mainstream smoke.
>
> An equivalent argument exists in relation to the plausibility of passive smoking as a cause of cancers of other sites known to be related to active smoking.
>
> 7.2 *Types of Epidemiological Evidence*
>
> There are two types of evidence by which to examine the relationship of passive smoking to cancer risk.
>
> First, with knowledge of the established cancer risks of active smoking and using the documented relationship between individual smoking behaviour and various biological indices of absorbed constituents of smoke (e.g. measures of nicotine and cotinine in blood and urine, thiocyanate and cotinine in saliva, and carboxyhaemoglobin in blood) to make direct estimations of the extent of non-smokers' exposure to smoke, it is possible to estimate the attendant risk of cancer. This approach presumes that the particular biological indices used are also indices of the carcinogenic potential of the inhaled and absorbed smoke. As indicated in Section 4, estimates based on biological measures indicate that passive smoking in the workplace typically entails exposures (for eight hours per day) equivalent to light active smoking. Light smokers are at approximately five times higher risk of lung cancer than non-smokers.
>
> The second, and more usual type of epidemiological evidence depends upon observing empirical associations between reported individual smoking habits and the occurrence of cancer. Such observations are made in either cohort (prospective) studies or case-control (retrospective) studies.
>
> During 1979-85, eleven epidemiological studies examining the association between passive smoking and lung cancer have been reported. Most show a positive association, albeit substantially less strong than that between active smoking and lung cancer. Among non-smokers, the relative risk of lung cancer in passively exposed versus unexposed persons varies from approximately 1.2 to 3.5. A dose-response relationship is present in four of nine studies that have reported such an analysis. One cohort study has examined and reported the change in lung cancer risk associated with cessation of exposure (i.e. spouse as ex-smoker); a reduction in risk occurred.
>
> During the same period, four epidemiological studies of passive smoking and non-lung cancers have been reported. Their findings have been less consistent than those pertaining to lung cancer.
>
> These variable results reflect not only the apparently smaller effect of passive smoking upon cancer risk than that of active smoking, but the associated small numbers of cases available for study, and the

deficiencies in the validity and precision of measurement of individual exposure to passive smoking. Not only might some of the individuals included as non-smokers be ex-smokers, but the actual determination of exposure dosage — from varied sources and across time — is intrinsically difficult. Further, for the 25-50 per cent of women and the great majority of men in Western populations who work outside the home, the spouse's smoking habit is a poor quantitative index of passive smoking exposure — particularly since the exposure concentration is estimated to be four times higher at work than in the home. Nevertheless, to the extent that exposure misclassification applies equally to all combined groups of study subjects, it may have led to underestimation of the relative risk associated with passive smoking.''

The report makes the following observations:

''The evidence that passive smoking causes lung cancer is strongly suggestive. It is plausible, moderately consistent, and demonstrates dose-response relationships. However, intrinsic difficulties in accurately classifying individual exposure, and insufficient numbers of study subjects in many studies, preclude a conclusive interpretation of these empirical data when considered in isolation from other corroborative scientific evidence.''

The report concludes with the following quotation from a report of the interdisciplinary working group of the International Agency for Research in Cancer:

'''Knowledge of the nature of sidestream and mainstream smoke, of the materials absorbed during ''passive'' smoking and of the quantitative relationships between dose and effect that are commonly observed from exposure to carcinogens, ... leads to the conclusion that passive smoking gives rise to some risk of cancer.' ''

Chapter 7 of the NH & MRC report is a statement of the findings of the working party. The Statement and Recommendations of the National Health & Medical Research Council itself are in Chapter 9 of the report, which reads, in part, as follows:

''Council notes that there is mounting epidemiological evidence that passive smoking may increase the risk of occurrence of lung cancer. Despite limitations in the amount of data available, and despite research difficulties in making satisfactory estimations of individual exposure, a consistent pattern of moderately increased risk of lung cancer in passive smokers has emerged. In view of this pattern, of the known and substantial increase in risk of lung cancer in active smokers (and the lack of threshold dose), and of the documented levels of bodily assimilation of passively-inhaled smoke, it is therefore prudent public health policy to infer an increased risk of lung cancer from passive smoking.''

(c) *The 1986 report of the United States Surgeon General*

In 1986 the United States Surgeon General issued a report entitled ''The Health Consequences of Involuntary Smoking''. The report was submitted to Congress on December 15, 1986. The report was prepared by the United States Department of Health and Human Services. The report lists the names of a number of individuals who prepared portions of the report. These persons held positions in American universities. Acknowledgement is also given in the report to the assistance of about fifty scientists and physicians. It will be convenient to refer to this report as the ''Surgeon General's 1986 Report''.

The content of the report reflects the contributions of over sixty scientists representing a variety of disciplines. The care with which the report was apparently prepared appears from the Introduction:

''Upon receipt of the final manuscripts from the authors, the Office and its consultants edited and consolidated the individual manuscripts into appropriate chapters. These draft chapters were subjected to an extensive outside peer review ... whereby each was reviewed by up to seven experts. Their comments were integrated and the entire volume was assembled. This revised edition of the Report was resubjected to review by 17 distinguished scientists outside the Federal Government, both in this country and abroad. Parallel to this review, the entire Report was also submitted to various institutes and agencies within the

U.S. Public Health Service for review and comment.''

The Introduction contains an overview of the report. After referring to the inhalation of tobacco smoke during active cigarette smoking as ''the largest single preventable cause of death and disability for the U.S. population'', the overview continues:

> ''The magnitude of the disease risks for active smokers secondary to their 'high dose' exposure to tobacco smoke suggests that the 'lower dose' exposure to tobacco smoke received by involuntary smokers may also have risks. Although the risks of involuntary smoking are smaller than the risks of active smoking, the number of individuals injured by involuntary smoking is large both in absolute terms and in comparison with the number injured by some other agents in the general environment that are regulated to curtail their potential to cause human illness.
>
> This Report reviews the evidence on the characteristics of mainstream tobacco smoke and of environmental tobacco smoke, on the levels of exposure to environmental tobacco smoke that occur, and on the health effects of involuntary exposure to tobacco smoke. The composition of the tobacco smoke inhaled by active smokers and by involuntary smokers is examined for similarities and differences, and the concentrations to tobacco smoke components that can be measured in a variety of settings are explored, as is smoke deposition and absorption in the respiratory tract. The studies that describe the risks of environmental tobacco smoke exposure for humans are carefully reviewed for their findings and their validity. The evidence on the health effects of involuntary smoking is reviewed for biologic plausibility, and compared with extrapolations of the risks of active smoking to the lower dose of exposure to tobacco smoke found in nonsmokers. This review leads to three major conclusions:
>
> 1. Involuntary smoking is a cause of disease, including lung cancer, in healthy nonsmokers.
>
> 2. The children of parents who smoke compared with the children of nonsmoking parents have an increased frequency of respiratory infections, increased respiratory symptoms, and slightly smaller rates of increase in lung function as the lung matures.
>
> 3. The simple separation of smokers and nonsmokers within the same air space may reduce, but does not eliminate, the exposure of nonsmokers to environmental tobacco smoke.''

The second conclusion does not, of course, relate to lung cancer.

The following statements are made in the report in relation to lung cancer:

> ''Exposure to environmental tobacco smoke has been examined in numerous recent epidemiological studies as a risk factor for lung cancer in nonsmokers. These studies have compared the risks for subjects exposed to ETS at home or at work with the risks for people not reported to be exposed in these environments. Because exposure to ETS is an almost universal experience in the more developed countries, these studies involve comparison of more exposed and less exposed people rather than comparison of exposed and unexposed people. Thus, the studies are inherently conservative in assessing the consequences of exposure to ETS. Interpretation of these studies must consider the extent to which populations with different ETS exposures have been identified, the gradient in ETS exposure from the lower exposure to the higher exposure groups, and the magnitude of the increased lung cancer risk that results from the gradient in ETS exposure.
>
> To date, questionnaires have been used to classify ETS exposure. Quantification of exposure by questionnaire, particularly lifetime exposure, is difficult and has not been validated. However, spousal and parental smoking status identify individuals with different levels of exposure to ETS. Therefore, investigation has focused on the children and nonsmoking spouses of smokers, groups for whom greater ETS exposure would be expected and for whom increased nicotine absorption has been documented relative to the children and nonsmoking spouses of nonsmokers.
>
> Of the epidemiologic studies reviewed in this Report that have examined the question

of involuntary smoking's association with lung cancer, most (11 of 13) have shown a positive association with exposure, and in 6 the association reached statistical significance. Given the difficulty in identifying groups with differing ETS exposures, the low-dose range of exposure examined and the small numbers of subjects in some series, it is not surprising that some studies have found no association and that in others the association did not reach a conventional level of statistical significance. The question is not whether cigarette smoke can cause lung cancer; that question has been answered unequivocally by examining the evidence for active smoking. The question is, rather, can tobacco smoke at a lower dose and through a different mode of exposure cause lung cancer in nonsmokers? The answer must be sought in the coherence and trends of the epidemiologic evidence available on this low-dose exposure to a known human carcinogen. In general, those studies with larger population sizes, more carefully validated diagnosis of lung cancer, and more careful assessment of ETS exposure status have shown statistically significant associations. A number of these studies have demonstrated a dose-response relationship between the level of ETS exposure and lung cancer risk. By using data on nicotine absorption by the nonsmoker, the nonsmoker's risk of developing lung cancer observed in human epidemiologic studies can be compared with the level of risk expected from an extrapolation of the dose-response data for the active smoker. This extrapolation yields estimates of an expected lung cancer risk that approximate the observed lung cancer risk in epidemiologic studies of involuntary smoking.

Cigarette smoke is well established as a human carcinogen. The chemical composition of ETS is qualitatively similar to mainstream smoke and sidestream smoke and also acts as a carcinogen in bioassay systems. For many nonsmokers, the quantitative exposure to ETS is large enough to expect an increased risk of lung cancer to occur, and epidemiologic studies have demonstrated an increased lung cancer risk with involuntary smoking. In examining a low-dose exposure to a known carcinogen, it is rare to have such an abundance of evidence on which to make a judgment, and given this abundance of evidence, a clear judgment can now be made: exposure to ETS is a cause of lung cancer.

The data presented in this Report establish that a substantial number of the lung cancer deaths that occur among nonsmokers can be attributed to involuntary smoking. However, better data on the extent and variability of ETS exposure are needed to estimate the number of deaths with confidence.''

After making extensive reference to the scientific literature as to the relationship between passive smoking and lung cancer the Surgeon General's Report adopts the following summary:

''Previous Reports of the Surgeon General have reviewed the data establishing active cigarette smoking as the major cause of lung cancer. The absence of a threshold for respiratory carcinogenesis in active smoking, the presence of the same carcinogens in mainstream smoke and sidestream smoke, the demonstrated uptake of tobacco smoke constituents by involuntary smokers, and the demonstration of an increased lung cancer risk in some populations with exposures to ETS leads to the conclusion that involuntary smoking is a cause of lung cancer.

The epidemiological evidence that involuntary smoking can significantly increase the risk of lung cancer in nonsmokers is compelling when considered as an examination of low-dose exposure to a known carcinogen (i.e., tobacco smoke). Eleven of the thirteen epidemiological studies to date show a modest (10 to 300 percent) elevation of the risk of lung cancer among nonsmokers exposed to involuntary smoking; in six studies positive associations were statistically significant. The studies showing no or non significantly positive findings were generally the weakest in terms of sample size (Gillis et al. 1984; Chan and Fung 1982; Koo et al. 1984; Kabat and Wynder 1984; Wu et al. 1985; Lee et al. 1986), study design (Kabat and Wynder 1984; Lee et al. 1986), or quality of data (Chan and Fung 1982).''

After detailed reference to the epidemiological studies referred to in the report, the summary concludes:

> "The magnitude of risk associated with involuntary smoking exposure is uncertain. Relative risks ranging from 2 to 3 were generally reported for the highest level of exposure based on the spouses' smoking habits, but since sample sizes in most studies are not large, the point estimates of effect are unstable, and confidence limits are broad and generally overlap from one study to another. An index of involuntary smoking based on the smoking habits of the spouse is a simplistic and convenient measure. There is no reason to believe, however, that the excess risk associated with involuntary smoking is restricted to exposure from spouses. Nonsmokers married to smokers are likely to be more tolerant of ETS exposure and to experience more exposure to environmental tobacco smoke (Wald and Ritchie 1984). Higher risk estimates for involuntary smoking have been obtained in studies restricted to squamous cell and small cell carcinomas of the lung.
>
> Although involuntary smoking can be established as a cause of lung cancer, important questions related to this exposure require further research. More accurate estimates for the assessment of exposure in the home, workplace, and other environments are needed. Studies of sufficiently large populations should also be performed. New data from such studies should yield more certain risk estimates and describe the magnitude of the lung cancer risk in nonsmokers."

The following statements appear in the report:

> "The appropriate framework for an examination of the lung cancer risk from involuntary smoking is that of a low-dose exposure to a known human carcinogen. Over 30 years of research have conclusively established cigarette smoke as a carcinogen. This Report presents evidence that the chemical composition of sidestream smoke is qualitatively similar to the mainstream smoke inhaled by the active smoker, and that both mainstream and sidestream smoke act as carcinogens in bioassay systems. Data related to environmental levels of tobacco smoke constituents and from measures of nicotine absorption in nonsmokers suggest that nonsmokers are exposed to levels of environmental tobacco smoke that would be expected to generate a lung cancer risk; epidemiological studies of populations exposed to ETS have documented an increased risk for lung cancer in those nonsmokers with increased exposure.
>
> It is rare to have such detailed exposure data or human epidemiologic studies on disease occurrence when attempting to evaluate the risk of low-dose exposure to an agent with established toxicity at higher levels of exposure. The relative abundance of data reviewed in this Report, their cohesiveness, and their biologic plausibility allow a judgment that involuntary smoking can cause lung cancer in nonsmokers. Although the number of lung cancers due to involuntary smoking is smaller than that due to active smoking, it still represents a number sufficiently large to generate substantial public health concern.
>
> It is certain that a substantial proportion of the lung cancers that occur in nonsmokers are due to ETS exposure; however, more complete data on the dose and variability of smoke exposure in the nonsmoking U.S. population will be needed before a quantitative estimate of the number of such cancers can be made."

(d) *The National Research Council report on Environmental Tobacco Smoke 1986*

The National Research Council is the principal operating agency of the National Academy of Sciences of the United States of America. It was requested by the United States Department of Health and Human Services to evaluate methods for assessing exposure to environmental tobacco smoke and to review the literature on the health consequences of such exposure. The Council responded to this request by appointing eleven scientists to serve on a committee. The committee's charge was to review the then existing scientific literature and to identify the then current state of knowledge with respect to known facts and areas of uncertainty. (Ex D3,p.v.) The committee membership represented the disciplines of toxicology, biochemistry, atmospheric science, epidemiology, bio-statistics and pulmonary physiology. For the most part, the members of the committee were drawn from American universities (including Harvard, Yale and Johns Hopkins), but its members also included Professor Nicholas Wald, Professor of Environmental and Preventative Medicine at St Bartholomew's Hospital, London, as well as Olav Axelson of the University Hospital, Linkoping, Sweden. According to its report, the committee conducted a public hearing on scientific studies relevant to its charge and reviewed the published scientific literature and received testimony from professional societies; medical, industry, consumer and public interest groups, academic scientists; and others involved in the generation and interpretation of scientific evidence on the health consequences of exposure to cigarette smoking. The public hearing was held on 29 January, 1986. The report is undated but was first printed in November 1986. I think it is a reasonable inference that the material upon which the report was based was available to the scientific community as at July 1986. It will be convenient to refer to this report as "the NRC report".

With respect to lung cancer the report (pp. 10-11) makes the following statement:

> "Considering the evidence as a whole, exposure to ETS increases the incidence of lung cancer in nonsmokers. Estimates of the magnitude of the increased risk vary. Among studies of various populations in Europe, Asia and North America, the risk of lung cancer is roughly 30% higher for nonsmoking spouses of smokers than it is for nonsmoking spouses of nonsmokers. There is consistency among the studies in that all of the studies individually include the 30% increased risk within the 95% confidence intervals. Patterns and extent of exposure may vary in different communities and countries. Based on presently available epidemiologic data, the estimate of the increased risk from the American studies is lower than the average for all the studies, though not significantly so. These estimates are almost exclusively derived from the comparison of persons identified as exposed, or unexposed, on the basis of their spouse's smoking habits.
>
> Certain errors in the reporting of smoking habits have probably contributed to the risks observed in the epidemiologic studies. Misclassification of current or exsmokers as nonsmokers would tend to produce an observed relative risk that is larger than the true risk. The effect was studied in detail using estimates of the extent of the errors involved and judged to contribute only a portion of the excess risk. Underestimation of the increased risk might also be introduced because the supposedly unexposed population had some exposure to ETS, although they were classified as unexposed in the studies. Taking both types of errors into account produces an estimate of the excess lung cancer risk for nonsmokers married to smokers compared with completely unexposed individuals that is similar to the relative risk observed in the epidemiologic studies considered.
>
> Since carcinogenic agents contained in ETS are inhaled by nonsmokers, in the absence of a threshold for carcinogenic effects, an increased risk of lung cancer due to ETS exposure is biologically plausible."

Chapter 12 of the report is entitled "Exposure to Environmental Tobacco Smoke and Lung Cancer". After observing that the risk of lung cancer in cigarette smokers is directly related to the number of cigarettes smoked and that, among smokers, an increase in exposure leads to an increase in risk, the authors state that passive smoking would, therefore, be expected to cause some increase in risk of lung cancer in active smokers, as well as in any other persons in whom the appropriate tissues are exposed. They continue:

> "The studies reviewed in this chapter have attempted to address the questions of whether an increase in risk of lung cancer does occur in nonsmokers exposed to ETS and whether the dose-response relationship is similar to that in smokers. In part, this depends on whether there is a threshold dose of cigarette smoke exposure below which there is no increase in risk. Biological theory and current evidence on low-dose exposure to carcinogens do not provide evidence for such a threshold, and it is generally thought that one is unlikely (Office of Science and Technology Policy, 1985). If there is no threshold, it follows that exposure to tobacco smoke at low concentrations, such as that experienced by nonsmokers exposed to ETS, will cause an

> increased risk of lung cancer. The risk, of course, will be expected to be very much smaller than that associated with active smoking because of the much lower exposure of the bronchial epithelium to tobacco smoke."

After a detailed examination of the scientific literature on the subject and a consideration of bias and misclassification factors which may have affected some or all of the studies reported in the literature, the following summary is made:

> "The weight of evidence derived from epidemiologic studies shows an association between ETS exposure of nonsmokers and lung cancer that, taken as a whole, is unlikely to be due to chance or systematic bias. The observed estimate of increased risk is 34%, largely for spouses of smokers compared with spouses of nonsmokers. One must consider the alternative explanations that this excess either reflects bias inherent in most of the studies or that it represents a causal effect. Misclassification can have contributed to the result to some extent. Computations of the effect of two sources of misclassification were presented. Computations taking into account the possible effects of misclassified exsmokers and the tendency for spouses to have similar smoking habits placed the best estimate of increased risk of lung cancer at about 25% in persons exposed to ETS at a level typical of that experienced by nonsmokers married to smokers compared with those married to nonsmokers. Another computation using information from cotinine levels observed in nonsmokers and taking into account the effect of making comparisons with a reference population that is truly unexposed leads to an estimated increased risk of about one-third when exposed spouses were compared with a truly unexposed population. The finding of such an increased risk is biologically plausible, because nonsmokers inhale other people's smoke and, as a result, absorb smoke components containing carcinogens.
>
> *What is Known*
>
> 1. A summary estimate from epidemiologic studies places the increased risk of lung cancer in nonsmokers married to smokers compared with nonsmokers married to nonsmokers at about 34%. Assuming linearity at low-to-average doses and a constant proportionality of nicotine and carcinogens in mainstream smoke and ETS, extrapolation from studies of active smokers using relative urinary cotinine places the risk at about 10%.
>
> 2. To some extent, misclassification (bias) may have contributed to the results reported in the epidemiologic literature. However, bias is not likely to account for all of the increased risk. The best estimate, allowing for reasonable misclassification, is that the adjusted risk of lung cancer is increased about 25% (i.e., RR = 1.25) in nonsmokers married to smokers compared with nonsmokers married to nonsmokers. When one allows for exposure to nonsmokers who report themselves as unexposed, the adjusted increased risk is at least 24%. The adjusted increased risk to a group of nonsmokers married to nonsmokers is at least 8% (i.e., RR = 1.08) compared with truly unexposed subjects. This excess risk may come about from exposures in the workplace or other public places."

(e) *The Froggatt Committee report 1988*

This report was made in January 1988 by the Independent Scientific Committee on Smoking & Health to the Secretary of State for Social Services (UK). According to the Committee's Report its responsibility is "to advise ... on scientific aspects of matters concerning smoking and health ..."

Chapter 3 of the report addresses questions related to the effect of exposure to ETS. In the following quotations from the report I have omitted footnotes which contain references to scientific literature:

> "64. Nicotine is virtually unique to tobacco and might be considered therefore as an index of ETS. Its uptake by non-smokers, as measured by its metabolites, indicates that some passive smokers may receive a dose equivalent to that received by smokers who smoke a small number of cigarettes. However, since sidestream and mainstream smoke differ in composition such measurements cannot be extrapolated to the whole range of potentially harmful constituents of the smoke. For example, when dimethylnitrosamine rather than nicotine is used as a marker, the estimation

of the uptake of tobacco smoke produces a greater equivalence. Recent work has also pointed to the role that ETS can play in enhancing concentrations of radon daughter products indoors. For these, and other reasons it is unwise to express ETS uptake in terms of an equivalent number of cigarettes actively smoked despite its undoubted convenience, a point made in our interim report in March 1987.

65. The mutagenicity of particulate material sampled from indoor and outdoor air has been studied using bacterial systems and smoking was found to be an important factor with its predominant effect on enzyme mediated mutagenesis, the number of revertants increasing with the number of cigarettes smoked.

66. Attempts have been made to evaluate relative risk by means of epidemiological studies, not surprising given the hypothesis of a zero threshold and that non-smokers absorb some of the carcinogenic agents produced in smoking, though the exact proportion is unknown. The commonest method is to investigate lung cancer incidence among non-smoking wives of husbands who are, or are not, smokers. Studies of adequate size with documented smoking histories of cases and spouses are few and our review has therefore covered surveys from many countries.

67. In our Third Report we concluded (para 35) that the reported association between passive smoking and lung cancer was speculative. Since then a number of new studies have been reported. The majority of reports conclude that passive smoking is associated with an increased risk of lung cancer in non-smokers. A minority conclude from their own data that any effect of passive smoking on the risk of lung cancer or other smoking-related disease in a non-smoker is negligible and that the increased risk noted in other studies is largely an artefact.

68. The published studies have been scrutinized by various groups of researchers to determine whether collectively they present a reasonably consistent picture from which the existence and magnitude of the relative risk might be assessed. The major problem is the extent to which individuals with lung cancer were misclassified as non-smokers when they were in fact smokers or ex-smokers. After making allowances for such misclassifications, and other artefacts, and then recalculating relative risks in each study, most of the scientific groups conclude that while none of the studies can on its own be accepted as unequivocal the findings overall are consistent with there being a small increase in the risk of lung cancer from exposure to environmental tobacco smoke, in the range 10 per cent-30 per cent though some other workers have however argued for a much lower relative risk, or no increased risk at all. The Committee, studying the same data, agrees with the former interpretation and so upholds the view expressed in its interim statement.

69. It is helpful to state exactly what is meant by a 10% to 30% increased risk. It means that people who have never smoked but who have been exposed to environmental tobacco smoke through most of their lives have a 10% to 30% higher risk of lung cancer than non-smokers not so exposed. If the risk in the latter group is, say, 10 per 100,000 per year (based on rates in non-smokers in the 35+ age range) the risk in the exposed group would be 11 to 13 per 100,000 per year. Thus there might be 1 to 3 extra lung cancer cases a year per 100,000 non-smokers regularly exposed to ETS. Since there are no firm data on the numbers of people who fall into that category, no more than a rough estimate of the actual number of lung cancer deaths arising in this way could be made. It might however amount to several hundred out of the current annual total of about 40,000 lung cancer deaths in the United Kingdom, a small but not negligible proportion. In view of this conclusion we recommend that—

FURTHER PUBLICITY SHOULD BE GIVEN TO THE RISK OF LUNG CANCER ARISING FROM EXPOSURE TO OTHER PEOPLE'S TOBACCO SMOKE.''

(iv) *Oral evidence*

I shall now refer to some of the oral evidence as to the alleged association between passive smoking and cancer.

(a) *Professor Stewart*

Professor Bernard Stewart is Associate Professor in the School of Paediatrics at the University of New South Wales, and is the Principal Research Fellow in the Children's Leukaemia and Cancer Research Unit at the Prince of Wales Children's Hospital. He is a bio-chemist with specialist experience in the field of carcinogenesis. For a number of years he was the senior Research Fellow in Carcinogenesis of the New South Wales State Cancer Council.

Professor Stewart has had a great deal of experience in the study of the carcinogenic qualities of tobacco smoke. He expressed the opinion that there was no doubt whatever that cigarette smoke had been shown "to the point of absolute certainty" to be carcinogenic for humans (T. 433). In his opinion, exposure for a short time to a high concentration of tobacco smoke is less dangerous to humans than exposure to a low concentration of smoke over a long period of time. The reason for this is that if exposure occurs over a long period of time the likelihood of malignancy is increased because cells tend to be pushed towards transformation or alteration i.e. to become cancerous, rather than being killed outright. According to Professor Stewart, there is no safe level of exposure to carcinogenic substances, whereas the same cannot be said of toxic substances. A chemical is carcinogenic if it has the capacity to cause normal cells to become malignant. Toxic chemicals are those which kill normal cells (T. 396). Carcinogenic chemicals may also have a toxic effect.

Professor Stewart explained his view that there is no safe level of exposure to carcinogens, as distinct from toxins, in the following words:

> "For the vast majority of toxins, for the vast majority of chemicals that adversely (affect) us as people, the adversity that the chemicals produce is related to the dose. If the dose is large then obviously the toxic chemical will cause death — or large enough. As the dose is reduced so the extent of pathology produced by that chemical is reduced and if the dose is reduced and reduced there comes a point where there is no discernible toxic effect at all. So that, for argument's sake, in respect of caustic soda. Although caustic soda is toxic, it will be possible to take a solution of caustic soda and dilute and dilute it until it was so diluted as to be consumed without causing any clinical injury to the oesophagus. Now that concept is [basic] to public health insofar as when measures to protect the community from toxins are taken, the concept of a safe level of exposure is crucial. That concept can be clearly distinguished from the same basis when one approaches carcinogenic hazards because carcinogenicity is not so related to dose. At two levels because the theory of carcinogenesis says that a single cell to be modified and give rise to a tumour in theory such a single modification could produce a lethal response. If you poison a cell in the oesophagus with caustic soda the death of one cell could not possibly cause the death of the whole person but if you produce a single malignant cell then in theory that cell can grow into a tumour and produce the death of the individual. So that is a conceptual basis for the idea that there is no safe dose for a known carcinogen. The other aspect of that concept is based on the investigation of that whole area. That is in addition to the conceptual basis of that idea, no safe dose, there is a body of experimental evidence pertaining to either people or experimental animals that have been exposed to lower and lower levels of carcinogen by one reason or another and all of that data taken as a whole has failed to indicate a safe level of exposure for the carcinogen under review. So it is a [basic] tenet of carcinogenesis that there is no safe level of exposure, a principle that lies at the very heart of all other areas of toxicology." (T. 397-8)

It is apparent from statements made in the written material which I admitted into evidence that Professor Stewart's view that there is no safe level of exposure to a carcinogen is shared by many distinguished scientists.

It was put to Professor Stewart in cross-examination that if his view is correct, one molecule of a carcinogen could cause cancer. Whilst he agreed that, in theory, this was correct, he said that the one molecule example was a trivialisation of the significance of minimal exposure to carcinogens. I think this is correct, particularly in the context of the present case. The reference to cigarette smoke in the statement in para. 3 of the advertisement is quite general. It would extend, for example, to cigarette smoke inhaled by a non-smoker working for many years beside and in close proximity to a heavy smoker. If it be true that environmental tobacco smoke contains carcinogenic chemicals, it would be quite unrealistic to regard such a non-smoker as being exposed to the risk of inhaling only one molecule of a carcinogen.

Professor Stewart drew support for his opinions from the findings contained in some of the primary articles and also the findings in the IARC report. He conceded in one part of his evidence (T. 521) that the available epidemiological evidence does not allow a judgment to be made on causality between lung cancer and exposure to environmental tobacco smoke. However, in the light of all his evidence, I did not understand this concession to be a concession that it has not been proved that cigarette smoke causes lung cancer in non-smokers. The concession he made was limited to the effect of the available epidemiological evidence, if considered in isolation from other evidence. It is plain from his evidence that he is firmly of the opinion that there is a considerable volume of evidence that cigarette smoke causes disease in non-smokers (T. 522). He thinks that exposure to tobacco smoke is an established carcinogenic hazard. According to him, this conclusion can be reached wholly on the basis of laboratory evidence without reference to the epidemiological studies. However, he thinks both types of evidence should be considered together. He said: "Complementarity of laboratory and epidemiological evidence, in respect of the carcinogenic hazard associated with exposure to environmental smoke is unequivocal. In view of these considerations, denial that evidence for a carcinogenic hazard from passive smoking has not been established is absurd" (see annexure E to his affidavit).

A consideration of the whole of Professor Stewart's evidence leads me to conclude that he is of the opinion that a causal link has been established between passive smoking and lung cancer in non-smokers, but that further epidemiological evidence would add weight to his opinion. In his affidavit he said:

> "In my opinion, understanding of the causation of lung cancer in cigarette smokers, taken together with knowledge of the nature of sidestream and mainstream tobacco smoke, of the materials absorbed during passive smoking and of the quantitative relationships between dose and effect that are commonly observed after exposure to carcinogens, leads to the reasonable presumption that passive smoking does carry some risk for lung and other cancers. In respect of lung cancer, this presumption is now confirmed by a variety of epidemiological and experimental evidence which are mutually supportive. Knowledge of the causal relationship between passive smoking and lung cancer is now sufficient as to warrant measures to limit human exposure to this risk factor as a necessary and practicable public health measure to reduce the burden of lung cancer in the community."

Professor Stewart said that undiluted sidestream smoke is characterised by significantly higher concentrations of many of the toxic and carcinogenic compounds found in mainstream smoke. According to him, a comparison of the chemical composition of smoke inhaled by active smokers with that inhaled by involuntary smokers suggests that the toxic and carcinogenic effects would be qualitatively similar. He said that since carcinogenic agents in environmental tobacco smoke are inhaled by non-smokers, in the absence of a threshold for carcinogenic effects, an increased risk of lung cancer due to environmental tobacco smoke is anticipated.

Professor Stewart conceded that active smokers are exposed to greater quantities of tobacco smoke constituents than involuntary smokers. However, he is of the view that exposures to respirable suspended particulates are higher for non-smokers exposed to environmental tobacco smoke than for non-smokers who are not so exposed.

It was put to Professor Stewart in cross-examination that the proposition that there is no safe dose for a carcinogen was a public health principle and that public health principles depend upon dictates of caution whereas scientific proof of a proposition depends on demonstration of its correctness (T. 491-2). The Professor agreed, but I do not think his agreement is tantamount to an admission that there is not scientific proof that there is no safe dose for a carcinogen. He specifically disagreed with the proposition put to him (T. 494) that the concept that there was no threshold for carcinogens was not universally accepted. He said he knew of no experimental studies that had satisfactorily demonstrated that there was any such threshold (T. 494).

Professor Stewart said there was no qualitative distinction as to carcinogens between the composition of mainstream smoke and sidestream smoke because both contained polycyclic hydrocarbons and both contained nitroso compounds or that group of nitroso compounds called nitrosamines (T. 416). However, under cross-examination Professor Stewart conceded that it has not been scientifically proven that nitroso compounds cause cancer in humans (T. 485). He said he believed there was a split within the scientific community on that issue. In his opinion nitroso compounds "would be appropriately characterized as a group 2A compound, that is they probably cause cancer in humans but it is not proven" (T. 485). Later, Professor Stewart elaborated:

> "... whether nitroso compounds cause cancer in humans. Now, that statement is by definition concerned with the causation of cancer in humans and can only be resolved by reference to epidemiology studies in humans. The animal data are suggestive but not definitive and the reason I appear to equivocate on it is that the generally appropriate generalization is certainly that nitroso compounds probably cause cancer in humans or nitroso compounds almost certainly cause cancer in humans but my studies on rats and mice or on rats are not relevant to the definitive determination that nitroso compounds cause cancer in humans. They only provide evidence consistent with such a proposition or even evidence that was strongly suggestive or almost leaving no room for doubt but they are not finally definitive ..." (T. 519-520).

I refer elsewhere to the contents of the IARC report and it is instructive to compare Professor Stewart's opinions with the conclusions reached in it. At p. 314 of the report, after reference is made to the three main sources of tobacco smoke i.e. mainstream smoke, sidestream smoke, and smoke exhaled to the general atmosphere by smokers, it is said:

> "Examination of smoke from the different sources shows that all three types contain chemicals that are both carcinogenic and mutagenic. The amounts absorbed by passive smokers are, however, small, and effects are unlikely to be detectable unless exposure is substantial and very large numbers of people are observed. The observations on nonsmokers that have been made so far are compatible with either an increased risk from 'passive' smoking or an absence of risk. Knowledge of the nature of sidestream and mainstream smoke, of the materials absorbed during 'passive' smoking, and of the quantitative relationships between dose and effect that are commonly observed from exposure to carcinogens, however, leads to the conclusion that passive smoking gives rise to some risk of cancer."

The report then makes the evaluation that:

> "There is sufficient evidence that tobacco smoke is carcinogenic to humans."

Reference to p. 24 of the report shows that the expression "sufficient evidence" of carcinogenicity indicates that there is a causal relationship between the exposure and human cancer. Thus Professor Stewart's opinions seem not to differ from those expressed in the report.

(b) *Professor McMichael*

Professor Anthony McMichael is Professor of Occupational and Environmental Health in the Department of Community Medicine at the University of Adelaide. He was the Chairman of the working party which produced the NH & MRC report. Prior to taking up his present appointment he was Senior Principal Research Scientist with the Commonwealth Scientific Industrial and Research Organisation. He was at one time Assistant Professor in the Department of Epidemiology in the University of North Carolina, U.S.A.

Professor McMichael is of the opinion that it is not true to say that there is little evidence that cigarette smoke causes disease in non-smokers. In his opinion, there is a considerable volume of evidence that cigarette smoke causes disease in non-smokers and the evidence is sufficient to constitute scientific proof that it does so.

Professor McMichael took a very active part in the preparation of the chapter in the NH & MRC report dealing with cancer. It is plain from his evidence that he shares the view expressed in the report. Indeed with respect to the statement made on p. 33 of the report that: "The evidence that passive smoking causes lung cancer is strongly suggestive" the Professor said that this was an understatement of the view which he himself held at the time.

The respondent sought to diminish the weight which should be given to Professor McMichael's evidence by showing that he had altered a draft report prepared for the consideration of the working party. I do not think it was shown that he did anything untoward in the handling of the draft report. Certainly he was responsible for the making of some alterations, but I am quite satisfied there was nothing improper in what he did. The members of the working party were all persons with high qualifications and great experience. I think it is reasonable to assume that they did not concur with Professor McMichael's views unless they shared his opinions as expressed in the final report.

Counsel for the respondent criticised Professor McMichael for showing a copy of the draft NH & MRC report to a body known as ASH, an acronym for Action on Smoking and Health. However, I can see nothing wrong with what he did in this regard. It is true that the draft was, at the time, a confidential document but as he pointed out there were many groups concerned with public health who knew of its existence, or at least knew that work was being done on the report. There is nothing to suggest that if the respondent had asked to see a copy of the draft report it would not have been shown it.

Professor McMichael's opinions have firmed since the publication in July 1986 of the NH & MRC report. He said (T. 969) that as at January 1987 his view was "a little firmer that there was a causal relationship demonstrated between passive smoking and lung cancer". It is apparent from his evidence that one reason why his opinion had firmed was the publication in late 1986 of an article by Professor Wald and others published in the *British Medical Journal*. Reference to this article, and to Professor Wald's evidence in respect of it, is made elsewhere in these reasons. Professor McMichael said he agreed with the conclusions in Wald's article.

It would not be right, however, to treat Professor McMichael's evidence as being merely an adoption and recapitulation of the views expressed by Wald and other writers of published scientific work. He made it plain that although he had regard to the views of others, he had arrived at his own opinions. Thus he said:

> "I do not depend centrally on Wald because Wald has done simply quantitatively in a way that I consider to be correct and appropriate the sort of thing that otherwise one has done, one does mentally or qualitatively in appraising the full set of results available." (T. 1347)

Professor McMichael's views are perhaps best captured in the following statements he made towards the conclusion of his evidence. The statements were made in the context of drawing a comparison between the evidence showing a link between the consumption of alcohol and breast cancer and the evidence showing a link between passive smoking and lung cancer. Although the statement is lengthy, I set it out in full because it encapsulates the gist of the arguments relied upon by the applicant on the question whether passive smoking causes lung cancer. He said (T. 1413-4):

> "With respect to ... tobacco smoke in human cancer, ... I would summarize the evidence in relation to active smoking and here we are talking not about 5, 10 or 20 or even hundreds of studies, but in totality thousands of human and animal experimental studies as showing very consistent and strong increases in risk of human cancer, particularly, cancer of the lung in epidemiological research — that is work spread now over three or four decades. An enormous range of corroborative evidence from animal experiments with tobacco smoke being encountered in different modes, either by inhalation or painting on the skin. A lot of work on the mutational capacity of cigarette smoke. Studies on the induction of genetic mutations in mammalian cells and in bacterial cells. With respect to the evidence on environmental tobacco smoke we have first up the epidemiological evidence, ... that is studies specifically of the risk of lung cancer in life-long non-smokers exposed to

environmental tobacco smoke, so we have that direct empirical evidence, although we have noted that the number of studies is not great. It is moving towards a total of around 20 now and if we were looking at those just on their own, and if they had arisen out of the blue, as it were, as has been the case for alcohol and breast cancer or methylxanthenes and breast cancer, that had arisen recently out of the blue, not against a background of all of this other corroborative scientific work and all of this other biological knowledge and theory, then we would be more cautious in drawing a causal inference. But because there is the overwhelming evidence from the studies of active smoking because we have from the toxicologists and chemists the evidence of the qualitative identity in terms of chemical constituents present, of active and passive smoke ... we would reasonably infer that that exposure has a capacity to produce cancers. ... we have a range of metabolic epidemiological studies in which it has been demonstrated that humans exposed to environmental tobacco smoke, whether at home, at work or in some other context, public transport and so, by measuring levels of cotinine in blood, urine, saliva and so on, it has been clearly established that non-trivial amounts of exposure are incurred by those individuals and that that is in some quantitative proportion to the types of exposures that might be estimated by direct environmental observation or by asking individuals, how much does your husband smoke and how much is it at work, et cetera. So we ... not only ... have those initial upfront studies from epidemiologists about environmental tobacco smoke in lung cancer, but we have this extraordinarily rich large and deep spectrum of scientific research, some of it bearing directly on environmental tobacco smoke, much of it bearing on active tobacco smoke which provides the sort of corroboration that in my judgment allows one to draw a reasonable inference of causality from the sort of evidence that has now accrued in relation to environmental tobacco smoke.''

Professor McMichael expressed the opinion that, qualitatively, environmental tobacco smoke and mainstream smoke have much the same chemical constituency (T. 928). He accepted that there were important quantitative differences, one of which was that at the point of origin the concentration of a number of chemicals is actually greater in sidestream smoke than it is in mainstream smoke. He said these chemicals include several chemicals which are carcinogenic.

Professor McMichael also shares the views of other witnesses in the case, and a view expressed in much of the literature, that there is no apparent threshold for carcinogens, i.e. no apparent safe dose or level of exposure below which there is no increase in the risk of lung cancer from tobacco smoke (T. 937).

The respondent sought to diminish the quality of some of the epidemiological studies referred to by Professor McMichael because the diagnosis of cancer in some of them depended upon cytological rather than histological examination. A histological examination involves taking a small piece of the tissue of the tumour of interest and examining it microscopically so as to form a judgment about its histology. Cytological examination involves taking specimen cells from the tumour and examining them microscopically. Professor McMichael accepted that histological examination provides a surer guide to a correct diagnosis than cytological examination, and that both are more reliable than diagnoses recorded on death certificates. There was no disagreement between the witnesses on this matter. However, in my opinion, the respondent's witnesses tended to place far too much emphasis on the absence of histological examination in some of the surveys.

Professor McMichael, in common with other witnesses, was cross-examined at length as to much of the detail in the epidemiological studies relied upon by the applicant. It is impracticable to traverse in these reasons all of the ground covered in the cross-examination. In his cross-examination of the applicant's witnesses, Mr O'Keefe Q.C. was able to identify many aspects of the studies upon which they could be criticised. He was also able to show that, within some of the studies, there were apparent inconsistencies. But Professor McMichael would not accept that the studies could therefore be discarded. He said repeatedly that what was of importance from an epidemiological point of view was consistency in epidemiological studies. As he said:

"It is always very important to look for consistency of findings across studies. There is a sort of hybrid vigour, if you like, or robustness that derives from making similar observations in different population settings and using different study designs." (T. 923)

This approach is also reflected in his appreciation of the importance of statistical significance. Lack of statistical significance in data derived from a study was regarded on the respondent's side as of almost crucial importance. However, Professor McMichael's opinion is that it is inappropriate to regard statistical significance as the sole criterion of the value of an epidemiological study. He regards statistical significance as only one aid to judgment in deciding how much weight should be attached to a study.

In Professor McMichael's opinion, the value of an epidemiological study cannot be ascertained by measuring it against set criteria. He said (T. 1238) that whilst there are recognised and important criteria for the drawing of judgments about causal inference, they are not and should not be seen as prerequisites to the drawing of such judgments. In his opinion, the drawing of causal inferences can quite reasonably proceed, and often does, in the presence of some only of the well recognised criteria.

Professor McMichael's view that it is the totality of all the evidence which is of importance can be seen from his view as to when a causal inference can be drawn. He said:

"[I] think we have to be aware again that we are talking about a continuum that moves from uncertainty to certainty in the drawing of these causal inferences, and that is not really a binary option that you either do or do not know that there is a causal relationship. It is very much a question of the accrual of evidence and the level of certainty that applies." (T. 1253)

Professor McMichael said that taking into account the totality of the scientific evidence he was satisfied that, as at mid-1986, there was sufficient evidence to allow the drawing of an inference of causality between exposure to passive smoking and the occurrence of lung cancer in humans. (T. 1269.) The above references to his evidence barely scratch the surface of it. I have not attempted to deal with the detailed evidence he gave, much of it in the course of cross-examination, about the epidemiological studies referred to in the primary articles. Indeed, it would be almost impossible to capture in these reasons the intricacies of that evidence. However, I should observe that I formed the opinion that Professor McMichael is highly skilled in the field of cancer epidemiology and that his opinions are entitled to great respect.

(c) *Dr Armstrong*

Dr Bruce Armstrong is Commissioner of Health for the State of Western Australia. Prior to that appointment he was Director of the National Health and Medical Research Council's Research Unit in Epidemiology and Preventative Medicine and Professor of Epidemiology and Cancer Research at the University of Western Australia.

Dr Armstrong is of the opinion that it is not true to say that there is little evidence that cigarette smoke causes disease in non-smokers. He thinks there is considerable scientific evidence that cigarette smoke causes disease in non-smokers and that the evidence is sufficient to prove this relationship on the balance of probabilities. In his opinion sidestream smoke is a rich source of toxic substances and contains a variety of known or suspected chemical carcinogens in amounts as much as thirty times higher than in mainstream smoke. (Annexure E to his affidavit.) He is of the view that there is no theoretical or empirical reason to postulate a low-dose threshold for tobacco smoke carcinogenesis. He holds the opinion that the products of tobacco combustion are readily measurable and that their inhalation and absorption in the human body is demonstrable by the measurement of cotinine in the urine of non-smokers.

Dr Armstrong adheres to the view he expressed in an article which he published in 1987. In that article he said:

"Knowledge derived from studies of 'active' smokers, evidence of exposure to tobacco smoke carcinogens through passive smoking and the results of studies of passive smokers themselves are concordant in suggesting that passive smoking gives rise to a small increase in the risk of lung cancer in non-smokers. The actual degree of increase in risk must, for the present, be considered as somewhat uncertain. Estimates of carcinogen exposure through passive smoking suggest that it may be as low as 14 per cent; studies of lung cancer itself suggest that it lies between 24 per cent and 61 per cent. Similar or perhaps greater absolute increases in risk of lung cancer due to passive smoking would be likely in current and ex-smokers but probably undetectable epidemiologically because of the associated high incidence of lung cancer due to active smoking.''

I did not understand there to be any material difference between Dr Armstrong's views on matters relevant to this case as at 1 July 1986 and as at the date he gave his evidence.

Dr Armstrong made a calculation in the article of the impact of the increased risk of lung cancer occasioned by passive smoking. Extrapolating from annual cancer mortality rates in the United States of America, he estimated that as at 1983 there were 60 deaths annually in Australia due to passive smoking. The estimate was higher making a different set of assumptions.

Dr Armstrong was asked his opinion as to the value which could be attached to an epidemiological study which disclosed only a low relative risk. He accepted that it is often stated in epidemiology that relative risks of 1.5 or below are difficult to interpret. However, he said that regard must be had to the ''totality of the evidence on the subject''. This includes evidence, if it exists, of a trend towards increasing risk of lung cancer with increasing passive exposure to tobacco smoking. He thinks such evidence is disclosed in the Trichopoulos and Hirayama studies. Other evidence to which regard must be had is evidence of biological plausibility. In his opinion there is an inherent biological plausibility of an association between passive smoking and lung cancer. He thinks that where evidence of this kind is available, a low relative risk is not particularly important.

He was prepared to agree that, notwithstanding his opinion to the contrary, another epidemiologist could properly have held the view as at the date of publication of the advertisement that the evidence associating environmental tobacco smoke with lung cancer was equivocal. But I do not take this to be a concession that his view was not correct. Concessions of a somewhat similar kind were made by other witnesses called by the applicant. I do not think concessions of this nature are of much significance. If an opinion is erroneous, the fact that it is honestly or ''properly'' held does not give it validity or diminish the strength of the evidence upon which a contrary opinion is based. If that evidence establishes the correctness of the contrary opinion, then the statement of the erroneous opinion may mislead or deceive a person to whom it is made.

Of course, it might be argued that if one scientist may properly hold a certain view on a matter, the correctness of the contrary view cannot be proved scientifically. I do not find this argument persuasive in so far as it is sought to be relied upon in the present case. The respondent failed to call one witness whose special expertise is in epidemiology and of whom it could be said that he ''properly'' held views contrary to those expressed by the distinguished epidemiologists called by the applicant. It is a fair assumption, I think, that such a witness would have been called by the respondent had he been available. In these circumstances, the concession made by Dr Armstrong and others was little more than an admission of the theoretical possibility that another epidemiologist may hold contrary views, rather than a concession that any competent epidemiologist does in fact hold contrary views.

Dr Armstrong was cross-examined at length as to the alleged deficiencies in the Hirayama and Trichopoulos studies. It is fair to say that he recognised that these and other epidemiological studies relied upon by the applicant had their limitations. But his recognition of these limitations did not cause him to alter his opinion that the totality of the evidence demonstrates a causal relationship between passive smoking and cancer.

Dr Armstrong did not agree with the proposition that an epidemiological study is not worthy of consideration unless it demonstrates a statistically significant association (T. 1463). He agreed that if one is considering a single epidemiological study then the statistical significance of the data revealed by it is of great importance but he thought this was not the case if one is considering consistency among studies.

He acknowledged (T. 1633) that a number of criticisms had been made of the Hirayama studies and he conceded that, to an extent, some of them were valid. He was exhaustively cross-examined as to the limitations of the Hirayama and other epidemiological studies and acknowledged (T. 1657) that the cross-examiner had been able to raise what he described as "issues of doubt and uncertainty" in some of those studies. But he maintained his opinion that on the balance of probabilities it was correct to say that environmental tobacco smoke causes lung cancer (T. 1657).

(d) *Professor Trichopoulos*

Professor Trichopoulos is Professor of Epidemiology at the Harvard School of Public Health. He was formerly Professor and Director in the Department of Hygiene and Epidemiology at the University of Athens Medical School. He has served as a consultant or adviser to the World Health Organisation on, inter alia, cancer aetiology and prevention, health statistics, and epidemiology of various diseases and conditions. He has also served as a member of the Panel of Social Medicine and Epidemiology of the European Economic Community and of the Community's Special Working Group on Epidemiology and Bio-statistics. He is the author or co-author of a large number of publications including one of the primary articles referred to above.

Professor Trichopoulos responded to some of the criticisms (see infra) made by Professor Tweedie of his study. One of Professor Tweedie's criticisms was that the study excluded patients with adenocarcinomas and alveolar carcinomas. His answer was that these cell types are less associated with lung cancer in active smokers and this justified their exclusion in a study of passive smokers. He also thought that Professor Tweedie's criticism of the use of controls from a hospital for orthopaedic disorders was not justified because there was no warrant for an assumption that the wives of orthopaedic patients smoked less than others.

He also disputed that bias would have played a significant role in the results of the data collected. He claimed that at the time the study was undertaken, the doctor who conducted the interviews did not believe that passive smoking caused lung cancer and there was no public awareness of a potential link between passive smoking and lung cancer such as might have affected the answers given by patients. He accepted that in only a minority of the cases was there histological confirmation of the diagnosis of lung cancer, but he claimed that cytological diagnoses were available for two-thirds of the patients, and that such diagnoses were scientifically acceptable. He did not accept that any potential misclassification on the basis of smoking status would have changed the results of the study.

Professor Trichopoulos accepted that a critic can always point to weaknesses in a specific study, but he said that: "in epidemiology, you don't take a specific study in isolation and expect it to provide final answers on every aspect of the question". He admitted that in one important respect the result of his study had been incorrectly published in *The Lancet*, the journal in which it appeared. However, he said this was a typographical error and was corrected in the subsequent issue of the journal. I accept Professor Trichopoulos' evidence on this point. In the Professor's opinion, what is important about the risk ratios reported in his study is that they are statistically significant and that bias and confounding factors are reasonably excluded.

In spite of lengthy cross-examination of Professor Trichopoulos to show that he was not free from bias on the question in issue, I did not form an unfavourable impression of him in that regard. It is true that he had great difficulty in confining his answers to matters directly relevant to the questions asked of him. But I am confident that Professor Trichopoulos has great experience in the field of epidemiology and is also a man of professional integrity whose judgments are not affected by bias.

Professor Trichopoulos was criticised for not producing documents showing the data upon which his study was based. I think he might have made more effort than he did to produce these documents. However, the documents he was asked to produce were not in his custody. They were in the possession of the University of Athens. The documents were brought into existence about ten years ago. Whilst it might have been wise for him to have written to the University requesting it to make the documents available to him so that he could produce them to the respondent, he was under no obligation to do so. Moreover, I do not find it hard to believe that he thought that the request made of him was unreasonable because the class of documents he was asked to produce was very wide. It is, I think, highly unlikely that the Professor and his co-authors study would have failed to have correctly analysed the data available to them.

Professor Trichopoulos agreed that his study had limitations but said that these were no different from those which he recognised himself in the text of his published article. He did not claim that his study, of itself, provided convincing evidence of a causal link between passive smoking and lung cancer. He agreed that only the convergence of results from different studies in different populations permits a reasonably sound conclusion to be drawn in that regard (T. 4146-7).

Professor Trichopoulos' evidence was limited because of a ruling I gave as to the matters upon which he could be examined in chief. The ruling was occasioned bv the fact that he was not called in the applicant's case in chief but only in reply.

(e) *Professor Janerich*

Professor Dwight Janerich is Professor of Epidemiology and Director of the Cancer Epidemiology Program and Cancer Prevention Research Unit at Yale University School of Medicine in New Haven, Connecticut. He is a past president of the American College of Epidemiology and has served on the Board of Directors of the College since 1979.

Professor Janerich was called to give evidence in respect of an unpublished thesis by Dr Luis Varela which was tendered by the respondent as part of its case. Dr Varela is now deceased. From 1982 to 1984 Professor Janerich was Director of the Division of Community Health and Epidemiology for the New York State Department of Health, where he was responsible for the design of the empirical study on which Dr Varela's thesis was based.

The Professor explained in some detail how the data analysed by Dr Varela was collected. I do not think any good purpose would be served by a detailed account of the way in which the study was designed or the data collected. It is sufficient to say that the study appears to have been well conducted.

Senior counsel for the respondent claimed, in effect, that it was not possible for him to cross-examine Dr Janerich because of the absence of the raw data upon which Dr Varela's thesis was based. I do not think that was the case. Dr Varela's thesis was tendered by the respondent. It is reasonable to assume it would not have been tendered if doubts were entertained as to its validity.

There were two classes of documents which counsel claimed he needed in order to cross-examine Professor Janerich. They were the form of questionnaire which was used in the collection of the data, and the completed questionnaires. Professor Janerich said that the copy of the questionnaire which was annexed to Dr Varela's thesis included all the questions which were relevant to the passive smoking issue. Dr Varela himself must have thought that this was the case because he referred to only that part of the questionnaire in the appendix to his study.

I am not persuaded that the documents, if produced, would have thrown any further light on Dr Varela's thesis or Professor Janerich's comments upon it. It was not Dr Varela who administered the questionnaires. This was done by interviewers employed by the New York Department of Health. Dr Varela used data collected by the interviewers. If the questionnaires had been produced, there would have been no means of checking them to ascertain whether the answers recorded by the interviewers were correct. It is reasonable to assume that the answers were correctly recorded. I think it must be assumed that the interviewers accurately recorded the answers communicated to them. There is no reason to think that the interviewers were biased, dishonest or incompetent.

Professor Janerich said that he basically agreed with the conclusions reached by Dr Varela in his thesis. Dr Varela concluded that the data he analysed did not show a statistically significant association between spousal smoking and lung cancer, but Professor Janerich thought there were possible explanations why this was so. He said that the evidence referred to in Dr Varela's thesis showed a positive effect and was, in his opinion, further evidence that environmental tobacco smoke can cause lung cancer. He said:

> "The New York study is population-based and from a large catchment area, which provides important assurances for the case-control design. The study was designed

to be representative of this catchment area, and we did everything we could to achieve that representativeness as the study was conducted. In my opinion, the positive finding from this study in respect of exposure to household smoking and the inability to detect a positive finding with other measures of exposure in no way detracts from the positive findings of earlier studies.''

In the light of Professor Janerich's evidence, which was virtually unchallenged, I do not think Dr Varela's thesis adds weight to the respondent's case.

(f) *Sir Richard Doll*

Sir Richard Doll was formerly Regius Professor of Medicine in the University of Oxford. He holds honorary degrees of Doctor of Science from Harvard, London, Oxford and other universities. He has an enviable reputation as an epidemiologist. Indeed, I think it is fair to say that many of the distinguished epidemiologists who were called in evidence regard him as something of an icon in the field of epidemiology. His academic and professional distinctions are too numerous to relate. Although he vacated his Chair at Oxford in 1979, he has maintained a close and active interest in epidemiology. He was the Director of the Imperial Cancer Research Fund's Cancer Epidemiology & Clinical Trials Unit between 1978 and 1983 and between 1987 and 1989. He is currently a member of the World Health Organisation Commission on Health and Environment. He is a former member of the Council of the Royal Society and in 1986 was awarded its Royal Medal. He was the first Warden of Green College, Oxford, which was established in 1979 as a post-graduate college with a special interest in clinical medicine. His researches include studies of the health effects of smoking, ionizing radiation, and of the causes of lung cancer.

Sir Richard Doll explained the nature of epidemiological research. He said that the results obtained from such research record only associations (or the absence of associations) and, as such, may be explained in several different ways. He said that if similar associations can be produced experimentally in animals in a laboratory, it is easy to conclude that they imply causation in humans. But in the absence of such evidence interpretation of the human evidence may be difficult. However, he made it plain that, in his opinion, epidemiological evidence alone may be sufficient to establish that a factor is a cause of a disease. He said (T. 3886):

> ''It is perfectly possible to draw a conclusion about causation in the absence of laboratory support. It is much more difficult and one has to require somewhat different conditions and you need a lot more thought and a lot of weight will be attached to the conclusion. Therefore, you have considerable responsibility in deciding upon the basis of epidemilogical evidence alone that a factor is a cause of disease. But it can be done and has been done frequently in the past ...''

Sir Richard Doll gave persuasive reasons supporting his opinion. He said such conclusions have been reached in the past despite the fact that intensive laboratory investigation has failed to demonstrate a similar effect in animals. He gave as an example a conclusion which he and Professor Bradford Hill reached in 1950 that smoking is an important factor in the cause of carcinoma of the lung. That conclusion was reached despite the fact that tobacco smoke had not, at that time, been recognised to be carcinogenic in animal experiments.

The evidence which was led from Sir Richard Doll was limited because he was called only in reply. I ruled that counsel for the applicant was not entitled to lead evidence from him as to the weight which could be attached to the data referred to in the primary articles.

Sir Richard was cross-examined for the purpose of demonstrating the extremely cautious approach he took when seeking to ascertain whether there was proof that chemically-treated oils imported into Spain as industrial oil and sold as pure olive oil were the cause of a toxic syndrome that affected many thousands of people in Spain in the summer of 1981. But I do not think I should infer from the cautious approach taken by Sir Richard in the Spanish oil disaster that he would not be satisfied that the epidemiological evidence demonstrates a causal link between passive smoking and lung cancer. Consistent with my ruling as to the evidence which could be given by Sir Richard, it was not possible for counsel for the applicant to ask his opinion on that matter. But counsel for the respondent could have sought Sir Richard's opinion on it. It should not be assumed that Sir Richard's view would have been adverse to the applicant when his view could have been elicited by the respondent, but was not.

Sir Richard Doll was co-author with Professor Peto of an editorial which appeared in the *British Journal of Cancer* in 1986, in which it is stated: "Exposure to ambient smoke must be assumed to cause some lung cancers in non-smokers, as they inhale the same chemicals as smokers, and it is now generally accepted that a safe threshold is unlikely to exist for most carcinogens." This statement suggests that Sir Richard regards the biological plausibility of a link between passive smoking and lung cancer as an important adjunct to the epidemiological studies. That element of biological plausibility was absent in the Spanish oil case.

It is true that in the same editorial, having referred to reports in a number of epidemiological studies of increased lung cancer risks in the non-smoking spouses of smokers, Sir Richard Doll and Professor Peto refer to those reports as "equivocal evidence". But as I read the article, this is a reference to the reported *estimates* of risk, not to the presence of carcinogens in tobacco smoke and the absence of a safe threshold for them. In a letter to the *British Journal of Cancer* written after the publication of the editorial, Doll and Peto, referring to their previous editorial, said that in it — "we concluded that the evidence that passive smoking confers an appreciable risk, although inconclusive, is suggestive enough to justify concern". I think it is apparent from a reading of both the letter and the editorial that the authors are firmly of the view that non-smokers are exposed to an appreciable risk from passive smoking. The evidence which they regard as being equivocal and inconclusive relates to the quantification of the risk, not its existence.

With reference to the concept of relative risk, Sir Richard Doll was asked whether he would agree that when a relative risk is 1.5 or below, one's confidence in causality is very much less than if it is above that number. He agreed with this proposition "in the absence of very strong other evidence" (T. 3934). He said he did not accept that a risk ratio of 2 or less was necessarily evidence of a weak association (T. 3951).

(g) *Professor Wald*

Professor Nicholas Wald is Professor and Head of the Department of Environmental and Preventive Medicine at St Bartholomew's Hospital Medical College in the University of London. He was previously Deputy Director of the Imperial Cancer Research Fund Cancer Epidemiology and Clinical Trials Unit in the University of Oxford. He is the author and co-author of a large number of publications, many of them related to research into the effects of tobacco smoking. He is a member of the United Kingdom Independent Scientific Committee on Smoking and Health, and has sat on various committees concerned with tobacco and health, including the United States National Academy of Science Committee on Passive Smoking, and the World Health Organization International Agency for Research on Cancer's Working Group on Tobacco. He was the Chairman of the United Kingdom Medical Research Council's Smoking Review Committee. He was also a member of the British Government's Committee on Carcinogenicity of Chemicals in Food, Consumer Products and the Environment.

Professor Wald was called by the applicant to give evidence of a statistical technique sometimes described as meta-analysis. It is a statistical technique employed to combine the results of individual epidemiological studies in order to derive a quantitative summarisation of data relating to a particular area of investigation.

Professor Wald was the co-author of an article ("the Wald article") which appeared in the *British Medical Journal* in November 1986 in which a meta-analysis is made of many of the epidemiological studies tendered in evidence. His co-authors were a highly qualified research assistant with expertise in computer programming, a lecturer in medical statistics and a senior lecturer in cancer research who was a mathematician and epidemiologist. In his oral evidence the Professor adhered to the views expressed in the article.

In meta-analysis information from several individual studies is pooled. Professor Wald said that the technique has a special value in situations where there are many studies each of which, on its own, may be too small to be expected to show an effect if there is one.

There are a number of different statistical techniques for performing a meta-analysis. A somewhat similar approach to that taken in the Wald article was taken by the National Research Council in its report.

The meta-analysis in the Wald article was carried out in order to ascertain whether there is an overall association between exposure to environmental tobacco smoke and lung cancer. Professor Wald and his co-authors included only studies in which exposure was assessed by whether the subject lived with a smoker. This was done because the view was taken that such individuals were likely to be more heavily exposed to environmental tobacco smoke than non-smokers living with non-smokers. They excluded three epidemiological studies from the analysis for reasons which the professor gave. However, two of the excluded studies were consistent with the overall result achieved and the third also reported a positive effect.

Professor Wald recognised that the value of an epidemiological study may be diminished by any one of a number of errors. Of these, misclassification bias appears to me to be the most significant and, since it is a matter of considerable importance in the case, I set out in some detail what he said about it. He said in his statement of evidence:

> "13. Examining the epidemiological evidence as a whole, particularly that relating to lung cancer among non-smokers who live with smokers compared with non-smokers who do not, there is clear evidence of an association between passive smoking and lung cancer. There are only two explanations for this association; it either represents a direct and causal effect of exposure to environmental tobacco smoke, or it may be due to systematic error (i.e. bias) or both explanations may in part apply. After careful consideration of all the potential sources of bias it can be concluded that only one source of bias must have, to some extent, exaggerated the magnitude of the observed association; this has become known as the misclassification bias. This bias will tend to introduce a spurious association between passive smoking and lung cancer. It arises from the combination of three effects. Firstly, some people who say that they are not smokers are in fact smokers, or have smoked in the past. Secondly, smokers tend to live with smokers. Thirdly, smoking is an important cause of lung cancer. It follows that in a group of reported non-smokers there will be some who, by virtue of having in fact smoked, will have a higher risk of lung cancer and also will be more likely to live with a smoker than would be the case if they were genuinely non-smokers. This will tend to produce an artefactual association between passive smoking and lung cancer among self-described non-smokers.
>
> 14. It is possible to estimate the magnitude of each of the effects that contribute to the bias, namely the proportion of misclassified smokers, the relative risk of lung cancer in those misclassified and the extent to which smokers live with smokers. With this information, together with estimates of the prevalence of smoking, one can estimate the magnitude of the bias. This reveals that the bias is very unlikely to explain the observed association between passive smoking and lung cancer. In my opinion, the observed association could only be completely explained in this way if unreasonably high estimates of the magnitude of the effects that contribute to the bias were used.
>
> 15. The validity of the misclassification bias depends on the close association between active smoking and lung cancer, an association that is accepted by scientists as being causal. Invoking the bias accepts this link between active smoking and lung cancer as well as the need to revise the observed relative risk between passive smoking and lung cancer to allow for the bias. It is illogical to accept it for one purpose but not for the other. It illustrates the importance of considering the evidence on lung cancer in relation to active and passive smoking together, recognizing the qualitative similarities in the two exposures and the expectation that a little of what causes a large increase in risk will still cause an increase in risk, albeit to a smaller extent. It also demonstrates how it is necessary when judging whether the association between passive smoking and lung cancer is causal to have an informed view on this issue with respect to active smoking and lung cancer. To hold a view on the former without holding one on the latter is logically untenable."

The meta-analysis carried out in the Wald article showed that there was a highly significant 35% increase in the risk of lung cancer among non-smokers living with smokers compared with non-smokers living with non-smokers. The relative risk of 1.35 was statistically significant at the 95% confidence interval. The authors of the study recognised that misclassification of some smokers as non-smokers had probably exaggerated the estimated increase in risk. Adjustment for this error reduced their estimated relative risk to 1.30. However, as people who live with non-smokers may still be exposed to other people's smoke they revised this estimate again to allow for the fact that a truly unexposed reference group was not used. The increase in risk among non-smokers living with smokers compared with the completely unexposed group was thus estimated by them as 53%, i.e. a relative risk of 1.53.

I have already referred to the fact that the National Research Council carried out a somewhat similar exercise. In the NRC report the relative risk of "exposed" non-smokers compared with truly "unexposed" non-smokers is stated to be 1.42.

The authors of the Wald article stated their conclusions in the following terms:

> "We conclude that breathing other people's tobacco smoke does cause lung cancer, and our conclusion rests on several observations. Firstly, carcinogens in tobacco smoke are released into the air. Secondly, tobacco smoke is breathed into the lungs by non-smokers. Thirdly, the general view is that exposure to carcinogens does not have a threshold below which there is no effect. Fourthly, people known to have an increased exposure to environmental tobacco smoke seem to have an excess risk of lung cancer, which is not explained satisfactorily by bias. Fifthly, the magnitude of the excess seems reasonable in view of the extent of exposure and, sixthly, there is a dose response relation between the extent of exposure and risk. In view of all these observations, we could not have concluded otherwise."

The authors estimated that about a third of the cases of lung cancer in non-smokers who lived with smokers, and about a quarter of the cases in non-smokers in general, may be attributed to exposure to environmental tobacco smoke.

Professor Tweedie (a witness called the respondent) identified potential sources of bias in most, if not all, of the epidemiological studies upon which the Wald meta-analysis is based. Professor Wald agreed that it is always possible that any epidemiological study may be affected by bias, but he did not think that this potentiality affected the validity of the exercise which he and his co-authors carried out. He said that the real issue is not whether there is a potentiality for bias. Rather, it is whether there is error of such character and magnitude that it has systematically disordered the results of the study in such a way as to lead to an association between passive smoking and lung cancer that would not otherwise have been observed. He said this had not been shown to have been the case. In particular, he did not think that Professor Tweedie's criticisms of the Hirayama and Trichopoulos studies showed them to be so flawed as to warrant their exclusion from the meta-analysis exercise. The voluminous evidence on this issue (and many other issues) is impossible to summarise in these reasons. However, I find Professor Wald's evidence on this matter most persuasive and I do not think that his meta-analysis was shown to be seriously flawed. As I have observed, the result of it is not greatly different from a similar exercise carried out by the National Research Council.

Dr Layard, another witness called by the respondent, expressed the opinion that the epidemiological studies upon which the Wald article is based lack consistency. Professor Wald holds a different view. In his opinion the undoubted variation in the point estimates in the studies is consistent with the sort of random variation that one would expect from a number of studies.

Dr Layard thinks that the utility of meta-analysis is very limited and that studies cannot be combined in a meta-analysis if the results in any of them may be due to bias or confounding. Professor Wald agreed that any epidemiological study which is so flawed as to make it uniformative should not be used as evidence, whether alone or in combination with other studies, in making a meta-analysis. However, he thinks that a study that is sufficiently sound to be considered as evidence on its own is eligible for inclusion in a meta-analysis. He agreed that a flawed study cannot be improved by inclusion in a meta-analysis. But he thinks that a sound study, albeit too small to show an effect on its own, can be used with other studies to show an effect. He agreed that meta-analysis cannot overcome bias, but said it can be used to overcome random error from small numbers in small studies.

Professor Wald was careful to point out that the risk ratio derived from a meta-analysis is a "summary estimate" of a given effect. That is to say, it is not the measure of the effect which will be applicable in all situations surveyed in all the epidemiological studies upon which the meta-analysis is based. In some social groups, exposure to environmental tobacco smoke may be more intense than in others and in these one would expect the effect of exposure to be greater. He illustrated his view by the observation that since room sizes in Japan are smaller on average than in the United States, exposure to environmental tobacco smoke in Japan is greater than in the United States. Hence one would expect that the relative risk estimate would be greater in the Japanese studies than in the American studies. But he thought that differences of this kind were no reason to conclude that the two sets of data cannot be combined to obtain an overall summary effect or to ascertain the overall level of statistical significance.

On a separate matter, Professor Wald said that cotinine is a reasonably sensitive measure of exposure to passive smoke and that it has many advantages in that respect over other markers (T. 4352). He accepted that estimates of doses of tobacco smoke based upon cotinine measurements need to be considered cautiously (T. 4404). He agreed that mainstream and environmental tobacco smoke differ in some respects, but thought that their similarities are more striking than their differences (T. 4404).

On another separate matter, Professor Wald expressed the opinion that Dr Varela's thesis, which formed part of the respondent's case, lent some weight to the conclusion that passive smoking causes lung cancer. He accepted that the data analysed by Dr Varela are consistent both with no association between lung cancer and exposure to environmental tobacco smoke in the home and with the positive association reported in both his meta-analysis and the NRC report. However, he drew attention to Dr Varela's examination of the association between exposure to environmental tobacco smoke as measured by the total number of smokers in the household expressed in terms of the number of person-years of passive smoke exposure. This examination showed a statistically significant association between such exposure and lung cancer. These apparently inconsistent results suggested to him that in some studies spousal smoking alone may be a poor way of categorising a person's exposure to environmental tobacco smoke.

As is apparent from the statement of the conclusions in the Wald article, Professor Wald's opinion that passive smoking is a cause of lung cancer is by no means based only on the statistically significant association he and his co-authors found between lung cancer and passive smoking. I think the difference between his views and those of the other epidemiologists called by the applicant, and the views of witnesses called by the respondent is explained by the broader approach taken by the former group of witnesses.

Professor Wald and the other witnesses called by the applicant tended to regard the separate items of scientific material (e.g. epidemiological studies, the "no threshold" for carcinogens theory, the presence of carcinogens in environmental tobacco smoke, and cotinine levels in non-smokers) as constituent parts of a mosaic, each piece itself representing some evidence that environmental tobacco smoke causes cancer in non-smokers. On the other hand, the respondent's witnesses tended to evaluate each piece of evidence in isolation. I think therein lies the explanation for much of the collision of opinion between the witnesses for the parties.

Professor Wald sees the epidemiologist as one of a team, the members of which collaborate in reaching a judgment. He said (T. 4251):

> "I am an epidemiologist. I am not a mathematician or a statistician, but epidemiologists by nature of their work collaborate closely with biologists, scientists, clinicians, statisticians and work together with them as a team, and in much of the work I do their components are performed by colleagues and the

responsibility for the different components will vary depending on the different skills. In computing the mathematical calculations that are involved in some of these analyses I rely heavily on statistical colleagues as do many — in fact all my epidemiological colleagues, Richard Doll, Prof. Trichopoulos and others. But at the end of the day I have to satisfy myself that what has been performed by my colleagues is sound and is a correct reflection of the scientific position and have to accept the responsibility for it, but I cannot say that I do every component bit of calculation. Indeed nor do they. They rely very much on other contributions in order to reach their judgments.''

I was left with the impression that Professor Tweedie and Dr Layard do not take the same approach to their discipline, which is the science of statistics. I am inclined to think that they tended to work within their own discipline and that, accordingly, they tended to take a narrower approach when considering whether the whole of the available data warranted a conclusion as to a causal link between passive smoking and lung cancer.

I have already observed that Professor Wald was a member of the National Research Council's Committee on Passive Smoking which produced the NRC report. He prepared the first draft of Chapter 12 of the report, which deals with exposure to environmental tobacco smoke and lung cancer. He said that his draft was worked on by others and also sent informally to scientific referees. Before the report was published it was sent to independent experts to judge whether it was in a satisfactory form. He said that he agreed with the general conclusions in the document as finally settled, and that he still adhered to the views expressed in it (T. 4362).

(h) *Dr Layard*

Dr Maxwell Layard is a partner in a firm of consulting statisticians based in California. He was formerly an Assistant Professor of Mathematics at the University of California. From 1973 to 1979 he was a statistician in the Mathematical Statistical and Applied Mathematics Section of the National Cancer Institute. From 1979 to 1983 he was Senior Biostatistician at the United States Veterans' Administration clinical trials centre in California where he was involved in the planning and management of medical trials and served as technical adviser to the centre on statistical and clinical trials methodology. He has served as a referee for papers submitted to several medical and statistical journals.

Dr Layard holds the opinion that the statement: ''There is little evidence and nothing which proves scientifically that cigarette smoke causes disease in non-smokers'' accurately summarises the epidemiological evidence available in July 1986 regarding environmental tobacco smoke and cancer. He is also of the opinion that the statement accurately summarises the epidemiological evidence available at the time he gave his evidence. His opinions are based on his review of the published reports of studies of environmental tobacco smoke and the incidence of cancer.

Dr Layard reviewed the same studies as were considered by the applicant's witnesses, and which are referred to in the primary articles. In his opinion they do not establish a convincing statistical association between environmental tobacco smoke exposure and lung cancer. He analysed the published data and formed the opinion that, collectively, they failed to satisfy the accepted criteria for epidemiological evidence which would enable them, if corroborated by other evidence, to support an inference of causation.

Dr Layard's opinion as to the matters which must be proved to demonstrate a causal association between an exposure and a health effect and his acknowledgement that the discipline of the statistician does not extend to all those matters appears in the following passage in his evidence:

> ''In assessing whether epidemiologic evidence reflects a causal association between an exposure and a health effect, it is first necessary to consider whether the data demonstrates a statistically significant association, that is, an association which is unlikely to be due to chance. If a statistically significant association has been demonstrated, it is then necessary to assess the validity and weight of the evidence in the light of criteria, such as strength and consistency of association, which refer to the epidemiologic studies themselves. However, even after these criteria have been considered, epidemiologic evidence must be

corroborated by other types of evidence before it is appropriate to draw a causal inference. The biologic plausibility of an observed association between exposure and health effect must be considered. Considerations of biologic plausibility involve such matters as knowledge of disease mechanisms, coherence with known facts about the natural history of the disease in question, and toxicologic experiments with animals which avoid problems of confounding and bias typically seen in epidemiologic studies. However, these considerations are outside the scope of my expertise, and I confine my comments in this statement to the interpretation of data from the relevant epidemiologic studies of ETS and cancer.''

It is plain from this passage that Dr Layard places greater emphasis on statistical significance than do the applicant's witnesses. Also his view that epidemiological evidence must be corroborated by other types of evidence before a causal inference can be drawn is not shared by many epidemiologists including Sir Richard Doll.

In Dr Layard's opinion, only the Trichopoulos and Hirayama studies reveal statistically significant associations and those studies are open to serious criticism. He thinks the studies as a whole do not establish a statistically significant association between exposure to environmental tobacco smoke and lung cancer. He acknowledged that the National Research Council had carried out a meta-analysis of all the studies (except that of Wu et al.) which he had considered and that its meta-analysis produced a combined relative risk of 1.34 which was statistically significant. But he disputed that it was appropriate to combine the results of studies in this way.

He said that the meta-analysis carried out by the National Research Council might be flawed because of publication bias in the literature. I recognise, as did the applicant's witnesses, that publication bias may occur in a given situation but I think it is quite unlikely to have occurred in the publication of studies dealing with the health effects, if any, of passive smoking. If studies had been produced by competent epidemiologists negativing any association between passive smoking and disease it is likely that, for the reasons given by Professor Wald (T. 4236-7 and Ex. SS, pp. 8-9) they would have found a publisher.

Dr Layard is also of the opinion that meta-analysis should not be used unless the several studies in the analysis are reasonably comparable with respect to demographic and social characteristics of the study populations, disease diagnosis and other factors. He thinks the studies display substantial diversity in these and other areas and that most of them are not methodologically sound or free from potential biases and confounding factors which might have distorted their results. He pointed to the fact that some of the studies show quite small associations and may have been the result of bias and confounding factors to the extent that they were not simply due to chance.

Dr Layard is very firm in his opinion that if a statistically significant association is not demonstrated by the data then it cannot be used as evidence in a process of drawing a causal inference.

As with the evidence of other witnesses, it is not possible in these reasons to give more than a summary of Dr Layard's evidence. He made the point that the relative risks revealed by most of the studies are, for the most part, fairly weak. This point is well made in the following table which forms part of his evidence:

Study	Sex	Number of Cases in Exposed Group	Relative Risk
Relative Risks 1 or Less			
Chan and Fung, 1982	F	34	0.75
Kabat and Wynder, 1984	F	13	0.79
	M	5	1.00
Buffler et al., 1984	F	33	0.80
	M	5	0.51
Gillis et al., 1984	F	6	1.00

Study	Sex	Number of Cases in Exposed Group	Relative Risk
Relative Risks Between 1 and 2			
Lee et al., 1986	F	22	1.03
	M	8	1.31
Garfinkel et al., 1985	F	92	1.12
Garfinkel 1981	F	88	1.17
Wu, 1985	F	29	1.20
Pershagen et al., 1987	F	33	1.20
Hirayama, 1984b	F	163	1.45
Akiba et al., 1986	F	73	1.52
Koo et al., 1987	F	51	1.55
Correa et al., 1983	M	2	1.97
Relative Risks Above 2			
Correa et al., 1983	F	14	2.07
Akiba, 1986	M	3	2.10
Trichopoulos et al., 1983	F	38	2.13
Hirayama, 1984a	M	7	2.28
Gillis et al., 1984	M	4	3.25

Dr Layard regards a relative risk of less than 2 as weak. There is a degree of disagreement between the epidemiologists as to what constitutes a weak association, but I think there would be general agreement that a relative risk below 1.5 is weak.

It is important to note the different approach taken by the statisticians (called by the respondent) and the epidemiologists (called by the applicant) to low relative risks revealed in the studies under consideration in the present case. The statisticians, as exemplified by Dr Layard, regard low relative risks as evidence only of a weak association. On the other hand, the epidemiologists, as exemplified by Professor Wald, took into account the strong association between active smoking and lung cancer and regarded the relative risks disclosed in the studies as evidence of a strong association at a low dose (Wald T. 4227). It is plain that the epidemiologists' interpretation of the data revealed in the studies is affected by their belief that there is a strong association between cigarette smoke and cancer in active smokers.

Dr Layard referred to inconsistencies in some of the results in the studies, the absence in many of them of dose response relationships and the possibility of various types of bias having given rise to apparent associations that might have been spurious. Moreover, he questioned the soundness of the methodology upon which the studies were based. He said that they were all open to criticism for flaws in their design and execution.

I think that Dr Layard was hypercritical in his approach to the studies. They all were carried out by apparently highly competent researchers. Scientists of high repute do not share Dr Layard's jaundiced view of them. Not only the applicant's witnesses but also the many highly skilled authors of the reports produced by the United States Surgeon General, the National Research Council, and the National Health and Medical Research Council failed to perceive in the reports many of the defects which Dr Layard found in them. In making this observation I do not overlook some of the highly relevant matters referred to by Dr Layard, e.g. internal inconsistencies in the Hirayama study.

A good deal of Dr Layard's practice is work undertaken on behalf of law firms who represent tobacco companies. Such work accounts for approximately 80% of his practice. The work includes the statistical analysis of published data relating to environmental tobacco smoke and health effects, and the presentation of papers which he has written at the request of law firms acting on behalf of tobacco companies. Plainly he has a very close association with the tobacco industry and depends upon it for most of his income. Not unnaturally, these matters were relied upon by counsel for the applicant as justifying the Court in taking a cautious approach to his evidence. I do not think that Dr Layard expressed opinions which he does not hold, but I do think his hypercritical approach to the epidemiological studies may not be dissociated with his close connection with the tobacco industry.

I think that even if all the epidemiological studies had been methodologically sound, free from bias of all kinds, free from confounding factors, and had consistently revealed statistically significant relative risks, Dr Layard would not have accepted them as proof that passive smoking is a cause of disease. When asked whether epidemiological studies had demonstrated a causal relationship between *active* smoking and disease he said that — "it would be more accurate to say that epidemiologic studies suggested the possibility of a causal relationship". (T. 2631)

Dr Layard concluded his proof of evidence with the statement that it is his opinion that little evidence and no scientific proof exists as of the present time that cigarette smoke causes cancer in non-smokers. He agreed with counsel for the applicant that in expressing this opinion he did not have regard to the evidence that exists in relation to biological plausibility because that is not an area within his area of expertise (T. 2650).

(j) *Professor Tweedie*

Professor Richard Tweedie is Dean, Information and Computing Sciences, at Bond University in the State of Queensland. He was formerly Associate Professor in the Department of Mathematics at the University of Western Australia and a Principal Research Scientist with the Division of Mathematics and Statistics in the Commonwealth Scientific Industrial Research Organisation.

Professor Tweedie's evidence fell into three broad categories. First, he gave an explanation of what he considered to be the requirements of scientific proof, particularly from the basis of statistical reasoning. Secondly, he made a detailed analysis of and comments upon the epidemiological studies referred to in the primary articles. Thirdly, he stated his conclusion as to the effect of the evidence after a consideration of those studies. His conclusion was expressed in the following terms:

> "Scientific proof requires consistent, significant results in repeated studies designed to test the hypothesis in question. Virtually the whole case for an association between lung cancer in women and exposure to ETS rests on the data from the study by Trichopoulos et al, and that study is seriously flawed.
>
> I cannot detect any scientific proof, in the papers I have read, of an increased risk in lung cancer from an association with exposure to ETS."

In his written proof of evidence the Professor did not express any opinion on the question whether or not it was correct to say that there is little evidence that cigarette smoke causes disease in non-smokers. At the conclusion of his evidence in chief he was asked his opinion on that matter and he said that he believed the statement to be accurate (T. 2444). He made it plain in cross-examination that he had considered only the question of lung cancer, and not any other disease. He also conceded that in considering the accuracy of the statement in the advertisement he had considered only whether or not there was any scientific proof to be found in the epidemiological studies. As this is a matter of some importance I set out some of his evidence with respect to it:

> "You did not direct your attention to other data that may be obtained, for example, biological data of exposure of animals to tobacco smoke? — I have read one or two papers on that subject but in terms of the effect on lung cancer in humans I did not read that as evidence.
>
> And you paid no regard to the biochemical analysis of tobacco smoke as between what is described as mainstream smoke, that is the smoke drawn from the filter and environmental tobacco smoke that is side stream smoke from the burning tip of the cigarette and exhaled mainstream smoke? — That is not correct. I actually did read two or three papers on that subject but as far as determining whether that is relevant to the effect on human beings I do not believe it can do other than add to the biological plausibility argument which is part of

scientific proof as opposed to whether or not it does in fact cause harm.

But your limited reading of that material, was that able to assist you in relation to the biological plausibility or did you not consider that aspect? — I do not believe I am expert at considering that. It certainly did not sway me to make a statement saying there is no biological plausibility.

I am sorry, say that again? It did not? — It did not lead me to make a statement saying there is no biological plausibility.

Thank you? — But I do not believe that is something I am expert in.

And I take it that nor did you examine the epidemiological data in relation to direct smoking and lung cancer? — I have not read any studies on that except insofar as some of the studies on exposure to ETS have some small amount of active smoking data in them.

But to the extent that that data exists, would you agree with me that it may assist another person to form some view as to the biological plausibility of some of the hypotheses that are being examined in the epidemiological data that you examined? — It would certainly seem to me to be a relative (sic) factor in deciding on the biological plausibility ...

And in that context, considering the phrase, there is little evidence and nothing that proves scientifically that cigarette smoke causes disease in non-smokers, you did not attempt to assess whether or not there was little evidence or more than little evidence, rather, you focused on the question of whether you could detect any scientific proof. Is that correct? — I focused on the question of whether I could detect any scientific proof in the question of lung cancer, yes, that is correct.'' (T. 2445-6)

The impression I gained from the Professor's evidence was that he had really concerned himself only with whether there was scientific proof, as distinct from little evidence, whether cigarette smoke causes disease in non-smokers.

Professor Tweedie made it clear that he thought that, on his approach, statistical significance was essential to scientific proof. That this is so appears from the following passages in his evidence (T. 2383):

``HIS HONOUR: As I understand your approach and I do understand it I think, you say that statistical significance is essential to scientific proof? — I believe absolutely that it is, yes.

If you are looking — I mean, once you resort to statistical analysis or epidemiological analysis you say that you have not got scientific proof unless your conclusion is based on statistically significant results; is that right? — I believe that very firmly, I think.''

It is apparent that Professor Tweedie's approach to the question of scientific proof is fundamentally different from that taken by the epidemiologists called in the applicant's case. In the first place, statistical significance to them is a guide to thought, rather than a prerequisite of proof. And in the second place, they take into account non-statistical considerations such as biological plausibility and reliance upon trends shown in epidemiological studies, even though the trends be observed in non-statistical results.

The different approach of the epidemiologist and the statistician can be seen in some evidence which Professor Tweedie gave as to the Hirayama study. He agreed that Hirayama found an odds ratio of 2.23 in respect of persons aged between 40 and 59 years who were married to smokers of 20 or more cigarettes per day, and that this result was statistically significant. However, since it was only one of a relatively small number of statistically significant results found by Hirayama amongst a greater number of non-statistical results, Professor Tweedie thought it might be the result of data-dredging. He thought that the result may show a true association between passive smoking and lung cancer, but the result had not been shown to be incompatible with chance. When he was asked whether he had gone through the various studies to ascertain whether the statistically significant results appeared generally to be in the cases where there had been a high level of smoking by the husband he said he had not done any analysis to check whether this was so. Similarly, when it was suggested that the statistically significant results in the studies also tended to be in older age groups he said he had not done an analysis to check that. He was thus unable to agree or disagree with the proposition that the statistically significant results accorded with biological plausibility of the development of lung cancer in that the disease is dose-related and is marked by a long latency period. Indeed, when cross-examined on this matter, senior counsel for the respondent objected to the questions on the ground that the Professor eschewed any medical knowledge when giving his evidence in chief (T. 2464).

Thus it will be seen that Professor Tweedie did not look for additional factors which the epidemiologists thought were of great importance in deciding whether there was a causal relationship between passive smoking and lung cancer.

It would be impossible in these reasons to capture the enormous detail of the criticisms made by Professor Tweedie of the studies referred to in the primary articles. The fact that I do not attempt to do so is no indication that I think that the studies are above criticism. But in general, I think he was over-critical of the methodology in most of the studies and gave more weight to potential flaws in them than was warranted.

In respect of the Hirayama study he thought it should be treated as hypothesis-generating and therefore unable to be used to prove or disprove the hypothesis itself. This is a criticism of the study which Professor McMichael regarded as unwarranted because of the existence of the hypothesis, which had been formed prior to the study being undertaken, as to the effect of mainstream smoke on smokers.

Professor Tweedie questioned the representativeness of the data in the Hirayama study. However, the relevance of this criticism was discussed by Professors McMichael and Wald (T. 1322 and T. 4302-3) and discounted. A similar attitude is taken in the Surgeon General's report (p. 75).

The possibility of misclassification because death certificates were used by Hirayama as an indication of lung cancer was stressed by Professor Tweedie. But as is pointed out by some commentators, there is no reason to believe that error in recording the causes of death of wives was influenced by the smoking habits of their husbands, and if any misclassification of this kind took place it was likely to be random.

Professor Tweedie also expressed concern as to the reliability of the Hirayama study because of the possibility of misclassification of smokers as non-smokers. He noted that when the study was carried out smoking by women was neither common nor accepted in Japanese society, and he thought many smoking women may have described themselves as non-smokers. However, as the Surgeon General points out in his report, there is some assurance of the reliability of the smoking data provided by the Japanese women in the Hirayama case from results obtained from other studies. This is not to say, of course, that no misclassification occurred. But the Professor seemed to me to take an excessively cautious approach on this matter, as with some other matters.

Professor Tweedie also pointed out that in the Hirayama study the smoking habits of the subject's husband was used as the indicator of exposure and that this is not necessarily an adequate measure of exposure. I agree that classifying non-smoking women upon the basis only of their husbands' smoking habits gives an imprecise measure of exposure. Obviously most non-smoking women will be exposed to passive smoke other than that generated by their husbands' smoking. Nevertheless, the classification based on the smoking habits of husbands seems to me to be a reasonable, if inexact basis of classification.

Professor Tweedie also thought there were many potential confounding factors in the Hirayama study which had been unaccounted for. Some of these were occupation, diet, medical care, family history, lifestyle and home environment. It may be almost impossible to totally exclude the possibility of some of these being potential confounding factors but this is not to say that the study does not have a value when taken in conjunction with other studies.

I have already referred to Professor Tweedie's criticism of the use of the statistically significant result found in respect of the 40 to 59 years age group where the husband smoked more than 20 cigarettes per day. He said it was data-dredging to use this admittedly statistically significant result. However, Dr Layard did not take the same view on this matter (T. 2658-9).

Professor Tweedie thought the Trichopoulos study afforded some support for an association between lung cancer and exposure to environmental tobacco smoke. He accepted that it was not hypothesis-generating and that some of the results were statistically significant. However, he thought that the study was so flawed as to render it incapable of providing data concerning an association between lung cancer and exposure to environmental tobacco smoke to which strong scientific credence can be given. He accepted that there was "some level of scientific credence in the study" (T. 2521).

Professor Tweedie's criticisms of the Trichopoulos study were put to Professor Trichopoulos when he gave evidence and I shall not repeat them or his answers to them. As Professor Trichopoulos acknowledged in his published article, his study had obvious limitations, in particular, that the numbers of cases were small.

The study by Garfinkel was said by Professor Tweedie to be flawed particularly by possible misclassification and the measurement of environmental tobacco smoke. The criticisms of this study are noted in the Surgeon General's report where it is observed that the misclassification which may have occurred could have led to an underestimate of the effect of passive smoking.

As I have observed it was not asserted by the applicant's witnesses that some of the criticisms levelled at the studies by Professor Tweedie did not have some justification. There is therefore little point in seeking to identify all those criticisms. However, even if all the studies had been free from the criticisms made of them by Professor Tweedie, he still would not have been persuaded that they proved a causal link between passive smoking and lung cancer.

Professor Tweedie carried out combined analyses for both the case control studies and for the cohort studies. The overall result for the cohort studies was significant at the 5% level, whilst the overall result for the case control studies was marginally insignificant at that level. He pointed out that the Trichopoulos study dominated the case control analysis, and the Hirayama study the cohort study analysis. When those studies were omitted, the results obtained were not statistically significant. However, I cannot see any justification for omitting them, nor did Professor Wald (Ex. SS, p. 11).

(k) *Professor Witorsch*

Professor Philip Witorsch is a physician and is currently Clinical Professor of Medicine, Adjunct Professor of Physiology, and Director, Section of Environmental Medicine and Toxicology in the Department of Medicine at the George Washington University School of Medicine and Health Sciences. He is also medical director at the Center for Environmental Health and Human Toxicology at the George Washington University Hospital. He is a Fellow of the American College of Physicians and of the American College of Chest Physicians and has served as an adviser and consultant to a number of Federal agencies in the United States, as well as to a number of industry and private groups, including the Tobacco Institute of the United States and the Tobacco Institute of Australia. Since 1985 he has been involved in the evaluation of data relating to a number of aspects of environmental tobacco smoke as a paid consultant to the Tobacco Institute of the United States of America.

He is the author of many articles which have been published in medical and scientific journals. Most of his time is now spent in clinical practice, medical teaching and scientific research.

Professor Witorsch is of the opinion that the statement made in para. 3 of the advertisement is an accurate characterisation of the evidence concerning environmental tobacco smoke that existed as at July 1986 and that it is still accurate when measured against the evidence that currently exists. He gave evidence as to the alleged association between passive smoking and lung cancer, respiratory disease in adult non-smokers, respiratory disease and respiratory function in children and cardiovascular disease. I shall consider in this section of my reasons only that part of his evidence as relates to the alleged association between passive smoking and lung cancer.

Professor Witorsch did not claim to have any special expertise in research into the causes of lung cancer. He said he was not an epidemiologist but that he did have some expertise in the field (T. 3114).

He is of the opinion that the quantitative and qualitative differences between mainstream and environmental tobacco smoke are such that one cannot reach meaningful conclusions regarding passive smoking and disease by extrapolating from experimental and epidemiological data relative to active smoking. He said that inhalation exposure patterns differ between active smokers and non-smokers exposed to environmental tobacco smoke in that active smoking involves intermittent high dose exposure through the mouth with the constituents being inhaled deeply and retained in the lungs, whereas passive smoking involves low dose exposure in which tobacco constituents are not necessarily deeply inhaled. He said that such differences in inhalation patterns may explain why only about 11% of the particulate portion of environmental tobacco smoke is retained by the respiratory tract, while retention of mainstream smoke particulates ranges from 50%-80%.

In his opinion results of epidemiological studies can suggest an association which, when taken together with other appropriate evidence, may provide support for the formation of a judgment as to a causal relationship between an exposure and a disease outcome. But he thinks they cannot, by themselves, prove that such a relationship exists. Consistent with this opinion, he holds the opinion that it has not been proved scientifically that mainstream smoke causes lung cancer in active smokers.

Professor Witorsch referred to the possibility of epidemiological studies being affected by matters such as bias and misclassification. He thinks that since there is an acknowledged tendency for smokers to marry smokers, some of the subjects in the studies who were considered to be non-smokers may actually have been current or ex-smokers, and that such misclassification could have resulted in artificial increases in the risk ratios reported. He said that some of the epidemiological studies concerning environmental tobacco smoke and the incidence of lung cancer suggest an association between the two, whilst others do not.

He commented on individual studies, pointing out that many of them gave results which were not statistically significant. He is of the view that all of the epidemiological studies have methodological and other problems that make it difficult to reach meaningful conclusions regarding the hypothesised association between environmental tobacco smoke exposure and increased incidence of lung cancer.

He thinks the studies were affected, in particular, by problems of inadequate verification of exposure to environmental tobacco smoke and inadequate validation of the smoking status or classification of the study subjects. In his opinion an acceptable biological or environmental marker of environmental tobacco smoke exposure is desirable in an epidemiological study so as to be sure that the exposed group is indeed exposed. He thinks that reliance upon questionnaires leads to a higher probability of exposure misclassification.

I have no doubt that acceptable biological or environmental markers would reduce the incidence of misclassification, but that is not to say that in their absence responses to questionnaires do not provide a sufficiently sound basis for classification.

Professor Witorsch made criticisms of the studies similar to those made by Professor Tweedie. For the most part, he referred to criticisms of the studies made by other persons and adopted them. This is understandable in view of the fact that he did not claim to be a specialist epidemiologist.

He questioned the meta-analysis exercises carried out by Professor Wald and the National Research Council because he thought they are based on a number of questionable assumptions, particularly the assumption that spousal smoking is a valid and reliable surrogate index for environmental tobacco smoke exposure.

Professor Witorsch made no mention in his proof of evidence of some matters which epidemiologists think are of great importance in reaching a conclusion whether there is a causal association between passive smoking and lung cancer, e.g. whether environmental tobacco smoke contains carcinogenic substances and whether there is no safe dose for carcinogens. In his opinion, the question whether exposure to environmental tobacco smoke is associated with an increased risk of lung cancer remains unresolved.

(1) *Professor Huber*

Professor Gary Huber has been Professor of Medicine in the Department of Medicine at the University of Texas Health Center since 1985. He has been associated with research, teaching, diagnosis and treatment in the field of pulmonary medicine since 1962. He has been interested in and associated with research into smoking, tobacco smoke and health since 1972 when he became Director of the Smoking and Health Research Program at the Harvard Medical School, Boston. This program was initiated jointly by the Harvard Medical School and by the major cigarette manufacturers in the United States, with the intent of developing a multi-disciplinary evaluation of the potential health effects of tobacco smoke.

Professor Huber is of the view that the statement made in the advertisement accurately describes the state of the evidence both as at July 1986 and at the present time. He thinks a major difficulty in studying the health effects of environmental tobacco smoke on non-smokers is that non-smokers are exposed to a mixture which is both qualitatively and quantitatively different from that to which active smokers are exposed. He also thinks it is not scientifically appropriate, in the present state of knowledge, to transpose theories concerned with active smoking and health into the field of health issues related to environmental tobacco smoke.

Professor Huber said that although different researchers have reported different levels of nicotine in the atmosphere of places in which smoking occurs, all of the levels reported are low and the majority of reported data indicates that, overall, tobacco smoke contributes very little to indoor environmental pollution. This is a judgment which appears to me to be inconsistent with common experience of some indoor environments.

He said that the constituent chemical components in environmental tobacco smoke include benzo(a)pyrene and other constituents which are found in minute quantities in mainstream smoke and in even smaller quantities in environmental tobacco smoke. These are hydrocarbons and can, when applied at high concentrations in condensate form, produce tumours. In his opinion, it has not been demonstrated and it is highly improbable that they present a risk of cancer in humans in the concentrations at which they are found in environmental tobacco smoke.

Professor Huber's evidence related mostly to relationships between environmental tobacco smoke and cardiovascular diseases, acute pulmonary effects, chronic pulmonary effects in adults and children, and asthma. He did not claim to have any special expertise in cancer epidemiology.

He agreed (T. 3724) that there are chemicals, such as vinyl chloride, that exist both in mainstream smoke and sidestream smoke and that vinyl chloride had been shown to be carcinogenic in humans. He would not agree, however, that a passive smoker who inhales environmental tobacco smoke may inhale smoke which contains vinyl chloride. He said that some things cannot be detected in environmental tobacco smoke that can be measured in sidestream smoke. He does not know whether vinyl chloride had been detected in environmental tobacco smoke or not. He agreed that it was possible that a small child being nursed by a woman smoking a cigarette might inhale a molecule of vinyl chloride.

When asked whether it is generally accepted that a safe threshold is unlikely to exist for most carcinogens, Professor Huber said that he did not know the exact answer to the question. When pressed with the question: "Do you agree that it is unlikely that there is a threshold of low dose exposure to carcinogens below which there is no increase in risk?", he answered: "I would think that there would be a threshold below which the risk is so small that it could not be measured." He agreed in cross-examination that in an article which was published in January 1990 and of which he was the co-author, the following statements appeared:

> "As summarized by the Surgeon General there is little disagreement that active smoking is associated with an increased risk for the development of lung cancer, with a causal and probable dose response relationship between tobacco smoking and the development of lung cancer."
>
> "Furthermore there does not seem to be any safe threshold for an absolute lower limit of tobacco smoking and the occurrence of lung cancer."
>
> "Depending on the extent of exposure the non-smoker may be exposed to clearly quantitatively lesser amounts of smoke but for some components qualitative exposure of the non smoker may differ little from the active smoker."

With respect to the last-mentioned passage he said he had since expanded his reading significantly and that, at the time he wrote the article, it was the best information he had. He also said that if he were to write the paper again, he would write it differently. I am bound to say that I found some of his answers unsatisfactory, as he did not persuade me that any significant body of scientific material had come to his notice since the paper was written.

Dr Huber claimed that the abovementioned statements had been taken out of context, and in this respect the following excerpt from his evidence is relevant:

> "MR FRANCEY: You complain, doctor, that the two sentences I read to you about threshold and similarity of the quality of smoke that non smokers are exposed to and smokers are exposed to were taken out of context. Can I ask you this then, that in writing that article by way of summary in relation to lung cancer you were of the view last year that some of the existing data show a positive association between passive smoking and lung cancer, although these data do not always necessarily meet strict criteria of causality in this association but considering the large number of persons exposed to passive smoking, even the most minimal potential association for the development of lung cancer in non smokers cannot, however, be ignored? — I would agree with that.
>
> And you would agree with it now? — Yes." (T. 3777)

I did not find Professor Huber a satisfactory witness in all respects. I thought, with all respect to him, that he was sometimes evasive in his answers. That this is so appears, I think, from the following passage in his evidence:

> "HIS HONOUR: ... In your opinion, does active smoking cause cancer in some smokers? — In a susceptible group within the smoking population.
>
> No, leaving that aside. If I just ... asked you the question, whether in your opinion, does active smoking cause lung cancer in some active smokers, what would your answer be? — My answer would be the same. My answer would be that there are associations and that there are a variety of complex aspects to that question. I am not trying to evade the question. I am trying to say it is a very complex issue and that people who smoke develop lung cancer.
>
> Would this be your answer and do not assent to it if it is not right, would your answer be there is a strong, perhaps very strong association between active smoking and the incidence of lung cancer ... (but) I cannot say that there is a causal relationship between the two? — There certainly is a strong association. I agree with that. I do not understand the nature of the potential causal relationship. I do not know what it is in tobacco smoke that might cause cancer in humans. I know that there are 40 or 50 carcinogens there that cause tumours in animals. I do not know which, if any of those might be responsible for the induction of cancer in humans. I do not know the mechanism by which that occurs. So I am left with a strong association between cigarette smoking and the development of cancer in some individuals and that is a strong association and the mechanisms and the details of which have defied science to this point. Does that answer your question?"

I think Professor Huber is excessively cautious in drawing conclusions from available data. Of all the witnesses called by the respondent, I found him the least impressive.

(m) *Dr Malmfors*

Dr Sven Malmfors is an independent consultant in toxicology and risk assessment. He resides in Sweden. He was, for a time, an Assistant Professor in the Department of Histology at the Karolinska Institute in Stockholm. Between 1972 and 1980 he was the head of the toxicology laboratory of a large pharmaceutical company. He left that position in 1980 to go into private practice as an independent consultant. He has worked part-time in the teaching of toxicology and the training of graduates in the science of toxicology. He is a past President of the Swedish Society of Toxicology.

In his capacity as a consultant, Dr Malmfors has spoken at seminars on behalf of the tobacco industry. Such seminars have been concerned with exposure to environmental tobacco smoke.

Dr Malmfors is of the opinion that the statement made in the advertisement was accurate at the time it was published and is still accurate. He said that a toxicological evaluation to determine the toxicity of a given chemical to humans requires the accumulation of data which may come from experimentation or epidemiology. Such experimentation may involve testing a biological system under artificial conditions in a laboratory, or experiments with animals or humans. He said if there are no experimental data other than epidemiological data, this is usually not sufficient from a toxicological point of view to establish a cause/effect relationship.

He drew attention to what he said were the qualitative and quantitative differences between mainstream and environmental tobacco smoke. He said that unless particular chemicals, either alone or in the same combination, can be shown to be present in both mainstream and environmental tobacco smoke, it is not scientifically proper to extrapolate from mainstream smoke components to environmental tobacco smoke components or to use the former to found a reasoning process based on analogy. He thinks that data derived from experiments concerning the effect of mainstream smoke on animals is not relevant to the question whether passive smoking causes cancer in humans. The results of such experiments cannot, in his opinion, be extrapolated to exposure to environmental tobacco smoke.

It seems to me that Dr Malmfors' requirements for the establishment of scientific truth are almost unattainable. Some idea of the degree of proof which he would require before being persuaded of a scientifically proved cause/effect relationship between environmental tobacco smoke and lung cancer may be gained from the opinions which he expressed as to the proof (or absence of it) of a cause/effect relationship between active smoking and lung cancer. His evidence included the following:

> "HIS HONOUR: Would you agree that tobacco smoke contains several agents which are cancer initiating and mutagenic? — Depends on under which circumstances. There are chemicals in mainstream smoke which under certain conditions initiate tumours and that is true.
>
> Well under conditions which obtain when a human inhales the smoke? — No, I consider those conditions different from those conditions where there are proof of [carcinogenicity] for those …
>
> I am not talking about ETS. I am talking about the active smoker? — Yes.
>
> Is the smoke which he inhales, smoke which contains several agents which are cancer initiating and mutagenic? — Yes, but the problem is that they are not cancer inducing and mutagenic everywhere under every condition. There are certain conditions which have to be fulfilled before that, in effect, can occur.
>
> Is it not your belief that those conditions are very often fulfilled and that that leads to what is said to be an increased incidence of lung cancer in active smokers? — I do not know which those conditions are so I cannot comment on that." (T. 2270)

He said (T. 2259) he was unable to point to any evidence that showed there was a safe dose for any of the carcinogenic substances in tobacco smoke. He agreed that epidemiological studies have reported an association between active smoking and the incidence of lung cancer in smokers but he said, quite positively, that he did not accept that direct smoking causes lung cancer. He conceded that it was possible that there may be important toxicological data obtained from research in connection with active smoking that might throw light on the effect of environmental tobacco smoke, but that he had not studied it. I am bound to say that I found this concession surprising coming from a scientist of his calibre who is so closely interested in the effects of environmental tobacco smoke that he addresses seminars on the subject on behalf of the tobacco industry. I think it reflects a very narrow scientific approach and a reluctance to consider all available data which might contribute to an understanding of the effects, if any, of passive smoking.

(n) *Professor Clayton*

Professor John Clayton is Professor Emeritus of Pharmacology and Toxicology at the University of Arizona. He held the positions of Professor of Pharmacology and Toxicology and Professor of Microbiology and Medical Immunology at the University from 1974 to 1989.

Professor Clayton referred to the quantitative and qualitative differences which he thinks distinguish mainstream smoke from environmental tobacco smoke. Based on toxicological data from animal inhalation experiments Professor Clayton's opinion is that the statement in the advertisement was accurate at the time it was published and is still accurate.

He thinks that in order to evaluate a hypothesis as to whether or not environmental tobacco smoke causes chronic disease such as lung cancer in humans, scientists must consider two major types of data: epidemiological and toxicological. In his opinion, epidemiology alone is not sufficient to establish a cause and effect relationship. He thinks that well designed and well conducted animal experiments are required in addition to epidemiological data before it can be scientifically concluded that a particular agent causes a specific chronic disease. He knows of no animal inhalation experiments investigating the effects of environmental tobacco smoke as at 1 July 1986. In the absence of such studies he thinks there was no pertinent toxicological evidence at that time and that therefore, it had not been proved scientifically that environmental tobacco smoke caused chronic disease in non-smokers.

Professor Clayton said that there had been two animal experiments since July 1986 in which attempts had been made to measure the effects of environmental tobacco smoke on hamsters. One experiment revealed pulmonary changes in the hamsters, but of a kind which could have been expected to occur under similar exposure to other agents, e.g. dust. The investigators who carried out the other experiment reported that overall there was no marked increase in tumour incidence in animals exposed to either mainstream smoke or sidestream smoke over the normal lifespan of a hamster.

With reference to three studies referred to by Professor Stewart in his evidence (Harris et al., Bernfeld et al. and Dalbey et al.) Professor Clayton said they were all studies concerned to simulate active smoking by exposure of mice, rats or hamsters to mainstream smoke, not environmental tobacco smoke. In any event, he thought there were other problems about the experiments, including that the concentrations of smoke used were very high and quite different from human exposure to environmental tobacco smoke. As to the theory that one molecule of a suspected carcinogen may initiate a carcinogenic process, the Professor said there was no way to prove or disprove this theory.

Professor Clayton is of the opinion that toxicology has not provided any proof that mainstream smoke causes lung cancer in active smokers. As he said: ''The toxicologist would say there is no demonstration that cigarette smoke inhalation causes lung cancer in humans.'' (T. 2941.) He accepted that some substances found in tobacco smoke, e.g. vinyl chloride and napthylamine are listed in the IARC report (Appendix Z at pp. 389-394) as being chemicals in respect of which there is sufficient evidence that they are carcinogenic to both animals and humans. But as I understood his evidence, he was not prepared to concede that this was indeed the case.

The respondent tendered as part of its case Chapter 4 of the 1982 report of the United States Surgeon General on the health consequences of smoking in which the statement is prominently made that — ''Cigarette smoking is the major single cause of cancer mortality in the United States''.

Professor Clayton's views do not rest easily with this statement.

(o) *Mr Leslie*

Mr George Leslie is an independent toxicologist and pharmacologist. Between 1974 and 1987 he was head of the Toxicology and Pathology Department of Smith Kline and French where he worked on many projects of a toxicological nature. He has been a full-time consultant in toxicology since 1987. He has lectured to students at a number of academic institutions, including London University and is an examiner of the candidates for the degree of Doctor of Philosophy in Pharmacology and Toxicology at the University of Wales. He has written many scientific papers.

Mr Leslie expressed the opinion that the statement made in the advertisement was accurate as at 1986 with respect to possible health effects on the embryo or foetus in a woman exposed to environmental tobacco smoke. I have had regard to what Mr Leslie said in his evidence regarding matters such as the nature of scientific proof and the distinction between proof of an association and proof of a cause and effect relationship. The bulk of Mr Leslie's evidence relates to matters other than the association, if any, between passive smoking and cancer in non-smokers and I shall not refer to it in the present context.

(p) *Professor Warren*

Professor Warren is Professor of Pathology at the University of New South Wales and has impressive qualifications as a pathologist. He described the histologic, cytologic and clinical techniques for diagnosing cancer of the lung and some of the limitations of these techniques. His evidence was essentially non-controversial. The limitations of which he spoke were recognised by the applicant's witnesses. I do not think they diminish the weight which I should give to their evidence and to the findings referred to in the primary articles.

(v) *Comments on the epidemiological evidence*

The respondent's witnesses, particularly Professor Tweedie and Dr Layard, criticised the methodology and quality of all the epidemiological studies upon which the applicant's witnesses relied. To a greater or lesser extent, the studies were said to be flawed because of a number of factors. These factors included reliability of the diagnoses of lung cancer, the adequacy of data provided by surrogate respondents, the representativeness of data, possible sources of bias and misclassification, the unreliability of using spousal smoking habits as an indicator of exposure to environmental tobacco smoke, and failure to account for confounding factors.

I think it is fair to say that the applicant's witnesses conceded, to a limited extent, that the results in some of the studies may have been affected by some of these factors, albeit not to the extent of making them unreliable. In their opinion, it was the pattern which emerged from the studies which was important. This opinion is reflected in Chapter 7 of the NH & MRC report where the following statement is made:

> "In reviewing the literature on passive smoking and lung cancer, it is important to include an overall assessment of the directionality and coherence of the findings from the various individual studies. Given the methodological impediments to making a conclusive finding in any one epidemiological study, then it is important to examine the pattern of findings. If, despite limitations and flaws in individual studies, substantial consistency emerges — as is the case for the reported evidence on passive smoking and lung cancer — then the prudent public health response must be to infer that a real effect is likely."

I have referred above to statements to the same effect by some of the applicant's witnesses.

Counsel for the respondent submitted that Dr McMichael had, in effect, conceded that there was no demonstrated causal link between passive smoking and lung cancer in a paper he submitted to the National Health & Medical Research Council Carcinogenic Substances Committee in March 1983 (Ex. 104). In that report, after a detailed discussion of the studies by Hirayama, Trichopoulos (1981 study only) and Garfinkel (1981 study only), he said that while the available epidemiological evidence suggested that passive smoking may increase the risk of lung cancer, the limitations in data and study design did not then allow a judgment on causality. But this paper was produced at a very early stage in the on-going investigation into the possible health hazard from passive smoking.

The intrinsic difficulties in appraising epidemiological studies of passive smoking and health are recognised in the scientific literature. Many of the limitations and criticisms of the studies referred to in the primary articles are dealt with in considerable detail in Chapter 2 of the Surgeon General's report. The Surgeon General's comments appear to me to be valid and I adopt them as part of these reasons. No useful purpose would be served by repeating them.

However, there are a few general comments I should make about the epidemiological evidence. In the first place, I think that more reliance can be placed upon non-statistically significant results than the respondent's witnesses were prepared to concede. I agree with Sir Richard Doll's view that statistical significance is "a guide to thought" rather than an absolute standard. If a positive relative risk is statistically insignificant because, say, the lower confidence limit is marginally below 1, do not think that it should be rejected from consideration for that reason alone. In such a situation, lack of statistical significance calls for the exercise of caution in evaluating the study, but that is not to say that it disqualifies the study from consideration.

On a related matter, I think that non-statistically significant data which, considered in isolation from other data, may be of little value in forming an epidemiological judgment, may well be valuable aids to judgment if they form part of a pattern of positive findings.

I agree that spousal smoking is an imprecise measure of total exposure to passive smoke because it accounts for only one of what may be many possible sources of tobacco smoke exposure. But with all its imprecision, it seems to me to afford a reasonable basis for measuring exposure.

The applicant's and the respondent's witnesses were generally agreed that what are known as the Bradford Hill criteria are standard criteria for evaluating epidemiological studies. However, the respondent's witnesses placed more store on the observance of all the criteria than did the applicant's witnesses. For instance, Dr McMichael thought the criteria should be applied only subject to a caveat. He said (T. 1238):

> "Well, it is a general caveat that, whilst those are well-recognised as useful and often important criteria in the drawing of judgments about causal inference, they are not and should not be seen as pre-requisites. In other words the drawing of causal inferences can quite reasonably proceed and often does in the presence of just several of these criteria."

It is this approach which appears to me to explain the differing views of the applicant's and the respondent's witnesses as to the evidentiary value of the studies referred to in the primary articles. I prefer the approach taken by the applicant's witnesses to that taken by the respondent's witnesses.

As to misclassification, I take the view that although the risk of it occurring is always present, the respondent's witnesses have tended to exaggerate its significance and not to have regard to the fact that it is often random in its distribution.

I think the respondent's witnesses tended to underestimate the biological plausibility of a causal link between passive smoking and lung cancer. I agree with Professor Trichopoulos' evidence that:

> "It is one thing to find strong statistical significance which comes out of the blue and it is quite different to find statistical significance [in] something which is suspected on the [basis] of biological grounds ..." (T. 4030)

Without wishing to derogate from the expertise of Professor Tweedie and Dr Layard as statisticians, I think their assessment of the value of the studies referred to in the primary articles tended to be over-technical. I have formed the opinion that the evaluations of the studies by the epidemiologists called by the applicant are to be preferred to the evaluations of them made by Professor Tweedie and Dr Layard.

It emerged from time to time in the evidence that a statistician is less likely to find evidence of proof in an epidemiological study than is an epidemiologist. Because of Dr Layard's close association with the tobacco industry, it seems highly unlikely that he is unaware of the epidemiological studies as to the existence of a causal link between active smoking and lung cancer. As I have already noted, Chapter 4 of the 1982 report of the Surgeon General (which was tendered by the respondent) contains a most positive statement that active smoking causes cancer in smokers. Yet when Dr Layard was asked whether he had formed an opinion on the question whether a causal relationship had been established between active smoking and any form of disease, he said (T. 2720) that he had not formed an opinion on that subject. When pressed why that was so he said: "I can only say that I do not feel that my knowledge of biological matters is sufficient for me to arrive at an informed conclusion on that subject."

I also think that Dr Witorsch and Professor Huber took an over-technical approach to the epidemiological evidence and were hypercritical of it.

(vi) *Is there more than a little evidence that cigarette smoke causes cancer in non-smokers?*

In my opinion, the applicant has established that, in relation to the disease of cancer, it was misleading and deceptive to state on 1 July 1986 that there was then little evidence that cigarette smoke causes disease in non-smokers. So far from there then being little evidence that cigarette smoke caused lung cancer in non-smokers, there was much evidence to that effect. That was the situation, even if only the data referred to in the primary articles is regarded as evidence for the purposes of the advertisement. Measuring that evidence by any standard, it cannot be fairly described as "little".

Unaided by the opinions of the experts who were called, I would have concluded that it cannot be described as "little". The opinions of the experts called in the applicant's case confirm my conclusion. I much prefer the opinions of the applicant's witnesses on this matter. The evidence of a link between passive smoking and lung cancer comes from epidemiological studies supported by strong biological plausibility. The epidemiologists called by the applicant were most impressive witnesses. Their opinions are shared by many other distinguished epidemiologists who took part in the compilation of the major reviews.

The respondent did not call one witness whose primary expertise was in the field of epidemiology. I do not overlook the fact that Professor Huber and Professor Witorsch have some experience in the field, nor that Professor Tweedie and Dr Layard are experienced statisticians. Nor is it a matter merely of counting heads. Rather it is a matter of judging, as best I can, which opinions are entitled to the most weight. I have no hesitation in preferring the opinions expressed by the applicant's witnesses.

I have reached the conclusion that the opinions of the experts called by the applicant are to be preferred to the opinions expressed by the experts called by the respondent. I think the applicant's witnesses had more experience in some matters upon which they disagreed with the respondent's witnesses. In particular, on questions concerning the carcinogenic qualities of tobacco smoke and the existence or otherwise of a safe level of exposure to carcinogens I found the evidence of Professor Stewart very persuasive and I prefer it to the respondent's evidence on the same matters.

As I have noted the applicant's witnesses said that the statement that there is little evidence that cigarette smoke causes cancer in non-smokers is incorrect. I did not understand the respondent's counsel to submit that evidence of this kind was inadmissible. However, it was submitted that the statements by the applicant's witnesses as to their own opinions on the question whether cigarette smoke causes disease in non-smokers is not evidence in the sense in which that word is used in the advertisement. It was submitted that any probative value attaching to the findings referred to in the primary articles was not increased by the applicant's experts expressing their concurrence with them. I think there is some substance in this submission, but I do not think it advances the respondent's case. The experts were entitled to explain the contents of the primary articles and to depose as to the strengths and weaknesses of the studies referred to in them. If, after examination of a primary article, it is seen to disclose some evidence of a causal relationship between passive smoking and lung cancer it is hardly necessary for an expert to express his opinion that it does so.

Of course, if it is relevant to have regard to the state of the evidence after 1 July 1986 and to major reviews as well as primary articles, the applicant's case becomes even stronger. As I have said earlier in these reasons, I think that the applicant is not confined to the state of the evidence as at 1 July 1986 and I also think that the major reviews are "evidence" as that word is used in the advertisement.

On the question of the relevance of articles published after 1 July 1986, I should make special reference to the Wald article on meta-analysis. Although the article was published after 1 July 1986, the studies which Professor Wald and his co-authors analysed were all published before that date. The meta-analysis which they carried out could as easily have been carried out on 1 July 1986. What the article did was to show the strength of the evidence as it existed at 1 July 1986, not as at the date of publication of the article. Hence, I think regard can be had to the article for the purpose of assessing whether it was misleading or deceptive to say, as at 1 July 1986, that the evidence which then existed was "little".

Since I am of the opinion that on no view of the meaning of the word "little" can the evidence that passive smoking causes disease in non-smokers be so described, there is no need to attach a precise meaning to the word. The essential message which the advertisement, as a whole, attempts to convey to the reader is that cigarette smoke may be annoying to some non-smokers but that (as stated in the penultimate paragraph) "... annoyance is neither a governmental nor a medical problem''. In substance, what the reader is told is that inhalation of cigarette smoke by non-smokers may be annoying to them but it is not a health problem. Having regard to the totality of the advertisement, the reference to ''little evidence'' seems to be a reference to evidence which is so inconsequential as not to support a reasonable apprehension that passive smoking may give rise to a medical or health problem.

It was submitted on behalf of the respondent that the evidence called by the applicant was not evidence that cigarette smoke causes disease in non-smokers. The evidence, so it was submitted, was no more than evidence of an association between cigarette smoke and disease. I am unable to accept that evidence of an association between passive smoking and lung cancer cannot be regarded as some evidence of a causal relationship between the two.

Nor do I accept the respondent's related submission that epidemiological evidence alone cannot establish a cause and effect relationship. The submission would be valid only if the standard of proof required to establish such a relationship is set at a virtually unattainable level.

(vii) *Is there scientific proof that cigarette smoke causes cancer in non-smokers?*

I have not so far considered whether the statement is erroneous in so far as it asserts that there is nothing which proves scientifically that cigarette smoke causes disease in non-smokers. As I have observed, I think that in the context of the advertisement the words ''nothing which proves scientifically that cigarette smoke causes disease in non-smokers'' mean ''nothing which affords compelling or convincing evidence that cigarette smoke causes disease in non-smokers''. Reading the statement in this way, I have come to the conclusion that it is erroneous.

The conclusion that cigarette smoke causes lung cancer in non-smokers cannot be drawn from any one epidemiological study or piece of evidence. But I think it can be drawn from the totality of the available data and by valid reasoning from it. A summary of the reasons which lead me to this conclusion is contained in the statement with which Professor Wald concluded his proof of evidence. I agree with what he there said, which was as follows:

> ''In our 1986 paper we concluded that breathing other people's tobacco smoke was a cause of lung cancer and our conclusion rested on several sources of evidence, not only the statistically significant association between lung cancer and exposure to environmental tobacco smoke. It also rested on other evidence, including the fact that carcinogens in tobacco smoke are released into the air and that tobacco smoke is breathed into the lungs by non-smokers. Non-smokers who are exposed to environmental tobacco smoke absorb tobacco products into their blood and tissues, and their urine contains chemicals that are mutagenic, that is chemicals that can induce change in the genetic material in a manner that is thought to be fundamental to the initiation of cancer. It is known that active smoking causes lung cancer, a strong effect in which the risk of lung cancer is some 14 times that in non-smokers. It is the accepted scientific view that exposure to carcinogens does not have a threshold below which there is no effect and therefore one would expect that non-smokers who inhale environmental tobacco smoke would have at least some increased risk of lung cancer. The conclusion that the excess risk is of the order of 30-50% is plausible in the light of the much higher risk of lung cancer due to active smoking. Given all the evidence I believe that the conclusion that breathing other people's smoke is a cause of lung cancer is scientifically sound.'' (Ex. SS, pp. 15-16)

It is obvious that Professor Wald's views that environmental tobacco smoke contains substances which are carcinogenic to humans and that there is no threshold level of exposure to carcinogens below which they cannot and do not cause cancer in humans, form an important part in his overall reasoning.

The expert witnesses called by the applicant all accepted the validity of these views. They are also shared by numerous distinguished authors of many of the primary articles and major reviews. Those few scientists (and they mostly have a professional association with the tobacco industry) who do not share their views claim that their validity has not been established. They do not go so far as to assert that the conclusions are invalid.

Once it is accepted:

(a) that passive smoking involves inhalation of environmental tobacco smoke which contains carcinogens;

(b) that there is no safe threshold level of exposure to carcinogens;

(c) that some of the studies referred to in the primary articles show a statistically significant association between spousal smoking and lung cancer; and

(d) that meta-analysis of the results in such studies discloses a statistically significant (adjusted) risk ratio of about 1.53 (Wald et al.) or 1.42 (NRC report) for non-smokers living with smokers compared with non-smokers not exposed to environmental tobacco smoke;

then my conclusion must be that there is compelling scientific evidence that cigarette smoke causes lung cancer in non-smokers. Although not based upon the findings made by the authors of the major reviews, my conclusion is consistent with those findings.

Counsel for the respondent submitted that such a conclusion cannot be drawn because some of the applicant's witnesses conceded that other scientists may hold a contrary view. I do not accept this submission. I did not understand any of the applicant's witnesses to concede that their opinions were or might be incorrect merely because some hypothetical scientist may hold a contrary opinion.

Moreover, the views held by other scientists may be formed upon the basis even that compelling evidence that passive smoking causes lung cancer does not establish proof for the purpose of the statement in the advertisement. Indeed, I have formed the view that the opinions of the respondent's witnesses are difficult to justify except on this basis. An extract from the evidence of Dr Leslie (T. 3470-1) illustrates this point:

"HIS HONOUR: ... assuming over a period of 50 years in every country of the world an odds ratio of 10 had been established ln respect of smokers who smoked two packets of cigarettes a day in relation to risk of cancer but no toxicology or other studies had been undertaken, all you had was there was a stream of consistent statistically significant results of that kind. That would be, what, no evidence that cigarette smoke caused cancer in smokers?

WITNESS: Well, it would be no direct evidence. It would be ...

HIS HONOUR: It would point to a relationship?

WITNESS: It would make you put the odds against it of there being a causal link as something astronomic but it still would not be proof."

It was also submitted that there are statements in the NH & MRC report which virtually concede the absence of scientific proof of a causal link between passive smoking and lung cancer. Reference was made particularly to the following statement made on p. 33 of the report:

"The evidence that passive smoking causes lung cancer is strongly suggestive. It is plausible, moderately consistent, and demonstrates dose-response relationships. However, intrinsic difficulties in accurately classifying individual exposure, and insufficient numbers of study subjects in many studies, preclude a conclusive interpretation of these empirical data when considered in isolation from other corroborative scientific evidence."

Dr McMichael said that the above passage understated the view of many scientists, including himself. More importantly, the passage on p. 33 is followed by a reference to conclusions contained in the IARC report. After referring to the statement in that report that: "The observations on non-smokers that have been made so far are compatible with either an increased risk from passive smoking or an absence of risk" Dr McMichael and his colleagues conclude the chapter in the NH & MRC report on passive smoking and cancer with the following statement, with which they apparently agree, in the IARC report:

"Knowledge of the nature of sidestream and mainstream smoke, of the materials absorbed during 'passive' smoking, and of the quantitative relationships between dose and effect that are commonly observed from exposure to carcinogens, however, leads to the conclusion that passive smoking gives rise to some risk of cancer."

It is to be noted that this passage in the IARC report is followed by the following statement:

"There is sufficient evidence that tobacco smoke is carcinogenic to humans."

As I have already observed, I regard the reference to "tobacco smoke" as a reference to all kinds of tobacco smoke, including environmental tobacco smoke. In IARC's lexicon, "sufficient evidence" of carcinogenicity indicates that there is a causal relationship between the exposure and human cancer — vide p. 24 of the IARC report.

As I understand what is said in these statements in the NH & MRC and IARC reports, the authors of them accept that the epidemiological studies which had been made prior to the making of the reports, taken in isolation from other scientific evidence, did not demonstrate that passive smoking causes lung cancer. But they appear to conclude that a consideration of the totality of all the scientific evidence leads to the conclusion that passive smoking gives rise to some risk of cancer, i.e. that some people will suffer from cancer as a result of their passive smoking.

Reliance was also placed by the respondent upon some statements made in Chapter 9 of the NH & MRC report, in particular the following passage:

> "Council notes that there is mounting epidemiological evidence that passive smoking may increase the risk of occurrence of lung cancer. Despite limitations in the amount of data available, and despite research difficulties in making satisfactory estimations of individual exposure, a consistent pattern of moderately increased risk of lung cancer in passive smokers has emerged. In view of this pattern, of the known and substantial increase in risk of lung cancer in active smokers (and the lack of a threshold dose), and of the documented levels of bodily assimilation of passively-inhaled smoke, it is therefore prudent public health policy to infer an increased risk of lung cancer from passive smoking."

It was argued that the language used in the latter part of the above statement indicated that the authors of it were not persuaded that there was a proven link between passive smoking and lung cancer. It should be noted that Chapter 9 of the report was not written by the members of the working party, who were the authors of the chapter on passive smoking and cancer. Chapter 9 is the work of the National Health and Medical Research Council itself. Dr McMichael said that the function of the Council is to advise the Australian Government on matters of public health policy and this no doubt explains the language used by the Council. I do not think the language used by the Council should be taken as qualifying the views of the authors of Chapter 7 of the report.

It was also submitted on behalf of the respondent that the authors of the NRC report did not reach a firm conclusion that passive smoking is a cause of lung cancer. I do not think this is the case. The National Research Council reached the conclusion that the relative risk of cancer incurred by "exposed" non-smokers compared with a truly unexposed non-smoker was 1.42. (This figure compares with Professor Wald's calculated equivalent relative risk of 1.53.) The authors of the report then make the following statement (p. 242):

> "We can say, therefore, that while the epidemiologic studies show a consistent and, in total, a highly significant association between lung cancer and ETS exposure of nonsmokers, the excess might, in principle, possibly be explained by bias. However, detailed consideration of the nature and extent of the bias shows that given some reasonable assumptions the bias would be insufficient to explain the whole effect. In fact, there are some types of bias that lead to underestimates of the effect. It must be concluded, therefore, that some, if not all, of the effect reported in spouse studies is causal."

This statement is made on the basis of the epidemiological studies alone. When regard is had to the generally accepted view that exposure to carcinogens does not have a threshold below which there is no effect, the findings in the NRC report do not stand in the way of the conclusion which I have reached that there is compelling scientific evidence that passive smoking does indeed cause lung cancer.

It follows from what I have written that the statement: "Yet there is little evidence and nothing proves scientifically that cigarette smoke causes disease in non-smokers" was erroneous when it was first made on 1 July 1986 and remains so.

8. *Respiratory disease in young children*

It is apparent from a consideration of the primary articles, the major reviews, and the oral evidence given by the applicant's and the respondent's witnesses that the applicant's case that cigarette smoke causes respiratory disease in non-smokers is at its strongest with respect to respiratory disease in children under the age of 12 months. For that reason I think it is unnecessary for the purpose of deciding the issues which arise in the present case to examine in detail the evidence as to the association between passive smoking and respiratory effects and pulmonary function in older children or in adults. If the applicant cannot, in respect of this part of its case, succeed in respect of children in the first year of life, it cannot succeed at all. I therefore do not propose to refer in any detail to the evidence as to the effect of passive smoking on older children or adults.

Before referring to the oral evidence in this part of the case I shall set out some of the statements made in the primary articles and the major reviews upon which the applicant places reliance.

(i) *The primary articles*

(a) *Harlap and Davies* — Infant admissions to hospital and maternal smoking

This article appeared in *The Lancet* in 1974. The authors of the article were from the Department of Medical Ecology at the Hebrew University, Jerusalem. The following summary of the study appears in the article:

> ''Admissions to hospital during the first year of life were recorded in a prospective study of 10,672 infants whose mothers' smoking habits were known. Infants with major congenital malformations, and those dying before their first birthday, were excluded. The infants of mothers who smoked had significantly more admissions for bronchitis or pneumonia, especially in the winter, and more injuries. They were also admitted more frequently, though not significantly so, for upper-respiratory-tract infections, gastroenteritis, childhood infectious diseases, and other diagnoses. The excess of bronchitis and pneumonia in the group exposed to smoke increased with increasing number of cigarettes smoked by the mother. It occurred within subgroups of birth-weight, social class and birth order. It was seen mainly in infants aged 6-9 months, while at older and younger ages there was no significant effect of maternal smoking. The findings support the hypothesis that atmospheric pollution with tobacco smoke endangers the health of non-smokers.''

There was a study population of 10,672. At the time of the interviews, 9.2% of the mothers were smokers and 7.4% had given up smoking earlier. The admission rate (per 100 infants) for bronchitis and pneumonia was 9.5 for children of non-smokers and 13.1 for children of smokers. The equivalent figures for admissions for upper respiratory tract infections were 4.8 and 5.3 respectively, but these last-mentioned figures were not statistically significant. The article contains a table giving admission rates (per 100 infants) by diagnosis in relation to maternal smoking and the number of cigarettes smoked daily. The table is as follows:

TABLE II — ADMISSION-RATES (PER 100 INFANTS) BY DIAGNOSIS, MATERNAL SMOKING AND NUMBER OF CIGARETTES SMOKED DAILY

Diagnosis	Non-smokers		Smokers			Total (10,672)
	Never smoked (8900)	Former smokers (786)	Cigarettes per day			
			1-10 (747)	11-20 (747)	21 + (60)	
Bronchitis and pneumonia	9.6	7.8	10.8	16.2	31.7	9.8
All other	15.5	15.1	16.4	17.3	23.3	15.6
Total	25.1	22.9	27.2	33.5	55.0	25.4

Differences among three categories of smokers: for bronchitis and pneumonia, P <0.001, for other diagnoses, not significant.

The authors included the following observations in their study:

> "Infants born to smokers were in hospital for an average of 384 days per 100 infants before their first birthday, 151 of them for bronchitis or pneumonia. These rates were 334 and 114, respectively, for the infants of non-smokers. However, there were no significant differences between the groups, exposed or not exposed to smoke, in average duration of each type of admission episode.
>
> Admissions for bronchitis or pneumonia increased in frequency with increasing number of cigarettes smoked by the mother (table II). There were no signifiant increases for any of the other diagnoses measured separately. Infants of mothers who had given up smoking had fewer admissions than those whose mothers had never smoked. This difference, which can be explained by the higher standard-of-living of those who gave up smoking, is not, however, statistically significant for any single diagnostic category. Infants born to former smokers spent fewer days in hospital in the first year of life (231 per 100 infants, 79 of them for bronchitis or pneumonia), and their admission episodes tended to be shorter for each diagnosis.
>
> Women who smoke gave birth to smaller infants, and birth-weight is an important predictor of admission to hospital in West Jerusalem. Admissions for bronchitis or pneumonia are more frequent in infants who are smaller or larger than average at birth; while for other diagnoses, increasing birth-weight predicts a decreasing probability of going to hospital. Table III shows that the excess of admissions for bronchitis or pneumonia in the passively smoking infants could not be wholly attributed to lower birth-weights, rates being higher than in the infants of non-smokers for all three birth-weight groups."
>
> ...
>
> "The excess risk associated with maternal smoking was not uniform throughout the first year of life ... In the first 5 months of life there were no significant differences between infants born to smokers or non-smokers in rates of admissions for bronchitis or pneumonia. Between the ages of 6 and 9 months, on the other hand, there were greatly increased rates of lower respiratory disease in the group exposed to smoke, both in the summer and in the winter. Toward the first birthday, differences between the two groups again disappeared."

In their discussion of the findings, the authors state:

> "This study relies on information on maternal smoking which was collected antenatally. It is not known how closely smoking in early pregnancy or mid-pregnancy correlates with habits after

the birth and in the baby's first year, but it seems reasonable to assume that for most mothers, smoking characteristics would have remained the same. However there would inevitably have been some smoking mothers who subsequently gave up the habit, and others, especially former smokers, who took it up later. As a result, this study tends to underestimate true differences between infants of smokers and non-smokers, rather than the opposite."

(b) *Colley et al.* — Influence of passive smoking and parental phlegm on pneumonia and bronchitis in early childhood

The authors were from the Department of Medical Statistics and Epidemiology at the London School of Hygiene and Tropical Medicine and from the Department of Community Medicine at St Thomas's Hospital Medical School, London.

This article appeared in *The Lancet* in November 1974. The following summary of the study appears in the article:

"The incidence of pneumonia and bronchitis has been studied in 2205 infants over the first five years of life. In the same period their parents' smoking habits and respiratory symptoms were recorded annually. The incidence of pneumonia and bronchitis in the first year of life was associated with parents' smoking habits; incidence was lowest where both parents were non-smokers, highest where both smoked, and lay between these two levels where only one parent smoked. Over the age of one year the association was not consistent. When parents' respiratory symptoms were also studied a close association was found with the incidence of pneumonia and bronchitis in the child; this was independent of parents' smoking habits and was an almost consistent finding throughout the first five years of life. In the first year of life exposure to cigarette smoke generated when parents smoked doubled the risk for the infant of an attack of pneumonia or bronchitis."

This study was conducted in Harrow, north-west of London, between 1963 and 1969 and involved all families living in six of the wards of the borough of Harrow who had an infant born in the period from July 1, 1963 to June 30, 1965. 2,205 familes were included in the study. After exclusions for some cases, such as multiple births, there were 2,149 infants eligible for study. It was a longitudinal study conducted over five years. The authors describe the methodology of their study in considerable detail. Some of the results of the study are stated to be as follows:

"The annual incidence per 100 children of pneumonia and bronchitis is given in table II by parents' smoking habit. Parents have been classified into one of four groups: (1) both parents non-smokers; (2) one parent smoker, the other non-smoker; (3) both parents smokers; (4) both parents ex-smokers, or one an ex-smoker, or parents who changed their smoking habits during the study. The incidence of pneumonia and bronchitis in the infant shows a gradient by parents' smoking habit in the first year of life. Incidence is lowest in infants with both parents non-smokers, highest where both parents smoke, and lies between these values where one parent smokes. This is a statistically significant gradient ($P < 0.0005$). In subsequent years there is no such clear gradient.

In table III parents have been classified both by their smoking habits and by their response to the question 'Did you usually bring up any phlegm from your chest first thing in the morning in the last winter?' In all categories except one, the incidence within a smoking category is higher among children where one or both parents have winter morning phlegm than in childen whose parents are both free of this symptom. Some of the incidence-rates in the children — in particular those whose parents are both non-smokers and who have winter morning phlegm — are based upon small numbers and therefore may not be wholly reliable. On the other hand, the incidence-rates in children where neither parent has symptoms, whether they smoke or not, are based upon substantial numbers. In them in the first year of life a consistent gradient is seen in the incidence of pneumonia and bronchitis in the childen in relation to the parents' smoking habits. The rates are lowest in children of non-smoking parents and highest where both parents smoke. In children over the age of a year there is, however, no consistent gradient.

Exposure of the child to cigarette smoke may be more precisely estimated from the total daily cigarette consumption of both parents. In table IV the incidence of pneumonia and bronchitis is given for parent pairs smoking between them 1-14, 15-24, and 25 or more cigarettes per day, by the presence of winter morning phlegm. A clear gradient of increasing incidence is seen in the first year of life that is independent of the presence of winter morning phlegm and is of the same size as that in table III. In the second year and thereafter the pattern is not consistent and thus does not suggest an effect of exposure to tobacco smoke at ages over one year."

Tables II, III and IV are reproduced below:

TABLE II — PNEUMONIA AND BRONCHITIS BY PARENTS' SMOKING HABITS

Year of follow-up	Annual incidence per 100 children (absolute numbers in parentheses) of pneumonia and bronchitis				
	Both non-smokers	One smoker	Both smokers	Both ex-smokers or one ex-smoker or smoking habit changed	All
1	7.8 (372)	11.4 (552)	17.6 (478)	9.2 (675)	11.5 (2077)
2	8.1 (358)	9.3 (494)	8.9 (438)	7.4 (758)	8.3 (2048)
3	7.0 (342)	10.2 (460)	9.1 (396)	8.9 (834)	8.9 (2032)
4	8.4 (323)	8.3 (408)	9.0 (357)	8.4 (882)	8.5 (1970)
5	7.5 (319)	6.7 (374)	6.5 (340)	6.6 (956)	6.7 (1989)

TABLE III — PNEUMONIA AND BRONCHITIS IN THE FIRST FIVE YEARS OF LIFE BY PARENTS' SMOKING HABIT AND MORNING PHLEGM

Year of follow-up	Annual incidence per 100 children (absolute numbers in parentheses) of pneumonia and bronchitis									
	Both non-smokers		One smoker		Both smokers		Both ex-smokers or one an ex-smoker or smoking habit changed		All	
	N	O/B	N	O/B	N	O/B	N	O/B	N	O/B
1	7.6 (343)	10.3 (29)	10.4 (424)	14.8 (128)	15.3 (339)	23.0 (139)	8.2 (546)	13.2 (129)	10.1 (1652)	16.7 (425)
2	8.1 (322)	8.3 (36)	7.1 (365)	15.5 (129)	8.7 (286)	9.2 (152)	6.5 (599)	10.7 (159)	7.4 (1572)	11.3 (476)

Year of follow-up	Annual incidence per 100 children (absolute numbers in parentheses) of pneumonia and bronchitis									
	Both non-smokers		One smoker		Both smokers		Both ex-smokers or one an ex-smoker or smoking habit changed		All	
	N	O/B	N	O/B	N	O/B	N	O/B	N	O/B
3	6.9 (305)	8.1 (37)	10.5 (353)	9.4 (107)	7.9 (242)	11.0 (154)	8.2 (661)	11.6 (173)	8.4 (1561)	10.6 (471)
4	8.0 (287)	11.1 (36)	7.5 (306)	10.8 (102)	7.6 (236)	11.6 (121)	8.2 (695)	9.1 (187)	7.9 (1524)	10.3 (446)
5	6.7 (285)	14.7 (34)	5.6 (267)	9.4 (107)	3.9 (208)	10.6 (132)	6.4 (737)	7.3 (219)	5.9 (1497)	9.1 (492)

N = neither with winter morning phlegm. O/B = one or both with winter morning phlegm.

TABLE IV — PNEUMONIA AND BRONCHITIS BY NUMBER OF CIGARETTES SMOKED PER DAY BY PARENTS AND WINTER MORNING PHLEGM

Year of follow-up	Annual incidence per 100 children (absolute numbers in parentheses) of pneumonia and bronchitis							
	Both non-smokers		One or both smokers* of following number of cigarettes per day**					
			1-14		15-24		25 and over	
	N	O/B	N	O/B	N	O/B	N	O/B
1	76 (343)	10.3 (29)	10.4 (269)	15.1 (53)	11.1 (171)	14.5 (76)	15.2 (323)	23.2 (138)
2	8.1 (322)	8.3 (36)	5.2 (231)	16.4 (55)	8.6 (151)	14.5 (62)	9.7 (269)	9.8 (164)
3	6.9 (305)	8.1 (37)	11.2 (206)	8.6 (58)	8.2 (146)	9.5 (42)	8.6 (243)	11.2 (161)
4	8.0 (287)	11.1 (36)	5.5 (163)	13.3 (45)	7.4 (136)	11.5 (52)	9.1 (243)	10.3 (126)
5	6.7 (285)	14.7 (34)	6.3 (144)	11.4 (44)	4.4 (133)	7.6 (53)	4.1 (218)	10.6 (142)

* Excluding parent pairs where one or both are ex-smokers or changed smoking habit.
**Includes tobacco and cigars expressed as cigarette equivalents (see Todd).
N = neither with winter morning phlegm. O/B = one or both with winter morning phlegm.

The authors also state:

> "The infants of mothers who smoke in pregnancy are, on average, lighter than those of mothers who do not smoke. As infants of low birth-weight are more likely to suffer respiratory illness than normal-weight infants, it is possible that the gradients in respiratory disease observed in the first year of life, and in particular the effects of passive smoking, may be due, indirectly, to maternal smoking during pregnancy. In this study, birth-weight, as expected, shows a gradient by parents' initial smoking habit, and to a lesser extent by winter morning phlegm. Thus parents who smoke have lighter infants than parents who do not smoke. The gradients in the incidence of pneumonia and bronchitis with parental smoking, and with winter morning phlegm, might therefore be partly attributable to differences in birth-weight. However, within different birth-weight categories the gradients for pneumonia and bronchitis with parents' smoking habits persist. Thus differences in birth-weight cannot account for the higher risk of pneumonia and bronchitis in the first year of life in children exposed to the cigarette smoke generated when their parents smoke at home."

In the discussion of their paper, the authors observe:

> "Passive smoking by the infant, after differences in birth-weight and parental respiratory symptoms have been allowed for, increases the risk to the infant of pneumonia and bronchitis in the first year of life. When both parents smoke, this risk is almost double that of infants with non-smoking parents. The findings confirm and extend those of Harlap and Davies. These workers did not, however, have information on fathers' smoking habits, nor did they take account of parents' respiratory symptoms.
>
> A picture has thus emerged of a serious risk to infants in the first year of life from exposure to their parents' cigarette smoke. In contrast, between one and five years of age, there does not appear to be any important effect of passive smoking in increasing the risk of pneumonia and bronchitis. Colley, in 6-14-year-olds also found no association between passive smoking and the prevalence of chronic cough.
>
> The estimates of children's exposure to cigarette smoke in this study are crude, being based either on whether parents were smokers or not, or on their total daily cigarette consumption. The smoke exposure of the childen may have been overestimated, since parents — in particular the father — will smoke outside the home, or at times when the infant is not present. The effects on the child may thus have resulted from exposure to levels of cigarette smoke less than those suggested by our study."

(c) *Leeder et al.* — Influence of family factors on the incidence of lower respiratory illness during the first year of life

This article was published in 1976 in the *British Journal of Preventive and Social Medicine*. The authors were from the Department of Community Medicine at St Thomas's Hospital, Medical School, London and the Department of Community Health at Bristol. The following summary of the study appears in the article:

> "In a study of a cohort of over 2000 childen born between 1963 and 1965, the incidence of bronchitis and pneumonia during their first year of life was found to be associated with several family factors. The most important determinant of respiratory illness in these infants was an attack of bronchitis or pneumonia in a sibling. The age of these siblings, and their number, also contributed to this incidence. Parental respiratory symptoms, including persistent cough and phlegm, and asthma or wheezing, as well as parental smoking habits had lesser but nevertheless important effects. Parental smoking, however, stands out from all other factors as the one most amenable to change in seeking to prevent bronchitis and pneumonia in infants."

The authors reported some of their findings in the following terms:

> "During the first year of life, the incidence of bronchitis and pneumonia varied according to several family factors. These illnesses occurred much more commonly in infants born to families which had several other childen already, and in those families

where the parents had respiratory disability or were smokers.

Children whose parents both had a history of asthma-wheeze had an incidence of bronchitis or pneumonia of 26.9% which was three times greater than that found in children of parents without such a history (9.4%) (Table III). The effect of parental smoking was not so great. The incidence of bronchitis or pneumonia in children of non-smoking parents was 7.2% compared with 17.7% when both parents smoked. When both smoking habits and asthma-wheeze were examined for combined effects on the incidence of bronchitis or pneumonia in the children, these contrasts widened. For example, the incidence of bronchitis or pneumonia was 6.7% in infants whose parents neither smoked nor had suffered from asthma-wheeze; this contrasted with an incidence of 39.3% when both parents smoked and had a history of asthma-wheeze.''

TABLE III

ANNUAL INCIDENCE PER 100 INFANTS OF BRONCHITIS OR PNEUMONIA IN THE FIRST YEAR OF LIFE BY PARENTAL HISTORY OF ASTHMA-WHEEZE AND SMOKING HABIT

		Parental Smoking Habit				
		Neither	One	Both	Habit Changed	Total
Parental asthma-wheeze	Neither	6.7 (451)	9.6 (502)	13.7 (314)	8.7 (241)	9.4 (1508)
	One	8.9 (101)	18.0 (178)	22.3 (139)	7.4 (81)	15.6 (499)
	Both	14.3 (7)	13.6 (22)	39.3 (28)	30.0 (10)	26.9 (67)
	Total	7.2 (559)	11.8 (702)	17.7 (481)	9.0 (332)	11.5 (2074)*

Populations in parentheses

*Total excludes 27 infants with missing first year data and an additional 48 with missing initial and first year data on parent pairs.

(d) *Sims et al.* — Study of 8-year-old children with a history of respiratory syncytial virus bronchiolitis in infancy

This article appeared in the *British Medical Journal* in 1978. The authors were from the University of Newcastle upon Tyne. The contents of the article are of only marginal significance for present purposes. In the study, 35 children known to have had respiratory syncytial virus bronchiolitis in infancy were examined at the age of 8 and their respiratory function tested. The results were compared with those in 35 controls matched for age, sex, and social class. The authors concluded, inter alia, that the parents of the children who had had bronchiolitis smoked significantly more cigarettes during the infant's first year of life than those of the control children.

(e) *Rantakallio* — Relationship of maternal smoking to morbidity and mortality of the child up to the age of five

The author of this article which was published in 1978 was from the Department of Paediatrics and the Department of Public Health, University of Oulu, Finland. The abstract of the article as published reads as follows:

''The effect of maternal smoking during pregnancy on the morbidity and mortality of the child up to the age of five was studied in 12 068 births. The children of the smokers were compared with those of controls of similar age, parity, marital status and place of residence. Perinatal mortality was no higher among the smokers, but postneonatal mortality from 28 days to 5 years was almost significantly (p <0.05) higher. The children of the smokers were highly significantly (p <0.001) more often hospitalized in pediatric departments, the difference being clearest below the age of one. The average duration of hospital admissions was longer among the children of the smokers, and similarly the numbers of visits to the doctor and hospital admissions to any hospital under the age of one were more frequent among the childen of the smokers. Respiratory diseases caused highly significantly more hospitalizations among these children.''

Table 6 in the article refers to the incidence of diseases during the first 5 years among the children of the smokers and the controls in the study. With respect to this table the authors state:

> ''Table 6 presents the frequency of all disease groups diagnosed in children's departments per thousand live births among the children of smokers and of their controls. If the child had been in hospital more than once for the same disease it was counted only once. Respiratory and skin diseases were more frequent among the smokers than among the controls, the difference being statistically highly significant ... Among the respiratory diseases the ratio of the incidence among the smokers to that of the controls was 2.2 in pneumonia, 1-8 in bronchitis, and 1.5 in others such as acute nasopharyngitis, sinusitis etc. ...
>
> Under the age of one year the difference in the diseases was in general greater between the heavy smokers and their controls than between the light smokers and their controls, but this was no longer true for the age from one to five.
>
> When the main causes of hospitalization in pediatric departments per thousand live births was calculated for both groups a statistically highly significant difference (p <0.001) was found only in the case of respiratory diseases, and an almost significant difference (p <0.05) in the case of skin diseases. The more frequent hospitalization of the children of smokers because of respiratory diseases was clearest below the age of one, but also existed at the age of one to five, the difference between the smokers and controls at that age being almost significant (p <0.05). Again the children of the heavy smokers were more affected than those of the light smokers under the age of one, but not at the age of one to five.''

(f) *Fergusson et al.* — Parental smoking and respiratory illess in infancy

The authors of this article which was published in 1980 were from the Department of Paediatrics, Christchurch Hospital, New Zealand.

The data for the study were collected during the third stage of a study known as the Christchurch Child Development Study. In the project a cohort of infants was studied at birth, at four months and at one year.

The summary of their article reads as follows:

> ''The relationship between parental smoking and respiratory illness in a birth cohort of 1180 one-year-old children was examined. Maternal smoking was associated with an increased incidence of lower respiratory illness but there was no statistically significant association between paternal smoking and lower respiratory illness. While children of mothers who smoked suffered more lower respiratory illnesses, their overall risk of respiratory infection was similar to that for children of nonsmoking mothers. The association between maternal smoking and infantile lower respiratory illness persisted when the child's social background, perinatal history, and postnatal diet were taken into account. The findings favour the view that prolonged exposure to cigarette smoke predisposes infants to develop lower respiratory symptoms when they contract a respiratory infection.''

In their discussion of their paper, the authors make the following statements:

> ''Previous studies have considered the effects of parental smoking on lower respiratory illness only. The findings reported here show that there is a complicated relationship between parental

smoking and all respiratory illness. Overall, the children of mothers who smoke do not have a greater risk of respiratory illness but they do have a greater risk of suffering respiratory illness affecting the lower respiratory tract. This finding suggests that the effect of maternal smoking is to irritate the infantile lung and thus facilitate the spread of infection to the lower respiratory tract.

In addition, previous research has examined the relationship between parental smoking and medical consultation for lower respiratory illness. Since medical consultations probably provide a biased sample of infant illness, there is the possibility that the apparent association between parental smoking and infant lower respiratory illness could have arisen from some bias in consulting practices. The results reported here show that this is unlikely to be the case: an association between maternal smoking and infantile lower respiratory illness has been shown to exist both for illness needing medical treatment and for maternal reports of lower respiratory symptoms, irrespective of whether these symptoms were treated by a medical practitioner.

Finally, the range of social and perinatal factors controlled in this study is greater than that considered in previous studies of the topic. On the basis of the findings reported here, it may be concluded that the association between maternal smoking and infantile lower respiratory illness cannot be explained by the confounding effects of such factors as adverse perinatal history, depressed social background, or bottle feeding.

There now appears to be suffient evidence to support the view that people in regular and prolonged contact with infants should not smoke, or if they must, they should not do so in the presence of infants.''

(g) *Fergusson et al.* — Parental smoking and lower respiratory illness in the first three years of life

The authors of this study (save for one additional co-author) were also the authors of the previous study. The article was published in 1981. The following summary of the study appears in the article:

> ''The relationships between parental smoking and the rates of lower respiratory illness during the first three years of life were examined for a birth cohort of 1265 New Zealand childen. Lower respiratory illness varied significantly with maternal smoking for the first year; there was equivocal evidence of a relationship between maternal smoking and lower respiratory illness in the second year; and by the third year the relationship had clearly disappeared. Paternal smoking had no significant effect on rates of lower respiratory illness at any time.
>
> Application of logistic regression showed that for the first year rates of lower respiratory illness were approximately linearly related to maternal smoking: increases of five cigarettes a day resulted in an increase of 2.5 to 3.5 incidents of lower respiratory illness per 100 children at risk. Statistical control for maternal age, education, family size, and family living standards showed that the relationship between maternal smoking and rates of lower respiratory illness was not significantly influenced by these factors.''

Table 2 of the report is as follows:

Table 2 Rates per 1000 children of bronchitis/pneumonia and lower respiratory symptoms in the first three years of life by maternal and paternal smoking (number of children in brackets)

Paternal smoking (cigs/day)	BRONCHITIS/PNEUMONIA			LOWER RESPIRATORY SYMPTOMS		
	Maternal smoking (cigs/day)			Maternal smoking (cigs/day)		
	0	1-10	11 +	0	1-10	11 +
FIRST YEAR	FIRST YEAR	FIRST YEAR	FIRST YEAR	FIRST YEAR	FIRST YEAR	FIRST YEAR
0	7.0 (588)	12.8 (78)	13.4 (112)	37.6 (588)	47.4 (78)	50.9 (112)
1-10	4.6 (66)	14.0 (43)	11.1 (18)	37.9 (66)	53.5 (43)	33.3 (18)
11+	8.8 (125)	12.7 (55)	19.7 (81)	42.4 (125)	43.6 (55)	53.1 (81)
SECOND YEAR	SECOND YEAR	SECOND YEAR	SECOND YEAR	SECOND YEAR	SECOND YEAR	SECOND YEAR
0	9.1 (584)	20.7 (87)	13.2 (114)	43.8 (585)	54.0 (87)	50.9 (116)
1-10	7.9 (76)	3.3 (30)	12.0 (25)	44.7 (76)	51.6 (31)	36.0 (25)
11+	11.1 (108)	15.9 (44)	11.9 (87)	55.6 (108)	52.2 (46)	50.8 (67)
THIRD YEAR	THIRD YEAR	THIRD YEAR	THIRD YEAR	THIRD YEAR	THIRD YEAR	THIRD YEAR
0	8.9 (605)	5.5 (73)	12.1 (116)	37.4 (805)	39.7 (73)	45.3 (117)
1-10	11.8 (76)	8.7 (23)	8.0 (25)	41.6 (77)	21.7 (23)	36.0 (25)
11+	10.2 (108)	13.5 (37)	6.1 (65)	36.1 (108)	40.5 (37)	41.5 (65)

In their discussion of their work the authors observe:

> "In confirmation of the findings of Colley et al. the correlation between parental smoking and childhood lower respiratory illness appeared to be most marked for the first year of life and showed a steady decline with increasing age. At one year, clear differences between the offspring of smokers and non-smokers were evident; at two years the evidence was equivocal, and by three years an association between maternal smoking and infant lower respiratory illness was clearly absent. However, these findings are not entirely consistent with reports which have shown greater rates of respiratory problems (morning cough and breathlessness) among children of school age with smoking parents. One hypothesis which satisfies the available data is that the effect of parental smoking on childhood lower respiratory illness and symptoms is two-fold. During early life, and particularly the first year, prolonged contact with cigarette smoke would appear to precipitate or exacerbate lower respiratory illness in children; this effect is relatively short-lived and disappears at the age of about 2. However, prolonged exposure to cigarette smoke over a period of years may have a compound interest effect in compromising the respiratory function of children, with the result that by the time middle childhood is reached, children of smokers have a greater rate of lower respiratory illness or symptoms."

(h) *Ekwo et al.* — Relationship of parental smoking and gas cooking to respiratory disease in children

The authors of this article, which was published in 1983, are from the University of Iowa Medical School.

The authors found that the risk of hospitalisation for respiratory illness in children before age 2 years was increased when at least one of the parents smoked. The authors concluded that, based on the findings of their report and from previously published findings, "one is led to conclude that parental smoking is associated with a risk of certain respiratory illnesses and symptoms among children living in the same environment".

(j) *Schenker et al.* — Risk factors for childhood respiratory disease. The effect of host factors and home environmental exposures

The authors of this article which was published in 1983 were from the Department of Medicine, Brigham and Women's Hospital and Harvard Medical School, Boston and the Department of Medicine, University of New Mexico School of Medicine.

Many of the findings of this study relate to matters of no present concern. However, the authors concluded that chest illness before two years of age showed a significant positive linear trend with the number of parental smokers.

(k) *Ware et al.* — Passive smoking, gas cooking, and respiratory health of children living in six cities

The authors of this study which was published in 1984 were from the Harvard School of Public Health, the Harvard Medical School and Brigham and Women's Hospital, Boston. Part of the summary which appears in the article is as follows:

> "As part of a longitudinal study of the respiratory health effects of indoor and outdoor air pollutants, pulmonary function, respiratory illnesss history, and symptom history were recorded at 2 successive annual examinations of 10,106 white children living in 6 cities in the United States. Parental education, illness history, and smoking habits also were recorded, along with the fuel used for cooking in the child's home. Maternal cigarette smoking was associated with increases of 20 to 35% in the rates of 8 respiratory illnesses and symptoms investigated, and paternal smoking was associated with smaller but still substantial increases. Illness and symptom rates were linearly related to the number of cigarettes smoked by the child's mother. Illness rates were higher for children of current smokers than for children of ex-smokers. The associations between maternal smoking status and childhood respiratory illnesses and symptoms were reduced but not eliminated by adjustment for parental illness history. Levels of forced expiratory volume in one second (FEV_1) were significantly lower for children of current smokers than for children of nonsmokers at both examinations and highest for children of exsmokers. Levels of forced vital capacity (FVC) were lower for children of nonsmokers than for children of current smokers at both examinations, but the difference was statistically significant only at the first examination. Both the increase in mean FVC and the decrease in mean FEV_1 among children of current smokers were linearly related to daily cigarette consumption. ... These results provide strong support for a causal effect of sidestream cigarette smoke on increased respiratory illness and reduced FEV_1 values in preadolescent children."

The authors explain the methodology of their study in considerable detail and make the following observations on their analyses of the data collected:

> "These analyses show a consistent association between parental cigarette smoking and increased respiratory illness during childhood. Of the children in this sample, 43% had mothers who were current smokers (table 4), 59% had fathers who were current smokers, and 68% had at least one parent who was a current smoker. Thus, effects of sidestream cigarette smoke of the size observed in this study would represent a substantial public health burden.
>
> Current maternal cigarette smoking was associated with a 20 to 35% increase in the risk of all respiratory illnesses and symptoms in the past year. A history of either parent smoking was associated with a similar increase in the reported prevalence of early childhood respiratory illness. Each

of these respiratory health indexes is linearly related to the current amount of cigarette smoking by either both parents or the mother alone. In all of these analyses, the association between impaired health and passive smoke exposure was stronger with maternal than with paternal or total parental smoking. Children of ex-smokers had respiratory illness and symptom frequencies that were typically between those of nonsmoking and currently smoking mothers. This was true for recent illness and symptom experience, as well as for early childhood illnesses. These findings are consistent, at least in part, with the hypothesis that exposure to cigarette smoke increases the risk of contemporaneous respiratory illness.''

After referring to the stronger association with maternal rather than paternal smoking for respiratory illness in childhood, the authors state:

> ''The somewhat stronger association of respiratory illness with maternal than with paternal smoking habits need not imply any special risk associated with maternal smoking. A more plausible interpretation is that the risk factor is exposure to sidestream cigarette smoke, and that children are more likely to be with their mothers than with their fathers at the times smoking occurs.''

(l) *Pedreira et al* — Involuntary smoking and incidence of respiratory illness during the first year of life

The authors of this article were from the Department of Paediatrics at the George Washington University School of Medicine, Washington, DC. The article was published in 1985. The following summary of the study appears in the article:

> ''A prospective study of 1,144 infants and their families was performed. Smoking and family histories were evaluated with respect to the incidence of lower respiratory disease during the first year of life. It was found that (1) tracheitis and bronchitis occurred significantly more frequently in infants exposed to cigarette smoke in the home, (2) maternal smoking imposed greater risks upon the infant than paternal smoking, (3) occurrence of neither tracheitis nor bronchitis showed a consistent relationship to the number of cigarettes smoked, (4) a family history that was positive for respiratory illness (chronic cough or bronchitis) significantly influenced the incidence of bronchitis, (5) too few cases of laryngitis and pneumonia were seen to warrant any opinions regarding the adverse influence of either smoking or a family history that was positive for respiratory illness, and (6) occurrence of bronchiolitis was not affected by the presence of a smoker nor influenced by a family history that was positive for respiratory illness. It is concluded that passive smoking is dangerous to the health of infants and that infants born to families with a history that is positive for respiratory illness (chronic cough or bronchitis) are at risk of developing bronchitis.''

(m) *Chen et al.* — Influence of passive smoking on admissions for respiratory illness in early childhood

The authors of this article were from the Department of Epidemiology, School of Public Health, Shanghai Medical University, Shanghai. The article was first published on 2 August 1986 in the *British Medical Journal,* but was accepted for publication in April 1986.

The following summary of the study appears in the article:

> ''An association was sought between passive smoking and in-patient admissions for respiratory illness in 1058 children born between 1 June and 31 December 1981 and living in the neighbourhoods of Nan-Jing Western Road and Yan-An Western Road in Jing-An District, Shanghai. The admission rate for first episodes of respiratory illness was positively correlated with the total daily cigarette consumption of family members during the children's first 18 months of life. The relative risk of developing a first episode of respiratory illness was 1.80 for children living in families including people who smoked 10 or more cigarettes a day compared with those living in non-smoking families. Multiple logistic regression analysis showed that the effect of passive smoking on in-patient admission for respiratory illness was independent of the child's birth weight, type of feeding, father's education, size of the home, and chronic respiratory disease among adults in the family. The adjusted odds ratios

> compared with the non-smoking group were 1.17 in families smoking 1-9 cigarettes daily and 1.89 in families smoking 10 or more cigarettes daily.
>
> These data suggest that exposure to household cigarette smoke of children in early life increases the risk of severe respiratory illness.''

(n) *Taylor and Wadsworth* — Maternal smoking during pregnancy and lower respiratory tract illness in early life

The authors of this article, which was received for publication on 27 February 1987, were from the Department of Child Health at the University of Bristol and the Departments of Paediatrics and Community Medicine at St Mary's Hospital Medical School, London.

The following summary of the study appears in the article:

> ''In a national study of 12743 children maternal, but not paternal, smoking was confirmed as having a significant influence on the reported incidence of bronchitis and admission to hospital for lower respiratory tract illness during the first five years of life. Reported rates of admissions to hospital for lower respiratory tract diseases were found to be as high in children born to mothers who stopped smoking during pregnancy as in those whose mothers smoked continuously both during and after pregnancy. Rates of admissions to hospital for lower respiratory tract diseases in children whose mothers started smoking only postnatally were no higher than in those whose mothers remained non-smokers. Postnatal smoking seemed to exert a significant influence on the reported incidence of bronchitis, but less than smoking during pregnancy.
>
> These findings suggest that maternal smoking influences the incidence of respiratory illnesses in children mainly through a congenital effect, and only to a lesser extent through passive exposure after birth.''

(ii) *The major reviews*

(a) *The Surgeon General's Report*

The Surgeon General examined a number of studies, based on a variety of different designs, examining the effects of involuntary smoking on the acute respiratory illness experience of children. Most of the studies contained in the primary articles are considered by the Surgeon General. He summarises his assessment of these studies as follows (p 44):

> ''In summary, the results of these studies show excess acute respiratory illness in the children of parents who smoke, particularly in children under 2 years of age. This pattern is evident in studies conducted with different methodologies and in different locales. The increased risk of hospitalization for severe bronchitis or pneumonia associated with parental smoking ranges from 20 to 40 percent during the first year of life. Young children appear to represent a more susceptible population for the adverse effects of involuntary smoking than older children or adults. The time-activity patterns of infants, which generally place them in proximity to their mothers, may lead to particularly high exposures to environmental tobacco smoke if the mother smokes.''

The Surgeon General's Report contains a table (Table I) in which the studies are summarised. Although the table contains some references which are elliptical, I set it out so as to show the material upon which the Surgeon General based his conclusions.

TABLE I — Early childhood respiratory illnesses and involuntary cigarette smoking

Study	Subjects	Findings	Illness rates per 100				Comments
			By cigarettes per day				
			0	1-10	11-20	20+	
Harlap and Davies (1974)	10,672 births, 1965-1968 Israel	Hospitalized, bronchitis/ pneumonia, first year of life RR = 1.38	9.5	10.8	16.2	31.7	Parental smoking history, maternal smoking only Longitudinal study
Colley[1]	2,205 births, 1963-1965 England	Questionnaire, bronchitis/ pneumonia, first year of life RR = 1.73 for one parent smoker RR = 2.04 for two parent smokers	7.6 10.3	10.4 15.1	11.1 14.5	15.2 23.2	= Asymptomatic parents = Symptomatic parents Neither controlled for sibling or smoker sex Longitudinal study
Fergusson et al. (1981); Fergusson and Horwood (1985)[2]	1,265 births, 4 months 1977, New Zealand	Questionnaire, doctor or hospital visits, bronchitis/ pneumonia; hospital records checked; assessed at 4 months, 1, 2, 3 and 6 years; RR =2.04 if mother smoked	7.0 7.0	12.8 4.6	13.4 8.8	Maternal only Paternal only	Effect significant for maternal smoking in first year of life only; effect present in first 2 years of life
			By number of smoking parents				
			0	1	2		
Ware et al. (1984)	8,528 children, aged 5-9, with two parents' smoking status known, six U.S. cities	Respiratory illness in last year	12.9	13.7	14.8		Adjusted for age, sex, and city cohort effect; significant trends Longitudinal study

TABLE I — Early childhood respiratory illnesses and involuntary cigarette smoking

Study	Subjects	Findings	Illness rates per 100			Comments
Said et al. (1978)	3,920 children, aged 10-20, France	Tonsillectomy and/or adenoidectomy, generally before age 5, as indicator of frequent respiratory tract infection	28.2	41.4	50.9	Children self-reported; not clear parent smoking habit at report time directly related to exposure approx 10+ years earlier Cross-sectional study
Shenker et al. (1969)	4,071 children, aged 5-14, United States	Chest illness before age 2 Chest illness > 3 days in past year	6.7 8.8	7.9 11.8	11.5 13.6	Trends for both significant Cross-sectional study
			Parent status			
			Nonsmoker		Current smoker	
175 Cameron et al.	158 children, aged 6-9, parents' telephone questionnaire, United States	Respiratory illness, restricted activity and/or medical consultation in last year	1.33		7.4	Illness reported not verified; not clear how reporting adult related to child Cross-sectional study
Leeder et al. (1976a, b)	2,149 infants, born 1963-1965, England	RR ~ 2.0 for infants with two smoking parents		Not provided		Parents' response bias unlikely, effects observed for infants of symptomatic parents; maternal v paternal smoking effects not investigated Longitudinal study
Sims et al. (1978)	35 children, hospitalized, RSV bronchiolitis; 35 controls, England	Borderline significant increase in maternal smoking, first year of life RR =2.65		Not provided		No significant effect for paternal smoking; average amount smoked greater for parents of cases than controls Case-control study

TABLE I — Early childhood respiratory illnesses and involuntary cigarette smoking

Study	Subjects	Findings	Illness rates per 100			Comments
Rantakallio (1978)	1,821 children of smoking mothers, 1,823 children of nonsmoking mothers, Finland	Significant increase in hospitalization for respiratory illness during first 5 years of life RR = 1.74		Not provided		Prospective followup of doctor visits, hospitalizations, deaths up to age 5; only maternal smoking evaluated Longitudinal study
Pullan and Hey (1982)	130 children hospitalized, RSV infection, first year of life; 111 nonhospitalized controls, England	Significant effect of maternal (RR = 1.96) and paternal (RR =1.53) smoking at time of study; significant maternal smoking effect during first year of life (RR = 1.55)		Not provided		Case-control study
Pedreira et al. (1985)	1,144 infants in pediatric practice, United States	Significant increase in respiratory illnesses among smoke-exposed children		Nonsmoker	Smoker	Pediatricians not blinded to exposure; no effect seen for croup, pneumonia, or bronchiolitis Longitudinal study
			Bronchitis	71	103	
			Tracheitis	21	40	
			Laryngitis	4	7	

[1] These data are considered in a more expanded analysis provided by Leeder et al. (1976a, b).

[2] Relative risk for children of smoking mothers versus children of nonsmoking mothers calculated from data provided by JM Samet (personal communication).

205
1110

The Surgeon General also examined studies as to the association between parental cigarette smoking and prevalence of chronic cough, chronic phlegm and persistent wheeze in children. His conclusion was as follows (p. 48):

> "In summary, children whose parents smoke had a 30 to 80 percent excess prevalence of chronic cough or phlegm compared with children of nonsmoking parents. For wheezing, the increase in risk varied from none to over sixfold among the studies reviewed. Many studies showed an exposure-related increase in the percentage of children with reported chronic symptoms as the number of parental smokers in the home increased. Misclassification as nonsmokers of children who are actively smoking could bias the results of these studies. Adolescent smoking may be reluctant to accurately report their smoking habits, and more objective measures of exposure may not help to distinguish active experimentation with cigarettes from involuntary exposure to smoke (Tager 1986). Although misclassification of children who are actively smoking as nonsmokers must be considered, many studies showing a positive association between parental smoking and symptoms in children, including children at ages before significant experimentation with cigarettes is prevalent. In addition, many studies (Bland et al. 1978; Weiss et al. 1980; Charlton 1984; Schenker et al. 1983; Dodge 1982; Burchfiel et al. 1986) found significant effects of parental smoking after considering active smoking by the children."

(b) *The National Research Council report*

At p. 9 of this report the following appears:

> "Respiratory symptoms, such as wheezing, coughing, and sputum production, are increased in children of smoking parents. These symptoms are more common in children of smokers than children of nonsmokers. The largest studies place the increased risk of 20 to 80%, depending on the symptom being assessed and number of smokers in the household. Also, respiratory infections manifested as pneumonia and bronchitis are significantly increased in infants of smoking parents. Some studies have reported that infants of smoking parents are hospitalized for respiratory infections more frequently than children of nonsmokers. Among children aged under 1 year studies are remarkably consistent in showing an increased risk of respiratory infections among children living in homes where parents smoke. There is a dose-response relationship that relates more to maternal smoking than paternal smoking. The association persists after allowing for possible confounding factors such as occupational data, respiratory illness in the parents, and birthweight. The mechanisms of the increased risk may either be a direct affect of ETS or due to a higher risk of cross-infection in such homes. Regardless of the mechanism, the exposure of small children to smoking in the home appears to put them at risk of respiratory illness."

In the body of the report particular attention is given to the possibility of under-reporting of active smoking on the part of children, recall bias leading to over-reporting of symptoms by parents, and the confounding variables of infections in parents. All three of these may lead to an over-estimation of symptom prevalences among children of smokers. However, after considering studies that have compared children of parents who smoke with children of parents who do not smoke and after referring to a finding that adjustment for parental symptoms or respiratory illness decreases the strength of the apparent association between exposure to environmental tobacco smoke and respiratory symptoms, but does not eliminate it, the authors state:

> "This finding leads to the reasonable conclusion that the exposures typical of ETS are sufficient to cause respiratory symptoms in some children. The increases in frequency of cough were 20 to 50%, and as high as 90%, when there were smoking parents. The increases in frequency of wheezing were more variable, which may indicate the difficulty in assessing this symptom. Furthermore, there appears to be a dose-response relationship between exposure and the likelihood of the child's developing respiratory symptoms or a respiratory illness."

(c) *The National Health and Medical Research Council report*

The following are extracts from chapter 5 of this report, which deals with Passive Smoking and Child Health. I have omitted references to some of the footnotes in the text of the report:

> "Several adverse health effects resulting from passive smoking during childhood have been demonstrated. Children who receive a heavy passive exposure to cigarette smoke have more symptoms and disability from respiratory tract infection than other children. Although many controlled studies have shown this increased prevalence of respiratory symptoms in children of smoking mothers, this observation is not universal.
>
> The best longitudinal cohort studies, adjusted for confounding variables, document that there is approximately twice the incidence of respiratory symptoms and disability due to respiratory disease in smokers' children in the first year of life, compared to children of non-smokers. In fact, no study negates this observation in the *first* year of life. However, the relationship is less certain at later ages."

The summary of the chapter in the report on Passive Smoking and Child Health is expressed in the following terms:

> "Smoking during pregnancy has a clear detrimental effect on the fetus. A consistent association of passive smoking with respiratory morbidity in children has been reported in a number of studies, based on different populations, using different study designs with a variety of outcome measures. There is strong evidence to suggest that maternal smoking is associated with increased lower respiratory symptoms in the first year of life. Associations of passive smoking with respiratory symptoms, reduced lung function, or asthma symptoms in later childhood have been suggested, but the changes are small. Additional longitudinal studies will be required to determine whether these changes are clinically significant.
>
> Smoking and non-smoking families differ in various respects and, although such differences have been recorded and adjusted for in many studies, it remains possible that some of the apparent effect of passive smoking arises from other environmental or behavioural confounding factors that have not been adequately controlled. Further, it is not known whether young children respond more to these irritants, nor whether observed effects of passive smoking reflect predominantly a small effect in large numbers or a larger effect in a susceptible subgroup.
>
> Passive smoking does appear to have some detrimental effect on health at most ages from conception to adolescence. A dose-response relationship with increasing maternal smoking rate found in a number of studies makes a causal link between passive smoking in infancy and respiratory illness, abnormal lung function in childhood, increased asthmatic symptoms and impaired growth seem likely. Further longitudinal studies should help clarify these observations."

(iii) *Oral evidence*

(a) *Professor Landau*

Professor Louis Landau is a respiratory physician. He has been Professor of Child Health in the University of Western Australia since 1984. He was at one time Principal Research Fellow at the Royal Children's Research Foundation, Melbourne and is a former Head of the Professorial Department of Thoracic Medicine at the Royal Children's Hospital, Melbourne. The Professor's clinical work is concerned exclusively with children with respiratory disorders. He has had considerable experience in clinical work.

In the course of his clinical experience over the past 15 years Professor Landau has examined and treated numerous non-smoking patients whose conditions and diseases were, in his view, directly or indirectly attributable to exposure to passive smoking. He is of the opinion that there is evidence which proves scientifically that cigarette smoke causes disease in non-smokers.

Professor Landau is of the opinion that tobacco smoke can harm children because of the effect of, inter alia, passively inhaled smoke. He said that measurements of cotinine in the secretions of children exposed to environmental tobacco smoke indicate significant intake of compounds which could exert a detrimental effect on their health. He said that although there is some variability in the measurements, there is a consistency of some effect and a dose-response to environmental tobacco smoke.

According to the Professor, children who receive a heavy exposure to cigarette smoke have more symptoms and disabilities from respiratory illness than others. He believes that the best studies, adjusted for confounding variables, document at least double the incidence of respiratory symptoms in the first year of life. In his opinion, cigarette smoke may also have an adverse effect on the health of children with pre-existing lung disease. He said that a dose-response relationship and the presence of high levels of cotinine in secretions from the children exposed to passive smoking make a causal link between passive smoking an, inter alia, respiratory disease seem very likely.

Professor Landau was the principal author of Chapter 5 of the NH and MRC report. He said that his views, as I have summarised them above, were held by him as at July 1986.

He gained particular support for his opinions from the primary articles by Harlap and Davies, and by Fergusson et al. However, he referred to many other primary articles in his evidence, and drew support from them.

As will be seen when I refer to the evidence of Dr Witorsch as to the relationship between passive smoking and respiratory disease in children, there does not appear to be much difference between his and Professor Landau's views as to the effect of passive smoking on children in the first year of life.

Professor Landau was cross-examined as to his views, but, in my opinion, they were not shown to be in any way erroneous. He was asked very little about the effect of passive smoking on children under the age of one year. He was cross-examined at some length as to the reasons why the first draft of part of the NH and MRC report had been altered. This part did not relate to respiratory symptoms in children in the first year of life. In any event, the Professor's explanation of the making of the alteration leaves me in no doubt that it was properly made.

Professor Landau was cross-examined at some length about the Harlap and Davies study. He agreed (T. 2136) that it pointed to the need for more and more detailed studies on the subject. However, he said the study gave information which needed to be confirmed and which was subsequently confirmed, by other studies.

Professor Landau limited his assertion that there was scientific proof that passive smoking causes disease to the causation of respiratory disease in children under the age of 12 months. But he said (T. 2060):

> "I think once we get beyond the first year of life the associations are strong, consistent, but it would be harder to use the definition of scientific proof in them ..."

(b) *Dr Le Soeuf*

Dr Peter Le Soeuf is Director of the Department of Respiratory Medicine at Princess Margaret Hospital for Children, Perth. He has had extensive experience in paediatrics. He was formerly a Research Fellow in the Respiratory Physiology Department of the Hospital for Sick Children, Toronto, Canada. He has been a Fellow in Paediatric Respiratory Medicine at the Royal Children's Hospital, Melbourne. He has held his present position for the last six years during which time he has been a Senior Lecturer in the Department of Paediatrics at the University of Western Australia. He is the co-author of a large number of learned articles mostly related to respiratory functions in children.

Dr Le Soeuf is of the opinion that there is very strong scientific evidence that the passive inhalation of cigarette smoke causes disease in young children. He bases his opinion on his professional and clinical experience as a paediatrician and upon his reading of the scientific literature. He said that in the course of his clinical experience and in his capacity as a consultant respiratory physician, he has examined and treated 40 young children whose condition or disease was in his view directly or indirectly attributable to exposure to passive smoking. He said there is an abundance of pathological, clinical and epidemiological evidence suggesting that passive smoking is an important and significant cause of respiratory illness in infants and young children.

In Dr Le Soeuf's opinion, the strongest evidence of a causal relationship between passive smoking and respiratory disease is found in studies of infants in the first year of life. He thinks that the studies of children in this age group had detected a relationship between parental smoking and respiratory problems. He said that a significant relationship between passive smoking and respiratory disease or impaired lung function in children beyond the age of infancy had also been found, but such relationship has not been found in every study involving older children. He summarised his view as follows:

> "In summary, there is a great deal of data from many different sources implicating passive smoking as a cause of respiratory disease in children. The strongest data is in the first year of life; every study in this age group has found that respiratory problems and passive smoking are significantly related. Overall, the data are so strong that in my opinion the possibility that passive smoking is not related to respiratory illness in young children is now excessively remote." (Annexure "E" to his affidavit)

Dr Le Soeuf said that as a consultant paediatric respiratory physician he has seen many children, mostly asthmatic children over five or six years of age, who report that cigarette smoke exacerbates their respiratory symptoms, and that accordingly they move away from smokers. He said that more than half the children he sees are unable to recognise the effect on them of smoke and are likely to remain in the vicinity of smokers. It is his opinion that there are several infants under his care who have required hospitalisation due to their parents' cigarette smoke.

Dr Le Soeuf has great experience in the treatment of children. He estimated that he sees about 500 each year. He agreed that his statement that he had treated 40 young children whose condition was directly or indirectly attributable to exposure to passive smoking was an assessment based on his general experience, rather than on case histories of particular patients.

Dr Le Soeuf was cross-examined at length as to the reliability of some of the studies upon which he placed reliance, particularly that of Harlap and Davies. But I do not think that it was shown that the studies were unreliable. Nor do I think that the cross-examination of him showed that his opinion as to the effect of passive smoking on very young children was unsound.

(c) *Dr Nolan*

Dr Terence Nolan is Senior Lecturer in the Department of Paediatrics at the University of Melbourne. Amongst his other qualifications, he holds the Degree of Doctor of Philosophy from the Department of Epidemiology and Biostatistics at McGill University. Dr Nolan lectures in Theoretical and Applied Epidemiology to students who are pursuing the Degree of Master of Science in Epidemiology.

According to Dr Nolan, the epidemiological evidence of adverse health effects due to passive cigarette smoking on infants and children is considerable. In his opinion, in most cases the avaliable evidence, apart from being abundant, is consistent, plausible and "temporally appropriate", i.e. one can be sure that exposure has preceded the onset of disease.

In his opinion, passive exposure to cigarette smoke increases the risk of respiratory illnesses, such as pneumonia, bronchiolitis, bronchitis, tracheitis and laryngitis in infancy and early childhood, at least during the first two years of life.

Dr Nolan is of the opinion that the findings referred to in the primary articles cannot reasonably be explained by bias in investigational methods, nor attributed to chance, nor reasonably explained by other factors.

Dr Nolan said that the opinions which he now holds were also held by him as at July 1986.

Dr Nolan made particular reference to the studies by Colley, Fergusson et al., Harlap and Davies, Pedreira and Rantakallio. Cross-examination did not, in my opinion, reveal any important deficiencies in these studies or show that Dr Nolan was not justified in placing reliance upon them. I formed the opinion that Dr Nolan was particularly skilled in his specialist field.

(d) *Professor Phelan*

Professor Peter Phelan has been Professor and Chairman, Department of Paediatrics, Melbourne University since 1983. He has been Chief Thoracic Physician at the Royal Children's Hospital, Melbourne since 1983. He has had a great deal of experience extending over many years in the treatment of children. For some years he was a Research Fellow in the Clinical Research Unit at the Royal Children's Hospital Research Foundation. He has been a visiting Professor in the Institute of Child Health at the University of London and an Honorary Consultant Physician at the Hospital for Sick Children, Great Ormond Street, London.

Professor Phelan said that there are many studies that indicate that the incidence of lower respiratory tract infection in children, particularly in the first one or two years of life, is increased amongst those exposed to cigarette smoke. Maternal smoking seems to have a much stronger effect than paternal smoking.

He said that evidence of an association between parental cigarette smoking, particularly domestic exposure, and respiratory illness in children is overwhelming. When challenged on this statement, he said that:

> "…. I think it is the volume, the consistency of the studies that I have referred to, and in many of them the very large numbers that together, in the view of experienced epidemiologists, say the evidence is overwhelming." (T. 1668)

He also said that it was his view that there is "extremely strong overwhelming evidence that there is an association between parental smoking and various types of respiratory illness in children" (T. 1669).

He was cross-examined about this statement and his evidence included the following (T. 1670-71):

> "Now, by 'overwhelming' do you mean to suggest to his Honour that competent, well-informed and reputable epidemiologists, expert in this area, namely, childhood respiratory disease and exposure to cigarette smoke could not consistently with those quality (sic) hold the view that it was less than overwhelming? — I cannot speak for every reputable epidemiologist with interest in this area. All I could say, I would find it very difficult to perceive how someone who has studied the subject could come to a different conclusion. But I cannot say that someone may not."

(The word "quality" in the above question is, I think, wrongly attributed in the transcript to the cross-examiner. The reference should be to "studies".)

> "Are you intending to suggest to his Honour perhaps that it is beyond debate so far as you are concerned? — Certainly, as far as I am concerned, it is beyond debate.
>
> For how long has it been beyond debate so far as you are concerned? — I think the studies became available from the mid-70s onwards, and certainly by the early '80s, and definitely by the mid-80s I believed it was a subject beyond debate, as far as I personally am concerned.
>
> What are the mid '80s? 1983 to 1988? 1987? — 1984, 1985.
>
> So, by 1984 or thereabouts, you tell his Honour, you regarded the question of an association between childhood respiratory illness and exposure to cigarette smoke as being beyond debate. Is that correct? — I believed at that stage that the evidence was very convincing.
>
> And when I refer to 'debate' I am, of course, referring to debate amongst honest, competent, relevantly expert scientists. Do you understand that? — I understand what you are saying and …
>
> Is that what you are saying, that by 1984, in your opinion, this question was beyond such debate? — I believed, with my recall of what evidence was available — and I would have to go back and check precise dates — but by the mid 1980s as I used (sic), that evidence was extremely convincing. Now, I cannot say that there would not be people who wish to take the opposite view. There are always in this world people who may wish to take an opposite view. But it certainly was a consensus of the people with whom I came in contact in the field of paediatric respiratory disease believed that evidence was convincing.
>
> Now, you have referred to people who will always take an opposite view. Do you mean by that to suggest to his Honour that people who disagree with your view are ornery persons who would disagree for the sake of disagreeing? — Not necessarily.
>
> Do you agree that there — it is true to say that, as at 1 July 1986, it was open to reputable, competent, well-informed epidemiologists and medical scientists, expert in the area of respiratory disease in children and exposure to cigarette smoke, to believe that there was, in fact, little evidence of an association? — I would not agree with that statement."

In his opinion, it would be extremely difficult for someone who stood back and objectively looked at the evidence to come to any conclusion but that there is an association between exposure to cigarette smoke in a domestic environment and respiratory illness in children (T. 1669).

Professor Phelan referred, as did the other witnesses in the applicant's case, to the many epidemiological studies tendered in evidence. I do not think any useful purpose would be served by further reference to them in these reasons. He noted some criticisms which could be made of some of the studies and took account of them. I much prefer his assessment of them to those made by the respondent's witnesses. He described the Fergusson et al. study as "a very well undertaken epidemiological study" (T. 1009-10). He was extensively cross-examined as to this study but I do not think his evaluation of it was shown to be wrong.

Pofessor Phelan was asked to explain how the views expressed in evidence could be reconciled with views he had expressed in a recent edition of a textbook of which he was co-author. In the book the following passage appears:

> "Uncertainty remains as to the reasons for the relationship between parental smoking, parental winter phlegm and childhood respiratory illness. It is possible that the relationship is due to a similar genetic background. The presence of parental phlegm could increase the risk of cross-infection. Passive inhalation of tobacco smoke itself may be a cause of respiratory damage. Whatever the mechanism, parental cigarette smoking is a major risk factor for lower respiratory infection in infants and children."

Professor Phelan said that he and his co-authors were too careful in writing that passage and that if he was writing it again he would have written it differently. The book was first published in 1975 and the second edition appeared in 1982. Professor Phelan said that, in retrospect, he thought that the section of the book from which the above quotation is taken should have been re-written.

I do not think the weight of Professor Phelan's evidence was lessened by the reference to the quotation from the book first written in 1975. For the purpose of this case, I am most concerned with his views as to the effect of respiratory illness in children in the first year or so of life. I do not think the statement in the third edition of his book, which refers to childhood respiratory illness in general, diminishes the weight of his evidence on the matter with which I am mostly concerned.

(e) *Professor Witorsch*

I have referred elsewhere to Professor Witorsch's qualifications and experience. The bulk of Professor Witorsch's clinical experience and academic research has been in the field of adult pulmonary disease (T. 3102).

Professor Witorsch said that an important assumption underlying the epidemiological studies into the possible association between environmental tobacco exposure and respiratory function in children is that parental smoking is an adequate and reliable surrogate for direct measurement of exposure to environmental tobacco smoke of the children whose respiratory condition is being examined. He agreed that a number of the studies reported an association between parental (usually maternal) smoking and an increased frequency of respiratory symptoms and/or illness in infants and children below the age of two years. He said that while individual studies suffered from various methodologic and other problems, the overall data nevertheless showed an association between maternal smoking and respiratory symptoms and/or illness in this age group of children. However, he thought there were no studies that establish any association between these findings and the development of respiratory disease or dysfunction in later life.

Professor Witorsch made some criticisms of the studies tendered by the applicant (especially one by Professor Landau and Dr Le Soeuf) and drew attention to the possibility of confounding factors. However, it is fairly clear from his evidence that whilst he has reservations as to the effect of passive smoking on children over the age of 12 months, he accepts that in their first year of life children of smoking mothers are more likely to have respiratory problems than children of non-smoking mothers. (T. 3085.) He also said that he did not see any substantial difference in the evidence on this matter between 1986 and the present time (T. 3086).

He thought that socio-economic factors may account, at least in part, for the increased frequency of respiratory symptoms and illness in young children associated with maternal smoking. Parental smoking is higher in lower income groups and is also positively correlated with a number of socio-economic related variables that can adversely affect childhood respiratory health, e.g. diet, housing, living density, ventilation, personal hygiene and other health habits, cooking and heating practices. He thought that in the studies associating parental smoking with respiratory health in young children adjustments for socio-economic status were either not performed or the complexities of them were not adequately taken into consideration. In this respect he pointed to the findings in the Harlap and Davies study that while there was an increased incidence of respiratory illness, there were also increased hospitalisations due to poisoning and injury in infants of smoking parents. This suggested to Professor Witorsch that the association reported in that study, and perhaps some of the other studies, may have been indicative of general parental neglect.

I do not think the socio-economic factors to which the Professor referred would have been likely to have so substantially affected the results of the study showing the effect of passive smoking on very young infants as to render those results unreliable.

(f) *Professor Huber*

I have referred to Professor Huber's experience and qualifications elsewhere in these reasons. He does not appear to have had any special qualifications or experience in relation to respiratory disease in young children.

The Professor commented upon many of the primary articles dealing with the association between environmental tobacco smoke and pulmonary functions. So far as they related to children, he said that the published results were neither uniform nor consistent and were difficult to interpret. In his proof of evidence he said little as to the effect of passive smoking on very young children, or as to the studies of such children. He made no mention of the Harlap and Davies study. With respect to the study by Fergusson et al., he thought that it did not define the precise nature of the outcomes which were being investigated. He said that in that study a child was defined as displaying symptoms of lower respiratory illness if he had received medical attention for bronchitis/pneumonia or if his mother reported "chesty colds or wheeze". He thought this definition lacked reliability and that in any event wheeze is usually not associated with lower respiratory tract illness. He also thought that the reliability of the index used to define bronchitis or pneumonia was unreliable.

I do not agree with these criticisms of the Fergusson et al. report which were not made by other witnesses. The authors of the Fergusson et al. report were paediatricians and might be expected to have defined with reasonable precision the nature of the outcomes they were investigating. In his analysis of the studies, the Surgeon General makes no mention of the criticisms raised by Professor Huber.

Professor Huber said (Ex. 60, p. 44) there is an approximately equal number of studies which report no significant association between parental smoking and respiratory illness in children, and cited a large number of articles in support of this argument. The two studies of which he made particular mention, viz a study conducted in Holland by Kerrebijn et al. and published in 1977 and a study by Schilling et al. carried out in the United States and published in 1977, related to respiratory symptoms in school-age children. The subject of the Schilling study were aged seven years or more and the children studied in the Kerrebijn study were attending school.

I have read all the studies referred to by Professor Huber and I do not think they provide data which is inconsistent with the findings by Harlap and Davies and by Fergusson et al. Professor Huber did not refer to any clinical experience which he had in treating very young children.

Upon examination, some of the studies referred to by Professor Huber, but not elaborated upon in oral evidence, do not support his opinions. For instance, in a study by Bouhuys the statement is made that:

> "Children of smoking parents may suffer unduly from respiratory disease. For example, infants of mothers who smoke have significantly more attacks of bronchitis and pneumonia than infants of nonsmoking mothers. Also, children of smoking parents who may or may not have symptoms themselves have more bronchitis and

pneumonia during their first year of life than children of nonsmoking parents. However, this was not true during four subsequent years of follow-up. But even older children may have an increased incidence of acute respiratory disease in homes where cigarettes are smoked. These studies have led to the conclusion that passive smoking (inhaling other people's smoke) is injurious to health.''

The studies referred to in the above quotation are ones which were not made by Bouhuys but it is plain that he adopts them. At the time of writing the paper, Bouhuys was Professor of Medicine and Epidemiology at Yale University Lung Research Center.

The Bouhuys study was concerned with children between the ages of 7 and 18. It is true that Bouhuys concluded that exposure to low levels of smoke produced by cigarette smokers does not result in chronic respiratory symptoms among children and adults. However, it is plain that this conclusion does not relate to children in the first year or two of life.

Another study referred to by Dr Huber was that by Gardner et al. This was a relatively small study of 131 infants. The authors found that the infants of parents who smoked were not at greater risk for viral infection or respiratory illness, the only exception to this being a significant relationship between pneumonia and parental smoking, especially in mothers at home. The authors state that their observations are in contrast with those of Harlap and Davies and Leeder. It was a much smaller study than the Harlap and Davies and Fergusson studies. Most of the studies referred to by Professor Huber seem to me to have very little, if any, relevance to a consideration of the effects of passive smoking on children in the first year or two of life.

I formed the opinion that Professor Huber sees difficulties and limitations in studies which are not perceived by competent researchers and specialists in the field.

(iv) *Does cigarette smoke cause respiratory disease in young children?*

In my opinion the only conclusion open on the evidence is that the statement that there was little evidence and nothing which proves scientifically that cigarette smoke causes disease in non-smokers, was demonstrably false in 1986 in so far as it applied to respiratory disease in children in the first year of life. The statement remains false to this day. In my view the falsity of the statement is demonstrated whatever meaning one gives to the terms ''little evidence'' and ''scientific proof''. I share the opinion expressed by Professor Phelan that the evidence, establishing a causal relationship between passive smoking and respiratory disease in very young children is overwhelming. The evidence is of such strength that it constitutes scientific proof.

The evidence is of two kinds, epidemiological and clinical. I cannot help observing that none of the witnesses called by the respondent were specialist paediatricians or epidemiologists. On the other hand, the applicant's witnesses included specialists in both fields. I think that the respondent would have called specialists in these fields, of whom there must be many in this country and overseas, had they been able to give evidence favourable to the respondent's case.

I was greatly impressed by the applicant's witnesses and prefer to accept their opinions whenever they are in conflict with the opinions expressed by the respondent's witnesses.

As I have observed, the applicant tendered many primary articles and called much oral evidence in support of its claim that passive smoking causes respiratory disease and loss of lung function in older children and adults. I make no finding one way or the other on this part of the applicant's case, since it is unnecessary to do so for the purposes of deciding whether the advertisement is misleading or deceptive. To have dealt adequately with the evidence on this issue would have greatly expanded these already lengthy reasons.

9. *Asthma*

It is part of the applicant's case that the statement in para. 3 of the advertisement is misleading or deceptive in so far as it applies to the disease of asthma. In order to evaluate this part of the case it is necessary to make brief mention of the nature and symptoms of the disease.

(i) *Meaning of ''asthma''*

Dr Breslin, to whose evidence I shall subsequently refer in greater detail, said that the standard definition of asthma is "paroxysmal generalised airways obstruction which varies spontaneously or as a result of treatment" (T. 569). He explained the disease in the following terms (T. 569-70):

> "Now, basically what asthma is it is a narrowing of the airways. The lungs are composed of two parts the breathing tubes that take air down into the spongy tissue or the lungs and the spongy tissue itself which is the lung substance. And asthma is a disease of the airways and not of the lung tissue.
>
> I liken it — the lung structure to say an inverted tree where you have got the trunk of the tree representing the trachea, the branches of the tree representing the remaining tubes that conduct air and the leaves of the tree being that part of the lung tissue where gas exchange takes place, oxygen is taken up by the body, carbon dioxode given off. The trunk of the tree is the trachea, the various branches are the bronchi, that gets smaller and smaller and smaller and smaller as they go out towards the leaves or alveoli and basically asthma is a disease of the conducting airways. It is not a disease of the leaves or alveoli. The basic abnormality in asthma is that out of the blue and from time to time in some patients and all the time in others the airways narrow down and then later on open up either spontaneously or as a result of treatment. Some people when a door slams leap out of their chair, some people cry easily, some people blush easily, asthmatics' airways narrow down easily. The reason they narrow down easily is because there are twitchy or hypersensitive. So one of the basic abnormalities in asthma is that the airways are twitchy. ... The airways are twitchy but having twitchy airways alone does not mean you have got asthma because there are normal people wandering around the community, probably some people in this room, who have twitchy airways but do not have asthma. In order to have asthma, the disease asthma, you need what I originally referred to in the definition and that is paroxysmal generalised airways obstruction. In addition to the twitchinesss you, as it were, need the door to slam and have you leap out of the chair as it were ..."

Having said that the airways vary from a centimetre in width at the trachea down to the width of a thread of cotton, Dr Breslin said (T. 571):

> "And these airways in asthmatics narrow down because they are twitchy and they narrow down to a variety of stimuli. So when a person has, firstly, twitchy airways and secondly, episodes of wheeze, chest tightness, shortness of breath and measurable objective changes of their lung function, then we call them asthmatic, they have the disease asthma. Having the twitchy airways in itself is not a disease because a lot of people without disease have that."

Dr Breslin's description of asthma was not challenged in cross-examination and I did not understand the respondent's witnesses to disagree with it.

(ii) *Oral evidence*

(a) *Dr Breslin*

Dr Antony Breslin is a consultant thoracic physician. Since 1973 he has been the Senior Specialist in Charge (Chest Diseases) at the Repatriation General Hospital Concord. He has for many years been a lecturer at the University of Sydney. He is a former chairman of the Thoracic Society of Australia (New South Wales) Branch and a member of the Court of Clinical Examiners, Royal Australasian College of Physicians. Dr Breslin has been specialising in respiratory disease and, in particular, asthma, for about 20 years.

Dr Breslin said that unless a person has attacks of asthma he does not have the disease of asthma (T. 650). It was put to him in cross-examination that there is a distinction between the disease of asthma and attacks of asthma but he refused to accept this distinction. He supported his refusal by drawing a comparison between asthma and epilepsy. He said:

> "You can have the propensity to epilepsy but if you do not have fits you do not have epilepsy. You can have the propensity to attacks but if you do not have attacks you do not have asthma."

In his practice as a respiratory physician Dr Breslin sees a large number of patients of all ages suffering from bronchial asthma. A very large proportion of these patients indicate to him that passive smoking is harmful to their asthma and produces a deterioration in their asthmatic condition.

In order to confirm whether the views of his patients could be supported objectively, Dr Breslin undertook a small study of asthmatic patients and exposed them to cigarette smoke. This study was carried out in 1984 and the results of it were published, in abbreviated form, in the *Medical Journal of Australia* in February 1985. The abstract of the study as published reads as follows:

> "A study of the effect of passive smoking on patients with asthma is presented. Six patients were exposed for one hour to the air in a room in which tobacco smoke was produced mechanically over that period. The effects on symptoms, lung function and airways sensitivity to inhaled histamine were then measured and compared with the same patient's responses during a control day when they inhaled smoke-free air. All six patients developed chest tightness and symptoms similar to an attack of asthma. The findings of respiratory and sensitivity tests suggest: (i) that passive smoking may trigger asthma attacks in subjects who suffer from asthma and (ii) that the airways of such subjects show increased histamine reactivity four hours after the passive smoke exposure."

Dr Breslin said that his clinical experience since he carried out his study in 1984 had served to confirm even more forcibly his opinion that passive smoking is a medical hazard. He said he was convinced that there is a large volume of evidence confirming that passive smoking "is a frequent and very troublesome trigger for bronchial asthma in many patients".

Dr Breslin said that about 20% of children under the age of 20 and about 10% of the total Australian population have asthma. His practice is to initially ask his patients what sort of things they have noticed trigger their asthma and then he subsequently asks them directly whether other things, which he nominates, trigger it. Thirty to 35 per cent of patients volunteer that cigarette smoke appears to have an effect on their asthma. When patients are specifically asked whether cigarette smoke has an effect on their asthma, the percentage of patients who respond positively rises to the order of 50% or 60% (T. 582).

Dr Breslin supported his opinion by reference to articles which had appeared in learned scientific journals. One such article by Dahms et al. was published in November 1981. The authors concluded that:

> "The results of this initial investigation indicate that patients with bronchial asthma do respond adversely when actively exposed to environmental tobacco smoke."

There is some inconsistency among the studies referred to by Dr Breslin. One reason for the inconsistencies, as is observed in the NRC report at p. 215, is the small sample sizes in the various studies. Further, as is noted in the report, the persons surveyed were not unaware of the presence of environmental tobacco smoke and therefore the authors could not exclude the possibility that pulmonary function changes could have been emotionally related to cigarette smoke exposure, especially in those patients who reported previous histories of adverse response to exposure to environmental tobacco smoke.

In the Surgeon General's 1986 report the statement is made that biases in observation and in the selection of subjects and the subjects' own expectations may have accounted for the divergent results. However, there is nothing in the major reviews to refute Dr Breslin's evidence that cigarette smoke causes attacks of asthma in some asthmatics.

Dr Breslin also referred to a study carried out by Kauffmann et al. the results of which were published in the *American Review of Respiratory Diseases* in 1986. He said the study showed that there was a statistically significant worsening of airways obstruction in asthmatic women as a result of exposure to cigarette smoke. Also, the study demonstrated that the greater the exposure to passive smoke, the worse was the effect on the asthma of the women.

Dr Breslin also referred to a study carried out by Murray et al., the results of which were published in July 1986. The authors summarised their findings as follows:

> "The effect of parental smoking was assessed in 94 consecutively observed children, aged 7 to 17 years, who had a history of asthmatic wheezing. The 24 children whose mothers smoked, when they were compared with children whose

> mothers did not smoke, had 47% more symptoms, a 13% lower mean FEV percent, a 23% lower mean FEF, and fourfold greater responsiveness to aerosolized histamine. A dose response was evident. There was a highly significant correlation between the results of the tests and the number of cigarettes the mother smoked while she was in the house. The differences between the children of smoking and nonsmoking mothers were greater in older than in younger subjects. The smoking habits of the father were not correlated with the severity of the child's asthma.''

FEV refers to forced expiratory volume. Thus FEV 1 represents the amount of air that a person can get out of his lungs in a forced manoeuvre from full inspiration in the first second. FVC means forced vital capacity, that is, the total amount of air that one can expel in one forced manoeuvre. Normally FEV 1 should be greater than 80% of the FVC. That is to say, normally if a person takes a full deep breath and then exhales rapidly and to completion he should be able to exhale more than 80% of the air in the first second. It is a characteristic of asthmatics that the ratio of their FEV 1 to their FVC during an attack of asthma is less than 80%. This is because their airways are obstructed. The use of histamine is one way of measuring the twitchiness of airways. If a normal person inhales histamine, his airways will narrow, but the airways of an asthmatic will narrow in response to a much smaller does of histamine than is required to produce a similar reaction in a normal non-asthmatic person.

Murray et al. made the following observation on their study:

> ''The evidence suggests that it is airborne cigarette smoke that causes the adverse effect. Not only is there a strong association between maternal smoking and severity of the child's asthma, but there is also evidence of a dose response. We found a significant correlation between all indicators of asthma severity and the logarithm of the number of cigarettes the mother smoked while she was in the home. There was also evidence that length of exposure had an effect. The older children, who had presumably been exposed to cigarette smoke for more years than the younger ones, were more severely affected. This finding is similar to that of Tager et al. They reported that the normal rate of increase in FEV_1 during adolescent growth is slowed in children whose mothers smoked. Further evidence, that it is passively inhaled smoke that is responsible for the changes, is the effect observed when the mother stops smoking. Vedal et al. report that children whose mothers are current smokers do but children whose mothers are exsmokers do not have significant differences in pulmonary function from those whose mothers are nonsmokers.
>
> In contrast to the smoking habits of the mother, those of the father had no significant correlation with the severity of the child's asthma. These findings agree with those in more recently published large epidemiologic studies. Several factors may account for this apparent paradox. One is our finding that the father, compared with the mother, smokes significantly fewer cigarettes when he is at home. Another is the possibility that the mother, more frequently than the father, is in the same room as the child when she smokes a cigarette. A third possibility is that the number of cigarettes smoked in the house are more accurately reported for the mother than for the father. The mother was usually the person who gave the information. Whatever the reason, the father's smoke did not appear to influence the child's asthma significantly. When we examined the effect of maternal and paternal smoking together, therefore, we found it to be less clear than when we examined the result of maternal smoking alone. This observation may explain the lack of effect of parental smoking on wheezing and spirometric values reported in some epidemiologic studies.
>
> ...
>
> Our findings indicate that maternal smoking aggravates asthma in children, the effect being clinically important as well as statistically significant.''

Dr Breslin also supported his opinion by reference to a study by O'Connell and Logan published in 1971. The summary of the findings in this study is as follows:

"The relationship between childhood asthma and parental smoking was studied in 400 cases. The incidence of parental smoking was about the same in asthmatic children's homes as in those of controls. Tobacco smoke aggravated the asthma in 50% of all the asthmatic children and in 67% of those whose parents smoked. Exposure to tobacco smoke was considered a significant factor in 10%. Elimination was usually followed by clinical improvement."

As part of their study, O'Connell and Logan noted the effect of the cessation of parental smoking. They identified 37 children whose parents' smoking had a significantly adverse effect on their asthma. Of these 37 families, 35 were followed up six months to two years later. Among them, 20 had succeeded in stopping the children's exposure to smoke and improvement had been obtained in 18 of the children. Smoke exposure had continued in 15 of the families and improvement had occurred in only 4 of those families. The improvement in these four cases was attributed to the elimination of contact with other factors. The authors noted that in general where smoke exposure was a significant factor in asthma, its elimination was followed by improvement and with continuance of exposure improvement did not occur.

O'Connell and Logan observed:

"From this study we assume that nearly two of every three children seen in the offices of Midwestern paediatricians come from homes in which one or both parents smoke and that, among asthmatic children from such homes, this daily air pollution aggravates the asthma at least occasionally in 67%."

Dr Breslin acknowledged that this study had the weakness of being retrospective. The authors carried out their study by examination of clinical files and records of 400 asthmatic children who were treated for their asthma in 1969, 1970 and early 1971.

Dr Breslin referred in his evidence to a study by Shepherd. This study was not confined to persons suffering only from asthma. It included sufferers from chronic bronchitis and pulmonary emphysema. Dr Breslin described this as a "critical fault" in the study. The study considered 14 volunteer asthmatic subjects who were exposed to environmental tobacco smoke in a room. All the subjects developed some symptoms but there were only very slight changes in respiratory function tests. Four of the fourteen who gave a positive pre-test history of their asthma being worsened by exposure to passive smoking showed small changes in their FEV, but the others did not. Dr Breslin thought it was hard to attach any significance to the study (T. 602-3).

Dr Breslin also referred to a study by Wiedemann et al. undertaken in 1983 but published in February 1986. The authors studied the acute effects of one hour of passive cigarette smoking on the lung function and airway activity of 9 young asthmatic volunteers. At the time of the study, the subjects were asymptomatic and had normal or nearly normal lung function. Passive smoking produced no change in their expiratory flow rate. The authors concluded that passive smoking presented no acute respiratory risk to young asymptomatic asthmatic patients. Dr Breslin observed of this study that it was made of subjects whom he described as "extremely mild asthmatics", none of whom was receiving any treatment. He drew a distinction between such persons and the type of persons referred to in the other studies.

Dr Breslin maintained that a person is an asthmatic if he gets attacks of asthma. He described asthma as a "recurrent condition" (T. 623). His clinical experience in treating asthmatic children was not challenged, nor was his evidence as to the percentage of his patients who informed him that tobacco smoke appears to have an effect on their asthma.

(b) *Professor Phelan*

Professor Phelan said that passive exposure to cigarette smoke seems to have a significant effect on asthmatic symptoms, and that cessation of smoking by parents leads to an improvement in asthmatic symptoms. As to the general nature of asthma, the Professor said (T. 989-90):

"I like to think of asthma as an inherited predisposition to the development of the condition or disease called asthma. It clearly is an inherited predisposition in the airways. Then various trigger factors can lead to narrowing in those airways that results in the symptoms of asthma and to be (sic) asthma is a disease causing symptoms that interfere with the patient's normal activities — cough, wheeze and breathlessness.

> Between those overt symptoms there may be some degree of airways narrowing persisting but it may not be of sufficient degree to affect their day to day activities and that term may then be called subclinical asthma or — the propensity to asthma in children, we do not have adequate data to say 'Is there changes present all the time in the child who has, say, three or four episodes of asthma a year.' To obtain that information would require to take pieces of the lining of the airways and that is ethically unacceptable in children. I think there is much evidence to suggest that three quarters of children probably have normal airways between their episodes and those episodes then are triggered by various factors.''

He later said (T. 990):

> ''... there are perhaps 20 to 30 per cent of the population [who] with appropriate trigger factors may develop allergic manifestations. It may be hay fever, it may be skin weals. Most of the time they are free of all symptoms but when they are exposed to a particular trigger factor, it may be a grass pollen, it may be an animal hair, they will develop symptoms of that condition. Now, they have allergic disease when they have those symptoms but when they are free of the symptoms I find it hard to call — say they have allergic disease as disease relates to something that is impairing bodily function.''

As well as referring to some of the epidemiological studies referred to by Dr Breslin, Professor Phelan referred to a study by Horwood et al. published in 1985. This was a study carried out in New Zealand in which no evidence was found to suggest that parental smoking played a significant role in the development of asthma in children up to the age of six years. Professor Phelan said that the number of children studied was small, there being only four girls with asthma from families in which both parents smoked. Nevertheless, he thought the study, particularly in respect of boys, showed a trend, i.e. when both parents smoked there was more asthma amongst the boys than when neither parent or only one parent smoked. The same trend was not apparent amongst girls.

(c) *Dr Le Souef*

Dr Le Souef said that as a consultant paediatric respiratory physician he has seen many children, mostly asthmatic individuals over five or six years of age, who report that cigarette smoke exacerbates their respiratory symptoms. These children usually add that they seek cleaner air by moving away from smokers. However, more than half the children he sees are younger than this and are unable to recognise and report such associations. He said that these younger children were then more likely to remain in the vicinity of smokers, particularly infants who are held by a smoker or are too young to be mobile. It is his opinion that there are several infants under his care who have required hospitalisation due to their parents' cigarette smoke.

(d) *Professor Witorsch*

Professor Witorsch drew a distinction between asthma and an attack of asthma. He thought that ''one is really a subdivision or a part of the other'' (T. 3093). He said that environmental tobacco smoke does not cause the disease of asthma but that it may produce or exacerbate symptoms in some asthmatics.

It seems to me that the difference between Professor Witorsch and Dr Breslin on the question of asthma is really one of semantics. They appear to agree that environmental tobacco smoke produces symptoms of asthma in some persons. But Professor Witorsch regards smoke as causing attacks of asthma, whereas Dr Breslin regards it as causing asthma.

I gained the impression that Professor Witorsch's experience in this field is much less than Dr Breslin's.

Professor Witorsch conceded that some individuals with asthma may have attacks that are precipitated by environmental tobacco smoke (T. 3092). He also agreed that when some asthmatic patients are asked what causes them to have acute attacks of asthma they include environmental tobacco smoke amongst the causes (T. 3099). He also agreed that the word ''disease'' can be taken to refer to, inter alia, acute disease and latent disease. I think it is difficult to say that an attack of asthma sustained by a person who suffers from an underlying condition of asthma does not constitute an episode of a latent disease.

(e) *Professor Huber*

I have referred elsewhere to Professor Huber's qualifications. Although they are extensive in the field of respiratory disease, he does not appear to have had any specialist experience in the field of asthma.

He is of the opinion that there is no reliable evidence that inhalation of environmental tobacco smoke causes asthma. He agreed that exposure to such smoke may provoke a reaction within the airways in some individuals who are already asthmatic. But he thought even that was uncertain. He thinks that when such reactions appear to occur it is unclear whether they are caused by an irritating effect of smoke on the airways or are psychological in origin. He said that even the sight of tobacco smoke may produce a reaction in some asthmatics. He thinks there is no evidence clearly indicating that a true allergic reaction occurs as a result of the inhalation of environmental tobacco smoke.

Professor Huber thinks that because psychological factors are known to produce bronchospasm in asthmatics, it is quite possible that the decrease in pulmonary function noted in some asthmatics in some of the studies can be related to the psychological factors associated with the experimental design used in the studies.

Professor Huber made no comment on Dr Breslin's evidence, based on his clinical experience, as to the proportion of his patients who identify tobacco smoke as being associated with attacks of asthma.

Professor Huber's evidence included the following (T.3735):

> "Do you hold any opinion as to whether it is wise for an asthmatic child to be kept for any period of time in a smoking environment, smoky (*sic*) meaning environmental tobacco smoke environment? — I would not recommend that they be in a smoking environment.
>
> Why would that be? — Because some of these children will react to the irritating effects of a smoking environment and have an exacerbation of their asthma. ..."

Further, at T.3737:

> "[E]xposure to environmental tobacco smoke can in some persons who are sensitive to it convert them from being someone with underlying asthma in respect of which they feel no symptoms to a person experiencing an acute attack of asthma in which they are constantly aware of symptoms? — Yes."

(iii) *Conclusion on asthma*

There is overwhelming evidence, which is really not disputed by the respondent, that passive smoking causes some people to experience attacks of asthma. It is unnecessary to have regard to any of the epidemiological studies to prove that this is the case. However, the majority of the studies support the opinions expressed by the applicant's witnesses. As I have shown, the respondent's witnesses themselves virtually concede that cigarette smoke may trigger attacks of asthma.

On the other hand, the applicant has not shown that cigarette smoke of itself causes what might be described as the underlying condition of asthma.

The real question on this part of the case is whether one should characterise an attack of asthma as "disease" for the purposes of the statement made in para. 3 of the advertisement.

Dr Nolan, was asked what was his understanding of the word "disease". He said that, broadly speaking, disease could be considered to be anything that is an unhealthy process. He said:

> "... in general I guess the term 'disease' implies a degree of disability or functional impairment, or discomfort, which is inconsistent with the notion of health." (T.749)

This seems to me to be a reasonably workable definition of the term, and coincides broadly with the ordinary meaning of the word and also with the meaning which I think would be attached to it by the reader of the advertisement. In the context of the advertisement, the most apposite meaning of the word as given in the *Shorter Oxford English Dictionary* is:

> "A condition of the body, or of some part or organ of the body, in which its functions are disturbed or deranged."

The *Macquarie Dictionary*, revised edition, gives as the primary meaning of "disease":

> "A morbid condition of the body, or of some organ or part; illness; sickness; ailment."

It seems to me that an attack of asthma fits easily within the dictionary definitions quoted above. Wheezing, which is one of the main symptoms of asthma, is plainly a condition of the body in which its functions are disturbed, often to a serious degree. I would think many lay persons would not distinguish between asthma and an attack of asthma. Those who did would, I think, regard the underlying condition of asthma referred to in some of the evidence as a latent disease and an attack of asthma as an acute manifestation of the disease. If such persons were told that there is little evidence and nothing which proves scientifically that cigarette smoke causes disease in non-smokers they may well be misled or deceived into believing that there is little evidence and nothing which proves scientifically that cigarette smoke causes attacks of asthma in non-smokers.

The likelihood of this happening is increased because, in its totality, the advertisement is directed at allaying the concerns of people that cigarette smoke may affect the health of non-smokers. Thus, people who are prone to asthma attacks could reasonably gain the impression from the statement made in para. 3 that they are not at risk of suffering attacks of asthma by reason of being exposed to cigarette smoke.

I accept Dr Breslin's evidence as to the nature and characteristics of asthma and of asthma attacks. I think there is much common sense in his approach that a person does not have asthma when he is not having an attack of asthma.

In my opinion the applicant's witnesses (particularly Dr Breslin) have a great deal more experience with asthma than the respondent's witnesses. Where there are differences in the opinions of the experts in this field, the opinions of the applicant's experts are to be preferred.

The evidence that cigarette smoke causes attacks of asthma is so overwhelming that I cannot accept that the draftsman of the advertisement held an opinion to the contrary. No rational basis exists for the holding of an opinion that there is little evidence and nothing which proves scientifically that cigarette smoke causes attacks of asthma. It was not suggested, nor could it have been, that any scientist could properly hold such an opinion.

I am satisfied that the applicant has established that the statement made in para. 3 of the advertisement is misleading and deceptive in so far as it applies to the disease of asthma. This is so whether the relevant date be regarded as 1 July 1986 or at any date thereafter.

10. *Otitis media*

(i) *Nature of the disease*

The disease of chronic secretory otitis media is also known as middle ear effusion and "glue ear". It occurs when cells in the middle ear secrete abnormal amounts of a gluey substance which is then trapped in the middle ear. The resulting blockage can cause temporary deafness in children, and may require surgery to ventilate and drain the middle ear. According to Dr Nolan the result of the disease process is deafness in children which in turn has been shown to interfere with child development and learning. He said it is quite a significant disability for a child to have. It may be prolonged but it is not a permanent effect on the nerve cells of the auditory nerve. The effect of the disease is to impede transmission of sound waves into the middle ear and then to the auditory nerve.

Dr Nolan thinks that it is probable that involuntary exposure to cigarette smoke causes chronic secretory otitis media.

(ii) *Primary articles*

(a) *Kraemer et al.* — Risk Factors for Persistent Middle-Ear Effusions: Otitis Media, Catarrh, Cigarette Smoke Exposure and Atopy.

The authors of this article came from the Children's Orthopedic Hospital and Medical Centre and the University of Washington School of Medicine, Seattle. It was published in the *Journal of the American Medical Association* in 1983.

The abstract published with the study reads as follows:

> "To ascertain risk factors for persistent middle-ear effusions (PMEE), we interviewed the parents of two groups of children. The first consisted of 76 children with PMEE who were admitted to the

hospital for tympanostomy-tube insertion. The second, a control group, consisted of 76 children admitted for other types of surgery, who were matched for age, sex, season, and surgical ward. Nearly all (97%) of the children admitted for insertion of tympanostomy tubes had one or more episodes of suppurative otitis media. Only 59% of the control children had previous ear infections. Frequent ear infections sharply increased the risk for persistent effusions. Catarrh, household cigarette smoke exposure, and atopy also occurred more frequently in children with PMEE. The risk for middle-ear effusions was greatest when these three factors were all present. The avoidance of daily exposure to domestic tobacco smoke and, if atopic, of specific allergens should be included in the medical treatment of children with PMEE.''

Table I on p. 1023 of the study sets out the relative risk of persistent middle-ear effusions according to the different variables about which information was obtained during interview. These variables included racial background, family size, frequency of catarrh, atopic disease, frequency of suppurative otitis media and household exposure to cigarette smoke.

An extract from the table dealing with household cigarette exposure is set out below:

Characteristic	No. (%) of PMEE Cases (N = 76)	No. (%) of Surgical Control Subjects (N = 76)	Relative Risk	95% Confidence Interval
Household cigarette smokers				
0	38 (50.0)	45 (59.2)	1.0	—
1	19 (25.0)	23 (30.3)	1.0	0.5-2.1
⩾2	19 (25.0)	8 (10.5)	2.8	1.1-7.0
Household cigarette use No. packs per day				
None	38 (50.0)	45 (59.2)	1.0	—
0.1-0.9	11 (14.5)	7 (9.2)	1.9	0.7-5.3
1.0-1.9	13 (17.1)	14 (18.4)	1.1	0.5-2.6
2.0-2.9	7 (9.2)	8 (10.5)	1.0	0.3-3.1
⩾3.0	7 (9.2)	2 (2.6)	4.1	0.9-19.2

This extract shows that a statistically significant relative risk of 2.8 was found for cases where there were 2 or more cigarette smokers in the household, but no increase in risk was found where there was one household smoker. It also shows that when exposure was measured by packs per day a linear dose response relationship was not apparent and no subgroup result was statistically significant. However when household cigarette use equalled or exceeded 3 packs per day, the relative risk of persistent middle-ear effusion was reported as 4.1 (95% C.I. 0.9-19.2).

A later table in the study shows the combined effects of nasal congestion, cigarette smoke exposure, and atopy. The authors reported that:

> ''[N]asal congestion alone elevated the risk nearly fourfold. When cigarette smoke exposure or atopy was added to nasal congestion, the risk increased. Children with all three factors were more than six times as likely to manifest PMEE.''

(b) *Black* — The Aetiology of Glue Ear — A Case-Control Study

The author of this study was from the Department of Community Medicine and General Practice at Oxford University. The article was published in the *International Journal of Pediatric Otorhinolaryngology* in 1985.

The abstract published with the study reads as follows:

> "A case-control study was carried out to investigate many of the proposed causes of glue ear in childhood. One hundred and fifty cases with two matched controls were found to be remarkably similar in nearly all medical and social aspects of their past and present lives, thus providing no support for many of the currently held views on the aetiology of glue ear. Of the 5 factors which were found to increase the risk of a child undergoing surgery for glue ear, only one of these is thought to be related to the development of the condition, rather than to the chances of its detection. This factor was parental smoking (RR 1.64) ..."

The author stated:

> "A significant association was found (RR 1.64; P <0.05) between glue ear and the smoking habits of all household members throughout the subject's life. This analysis assumes a constant level of exposure to smoke throughout the subject's life. Further study would be required to determine whether or not the risk of smoke is associated with any particular stage of childhood." (p. 131)

The statistically significant result of 1.64 emerged after original insignificant results were subjected to further (matched pair) analysis. It was suggested to Professor Landau in cross-examination that this was a weak association and that the author was attempting to use two reported weak associations to argue for a strong association. Professor Landau said that the conclusion of a strong association was based on the consistent findings. However, he agreed that the Black study (and also Kraemer's) showed no more than that cigarette smoke was a risk factor for glue ear.

The respondent led no expert evidence directly on the issue of otitis media and environmental tobacco smoke.

(iii) *The major reviews*

The authors of the N.R.C. report state (at p. 274):

> "Household exposure to ETS is linked with increased rates of chronic ear infections and middle-ear effusions in young children. For children with nasal allergies and recurrent otitis media, ETS exposure may synergistically increase their risk of persistent middle-ear effusions."

The authors of the Surgeon General's report after referring to five studies (Black, Kraemer et al., Pukander, Said et al. (1978) (Ex E333) and Iverson et al. (1985) (Ex E192)) conclude:

> "These studies are consistent in their demonstration of excess chronic middle ear effusions, a sign of chronic ear disease, in children exposed to parental cigarette smoke. Potential confounding factors for middle ear effusions should be examined carefully in future studies. The long-term implications of the excess middle ear problems deserve further study."

(iv) *Conclusion*

The number of studies which have examined the association between otitis media and passive smoking is limited and there are some questions as to the consistency of data and the methodology of the studies. Nevertheless the studies by Black and Kraemer offer substantial support for the hypothesis that exposure to environmental tobacco smoke causes recurrent otitis media in children. Dr Nolan and Professor Landau are both distinguished medical researchers and their views are entitled to respect. The studies on which they rely were produced or published by institutions of international standing.

In contrast, the respondent offered no detailed expert evidence on this question.

I am not satisfied there is scientific proof of a causal association between passive smoking and otitis media, mainly because of the cautious note of Professor Landau's answers in cross-examination. Nevertheless, I am persuaded on the strength of the oral evidence and the primary articles that there was, in 1986, more than a little evidence that passive smoking causes recurrent otitis media in children.

11. *Does the advertisement state fact or opinion?*

It was submitted on behalf of the respondent that the statement in the advertisement would be understood by the reader as being no more than an expression of opinion and that s. 52 of the Act does not operate to restrict publication of opinions on scientific issues.

The statement made in the advertisement is not expressed to be an opinion. It is an assertion of the state of the evidence on the question whether cigarette smoke causes disease in non-smokers.

The statement must be read in the context of the whole of the advertisement. The paragraphs which immediately follow para. 3 contain statements which support the view that what is said in para. 3 itself is a reference to the state of the evidence, as distinct from the expression of an opinion, as to the existence of a causal link between cigarette smoke and disease in non-smokers. The references to the work of the Institute of Cancer Research, the American Cancer Society and the Harvard School of Public Health are calculated to cause the reader to believe that the published views of those bodies represent the state of the evidence as to a link between cigarette smoke and disease in non-smokers. The reference to major reviews is calculated to induce the same belief in the reader. That is to say, what the reader is told in para. 3 is not that some innominate person or body holds an opinion as to the relationship between cigarette smoke and disease in non-smokers, rather he is told what the state of the evidence is on the subject. In my opinion most readers would read the advertisement in that way. To put the matter at the very lowest, and to borrow words used by *Deane* J. in *Tillmanns Butcheries Pty Limited v. Australasian Meat Industry Employees' Union* (1979) ATPR ¶40-138 at 18,499; (1979) 42 FLR 331 at 346, there is a real or not remote chance or possibility regardless of whether it is less or more than 50% that readers would understand the statement in para. 3 in that way.

In any event, I find it impossible to believe that a person who, on 1 July 1986 or at any time subsequently, acquainted himself with the available evidence as to the relationship between cigarette smoke and disease in non-smokers could conclude that it was "little". The evidence in the primary articles alone is such as to deny a rational basis for the use of the phrase "little evidence", even if it be treated as a statement of opinion. In *Global Sportsman Pty. Limited v. Mirror Newspapers Pty Limited* (1984) ATPR ¶40-463 at 45,344; (1984) 2 FCR 82 at 88 the Court said:

> "Many statements, for example, promises, predictions and opinions, do involve the state of mind of the maker of the statement at the time when the statement is made. Precisely the same principles control the operation of subsec. 52(1) with respect to the making of such statements. A statement which involves the state of mind of the maker ordinarily conveys the meaning (expressly or by implication) that the maker of the statement had a particular state of mind when the statement was made and, commonly at least, that there was basis for that statement of mind. If the meaning contained in or conveyed by the statement is false in that or in any other respect, the making of the statement will have contravened s. 52(1) of the Act. Compare *Lyons v. Kern Konstructions (Townsville) Pty. Limited* (1983) ATPR ¶40-343; (1983) 47 A.L.R. 114."

Had there been persuasive material which existed as at 1 July 1986 which cast serious doubt upon the evidence called by the applicant in respect of all the diseases the position may well have been different. In that case there would have been room for an argument that there was a basis for the making of the statement in the advertisement, whether that statement be regarded as one of fact or one of opinion. But that is not the case.

12. *Laches, acquiescence and delay*

Although this defence was pleaded, it was not developed at any length by counsel for the respondent. The advertisement appeared on 1 July 1986 and on 25 July 1986 the applicant complained to the Trade Practices Commission. It was reasonable for the applicant to await the outcome of its complaint to the Commission before commencing its own proceedings. It was not until the early part of 1987 that it became apparent to the applicant that the respondent was not prepared to fully retract the statements made in the advertisement. The application in this Court was filed on 11 June 1987.

In these circumstances, I think there is no substance in the defence based on laches, acquiescence and delay. The delay in commencing the proceedings was not great, nor was the respondent prejudiced by such delay as occurred.

13. *Discretion*

There is no reason why in the exercise of the Court's discretion the applicant should be refused relief to which it is otherwise entitled. On the contrary, there is a strong public interest in the respondent being prevented from making the statement that there is little evidence and nothing which proves that cigarette smoke causes disease in non-smokers. Active smokers are likely to be misled or deceived by the statement into believing that their smoking does not prejudice the health of non-smokers, particularly small children. Non-smokers are likely to be deceived or misled by the statement into believing that cigarette smoke does not affect their own health or the health of their children. These are serious matters.

In the early stages of the litigation the respondent made an open offer of settlement which was rejected by the applicant. It was made plain by counsel for the respondent that the rejection would be relied upon on the question of costs should the respondent lose the proceedings. However, I did not understand counsel for the respondent to argue in final address that the rejection of the offer of settlement was relevant to the question of discretion. Whilst I have some difficulty in seeing how the rejection of the offer of settlement could affect the exercise of my discretion to grant relief, I am prepared to reconsider the question should the respondent wish to put any further submission on that matter.

14. *Relief*

The applicant seeks not only injunctive relief but also an order that the respondent publish a correcting advertisement. It is entitled to injunctive relief in appropriate terms, but I do not think I should make an order that the respondent publish an advertisement correcting what was said in the advertisements published on 1 July 1986 and in January 1987.

So much time has passed since the advertisements were published that it is unrealistic to think that members of the public who might read a correcting advertisement would have any clear recollection of what was said in the original advertisement. I think the fact that the respondent will be enjoined from making the offending statement in the future is sufficient vindication of the interests of the applicant and of the general public.

I direct the applicant to file and serve draft minutes of the orders it seeks within fourteen days of this date. I direct the respondent to file and serve within twenty eight days of this date draft minutes of orders it proposes that the Court should make. I reserve the question of costs. The matter is to be relisted on a date to be fixed for argument on question of costs and for settlement of minutes of orders.

THE COURT GIVES THE FOLLOWING DIRECTIONS:

1. The applicant is to file and serve draft minutes of the orders it seeks within 14 days of this date.

2. The respondent is to file and serve within 28 days of this date draft minutes of the orders it proposes the Court should make.

3. Reserve question of costs.

4. Matter to be relisted on a date to be fixed for argument on costs and for settlement of minutes of orders.

[¶41-114] AUSTRALIAN FEDERATION OF CONSUMER ORGANISATIONS INCORPORATED v TOBACCO INSTITUTE OF AUSTRALIA LIMITED
Federal Court of Australia
Judgment delivered 15 April 1991

Trade practices — Misleading or deceptive conduct — Costs — Tobacco industry — Action by public interest group to restrain advertising — Injunction granted — Costs on indemnity basis — Whether circumstances justify special order — Federal Court of Australia Act 1976, sec 43.

On 7 February 1991 the Federal Court found that the respondent had engaged in misleading or deceptive conduct in contravention of sec 52 of the Trade Practices Act 1974. See (1991) ATPR ¶41-079.

By way of a separate decision Morling J made final orders which are set out below, together with his Honour's reasons. Morling J observed that the orders did not restrain the respondent from making statements of opinion.

By way of another separate decision Morling J made an order for costs which is also set out below, together with his Honour's reasons. The applicant sought an order for costs which would indemnify it for all costs except in so far as they were of an unreasonable amount or were unreasonably incurred.

***Held:* respondent to pay applicant's costs on indemnity basis.**

1. The cases in which orders for costs have been made on a solicitor and client or indemnity basis by reason of the undeserving conduct of a litigant were distinguishable from the present case.

2. As to whether the respondent should have accepted the applicant's offer of settlement:

The respondent was not obliged to accept the applicant's offer, but its failure to do so led to the applicant incurring very great costs which might have been avoided.

3. As to whether a public interest group action justified the order sought:

What was relevant was that the proceedings were brought for the purpose of restraining the respondent from making misleading statements on important matters of public health.

It would not be in the public interest for a litigant in the position of the applicant to be heavily out-of-pocket in consequence of the public-spirited action it had taken.

In a sense, these proceedings were in the nature of a test case on the issue whether passive smoking was a hazard to the health of non-smokers.

The proceedings instituted by the applicant served the public interest, and in a very important respect.

In all the circumstances of the present case, it was appropriate that the respondent should pay the applicant's costs on an indemnity basis.

[*Headnote by the CCH TRADE PRACTICES EDITORS*]

Before: Morling J.

Morling J:

Reasons for final orders

In explanation of the final orders I have made to-day I make the following observations:

(i) I think it is appropriate that order 1 should be made since the statements made in paras 3 and 5 of Exhibit A should be read in the context in which they were published. Order 1 does not, of course, restrain the respondent from making most of the statements which appear in Exhibit A. It merely prevents the re-publication of the advertisement in its entirety.

(ii) The orders in para 2 are framed upon the basis that the statements in para 3 of Exhibit A are made as statements of fact. I have framed the orders in the present tense since I think they are justified by the evidence as it presently stands. It will be open for the respondent to apply for a variation or discharge of any of the orders should they be thought to be inappropriate in the light of new evidence which may come to the knowledge of the respondent. To frame orders in this fashion appears to me to conform with usual practice. Thus, in a case where a rival trader proves that a competitor is making a misleading or deceptive statement about his [the competitor's] product, the appropriate order is to enjoin repetition of the statement, leaving it to the competitor to apply for a variation or discharge of the injunction should he be able to demonstrate by further evidence that the statement has ceased to be misleading or deceptive.

(iii) I have used the words "attacks of asthma" rather than "asthma" in orders 2(f) and (g) because both parties have suggested those words in their draft minutes.

(iv) The order for costs in para 5 has been made for the reasons which appear in the separate reasons which I publish to-day.

(v) It will be observed that the orders do not restrain the respondent from making statements of opinion. The reason for this is that I have found (1991) ATPR ¶41-079 at 52,262 that the statement made in the advertisement is not expressed to be an opinion. Had I accepted the respondent's argument that the statement in the advertisement was a statement of opinion, having regard to my findings on pp. 52,252, 52,258-52,259 and 52,262-52,263 I would have made orders in the following terms:

> "The respondent its servants and agents be restrained from making statements in trade or commerce that:
>
> (a) it is the opinion of the respondent that there is little evidence and nothing which

proves scientifically that cigarette smoke causes disease in non-smokers;

(b) it is the opinion of the respondent that there is little evidence and nothing which proves scientifically that cigarette smoke causes respiratory disease in children under the age of one year;

(c) it is the opinion of the respondent that there is little evidence and nothing which proves scientifically that cigarette smoke causes attacks of asthma.''

I think such orders would have been appropriate in the light of what is said in *Global Sportsman Pty Limited v Mirror Newspapers Pty Limited* (1984) ATPR ¶40-463 at 45,347; 2 FCR 82 at 88.

The Court orders that:

1. The respondent its servants and agents be restrained from publishing or causing to be published, in trade or commerce, the advertisement which is Exhibit A in these proceedings.

2. The respondent its servants and agents be restrained from making statements in trade or commerce that it is the fact that:

(a) there is little evidence and nothing which proves scientifically that cigarette smoke causes disease in non-smokers;

(b) there is little evidence that cigarette smoke causes lung cancer in non-smokers;

(c) there is nothing which proves scientifically that cigarette smoke causes lung cancer in non-smokers;

(d) there is little evidence that cigarette smoke causes respiratory disease in children under the age of one year;

(e) there is nothing which proves scientifically that cigarette smoke causes respiratory disease in children under the age of one year;

(f) there is little evidence that cigarette smoke causes attacks of asthma in non-smokers;

(g) there is nothing which proves scientifically that cigarette smoke causes attacks of asthma in non-smokers;

(h) there is little evidence that cigarette smoke causes otitis media in children.

3. The respondent its servants and agents be restrained from making statements in trade or commerce that the conclusions drawn in the article ''Relationship of Passive Smoking to Risk of Cancer and other Smoking-Associated Diseases'' by Lee, Chamberlain and Alderson were based on statistical detail in a study involving 12,000 people.

4. The respondent pay the applicant's costs on the basis that such costs are to include all costs except insofar as they are of an unreasonable amount or were unreasonably incurred so that, subject to such exceptions, the applicant will be completely indemnified by the respondent for its costs.

Reasons for costs order

The applicant seeks an order that the respondent pay its costs on an indemnity basis.

The power of the Court to make orders for costs is found in s. 43 of the *Federal Court of Australia Act* (''the Act'') which gives a general power to award costs and provides, in subs. (2) that:

> ''Except as provided by any other Act, the award of costs is in the discretion of the Court or Judge.''

The discretion to award costs is unfettered, but must be exercised judicially. Speaking of a similar discretion contained in Order 65, rule 1 of the rules of the Supreme Court of South Australia, *Bray* CJ said in *Cretazzo v Lombardi* (1975) 13 SASR 4 at 11:

> ''Order 65, rule 1 provides generally that all costs shall be in the discretion of the court or judge, subject to a proviso irrelevant for the present purpose. Time and again attempts have been made to fetter that general discretion by the imposition of judge-made rules. Time and again those fetters have been released by appellate courts. I think the guiding principle still stands as it left the House of Lords in the famous case of *Donald Campbell & Co v Pollak* [1927] AC 732, that the general discretion is absolute and unfettered, except that it must be exercised judicially, not arbitrarily or capriciously, and that it cannot be exercised on grounds unconnected with the litigation.''

This passage was quoted with approval by *Fisher* J in *Trade Practices Commission v*

Nicholas Enterprises Pty Ltd (1979) 28 ALR 201 at 206-207. See also *Australian Transport Insurance Pty Ltd & Anor v Graeme Phillips Road Transport Insurance Pty Ltd & Anor* (1986) ATPR (Digest) ¶46-004; 71 ALR 287 at 288 where *Woodward* J said that the general power given by s. 43 of the Act to award costs authorised the making of an order for costs on a solicitor and client basis in an appropriate case where there is some special or unusual feature in the case to justify the exercise of the discretion. See also *Fountain Selected Meats (Sales) Pty Ltd v International Produce Merchants Pty Ltd* (1988) 81 ALR 397 at 400-401. In *Thors v Weekes* (1989) 92 ALR 131 *Gummow* J made an order for costs on a solicitor and client basis and observed (at p. 152) that in an appropriate case costs may be awarded on an indemnity basis.

In *Mudginberri Station Pty Limited v AMIEU* (1986) ATPR ¶40-734, I declined to make an order for payment of the successful applicant's costs on a solicitor and client basis. I expressed the view (at p. 47,993) that it was very unusual for an order for costs to be made on that basis and that, in my experience, such an order had not previously been made in a case arising under the *Trade Practices Act*. I think what I said in that case was correct, but I do not think it is of relevance in the present proceedings. *Mudginberri* was a case in which the applicant sought relief to protect its private commercial interests. It had none of the features of the present case.

In *Concrete Constructions Pty Ltd & Anor v Plumbers and Gas Fitters Employees' Union of Australia & Anor (No. 2)* (1987) ATPR ¶40-775; 72 ALR 415, the successful applicants sought an order for costs on an indemnity basis. The proceedings were brought by the applicants for the purpose of obtaining the respondent's compliance with orders made by the Court pursuant to s. 45D of the *Trade Practices Act 1974*. At ATPR p. 48,477; ALR p. 438-439, *Wilcox* J said:

> "The applicants each seek an order for costs in their favour on an indemnity basis, that is costs to be taxed as between solicitor and own client. Such an order is not uncommon in contempt proceedings, reflecting the view that a party should not be further prejudiced — by being required to bear the difference between party/party costs and solicitor/client costs — by the failure of the opponent to comply with an order of the court. The relevant policy was expressed by *Holland* J in *Degmam Pty. Ltd. (in liq) v Wright (No. 2)* (1983) 2 N.S.W.L.R. 354 at 358:
>
> 'It is, in my experience, quite common to find, in cases where an application is made to the court for committal for contempt such orders being made in an endeavour to ensure that the party that has been enforced to take that extra step, in order to obtain his rights, after they have been adjudicated by the court, may be relieved entirely of the expense of doing so and, although there is nothing in the rules about it, it is in my experience common to find an order designed to give a party a complete indemnity against such costs, usually by an order that the contemnor pay the other party's costs on a solicitor and client or solicitor and own client basis but the object is to ensure an indemnity.' "

Wilcox J made an order for costs on a solicitor and client basis, although it appears from p. 438 that he was asked to make an order on a solicitor and own client basis. An order of the latter kind is more or less equivalent to an order for costs on an indemnity basis: see *EMI Records Ltd v Ian Cameron Wallace Ltd* (1983) 1 Ch 59 at 65.

In the present case the applicant seeks an order for costs which will indemnify it for all costs except insofar as they are of an unreasonable amount or were unreasonably incurred. This is the type of order made by *Holland* J in *Degmam*, supra. The costs covered by such an order are described by Sir Robert *Megarry* V-C in *EMI Records* at p. 71.

Special provision is now made in the rules of the Supreme Court of New South Wales for orders for costs to be made on an indemnity basis in cases where the plaintiff makes an offer of settlement which is not accepted by the defendant and the plaintiff subsequently obtains an order from the Court no less favourable to him than the terms of the offer — vide Part 52 rule 17. Quite apart from this rule, it has been held in the Supreme Court that a letter of offer in which a party has offered as much as, or more than, that to which the opposing party ultimately establishes his entitlement following the hearing, should be taken into account by the court in determining whether to make a special costs order: *Messiter v Hutchinson* (1987) 10 NSWLR 525. For informative observations as to the inadequacy of costs taxed on a party and party basis to protect a successful litigant, see *Qantas Airways Limited v Dillingham Corporation* (14 May 1987 per *Rogers* J — Supreme Court of New South Wales, unreported).

I was referred to a number of cases in which orders for costs have been made on a solicitor and client or indemnity basis. Those orders have usually been made in circumstances where the conduct of the parties against whom the orders have been made has been deserving of criticism: see, for example, *Degmam v Wright* (supra), *Packer v Meagher* (1984) 3 NSWLR 486, and *Australian Guarantee Corporation v De Jager* (1984) VR 483. The respondent fought these proceedings fiercely and left no stone unturned in resisting the application. But I do not think the conduct of its case is deserving of criticism of the kind referred to in the authorities relied upon by the applicant. Accordingly, the cases in which orders for costs have been made on a solicitor and client or indemnity basis by reason of the undeserving conduct of a litigant are distinguishable from the present case.

Three substantial matters were relied upon as justifying the making of the order sought. First, it was argued that the applicant made an offer to settle the litigation which was rejected by the respondent and which, if it had been accepted, would have left the respondent in a better position than it is in as a consequence of the Court's findings. Secondly, it was argued that the applicant performed a significant public service in bringing the proceedings and that it should not be placed in the position of being considerably out-of-pocket, as it will be if the order for costs is made on a party and party basis. Thirdly, it was argued that the conduct of the respondent's case was so lacking in merit as to justify the making of a special order for costs.

What I have already said about the manner in which the respondent's case was conducted is sufficient to dispose of the last-mentioned submission. However, in my opinion it would be wrong to hold that an order for costs on an indemnity or solicitor and client basis should only be made in circumstances where the conduct of the party against whom the order is made is deserving of criticism. To so hold would be to fetter the discretion referred to in s. 43(2) of the Act in a manner not justified by the words of the sub-section.

I therefore turn to consider whether in the exercise of the discretion I have under s. 43(2), it would be proper to accede to the first two arguments advanced by counsel for the applicant as justifying a special order as to costs. As to the first argument, I am satisfied that before heavy costs were incurred the applicant made an offer of settlement which, in the light of my findings, it would have been prudent for the respondent to accept. I do not think it is correct to say, as was submitted by counsel for the respondent, that the applicant's offer of settlement sought much more than the relief it ultimately obtained. The respondent was not obliged to accept the applicant's offer, but its failure to do so led to the applicant incurring very great costs which might have been avoided.

The applicant's second argument requires careful consideration. So far as I am aware, there is no precedent for the making of an order for costs on an indemnity basis in favour of a public-interest group such as the applicant. But lack of precedent should be no bar to the making of the order: cf the observations of *Bray* CJ in *Cretazzo v Lombardi*, supra. Counsel for the respondent submitted that a public-interest group should be in no better position on the question of costs than an ordinary litigant: *John Fairfax & Sons Ltd v Palmer* (1987) 8 NSWLR 297 at 306 and 309 was relied upon. In that case it was held that the status of the plaintiff (a well known physician) was irrelevant in determining whether a special order for costs should be made in his favour in a defamation action. I do not think that case is of much relevance in the present context. The plaintiff in *Fairfax* sued to vindicate his own reputation and to recover damages for himself. There is no parallel between that litigation and the present proceedings.

In any case, it is not the fact that the applicant is a public-interest group which is of relevance. What is relevant is that the proceedings were brought for the purpose of restraining the respondent from making misleading or deceptive statements on important matters of public health. I would have taken the same approach to the question whether a special order for costs was justified in the present proceedings if the applicant had not been a public-interest group, but, say, a medical society whose members were concerned about the respondent's advertising.

The applicant must have incurred very considerable costs in prosecuting these proceedings. In a real sense, the costs were incurred in the public interest. It is very much in the public interest that the respondent be restrained from making statements which might mislead members of the public on matters affecting their health. I do not think it would be in the public interest for a litigant in the position of the applicant to be heavily out-of-pocket in consequence of the public-spirited action it has taken.

Counsel for the respondent submitted that I should not have regard to what was said from the bar table as to the extent of legal aid which the applicant has received. The state of the applicant's finances was referred to during the course of the hearing of an application for security for costs, which the respondent subsequently withdrew. However, I do not think the extent of the applicant's financial resources and the degree of legal aid it has received are significant for present purposes. I think its claim for a special order for costs rests on a more secure footing than its limited financial resources.

In *Baltic Shipping v Dillon* (1991) ATPR (Digest) ¶46-068 the court was concerned with the question whether it was appropriate to make an order for costs on a solicitor and client basis in an Admiralty matter in the New South Wales Supreme Court. Rule 126 of that Court's Admiralty Rules confers a discretion as to costs not dissimilar to the discretion conferred by s. 43(2) of the Act. It provides:

> "126. In general, costs shall follow the result but the judge may, in any case, make such order as to costs as to him shall seem fit."

Kirby P (with whose reasons *Gleeson* CJ concurred) was of the opinion that it was not a prerequisite of the making of an order for costs on a solicitor and client basis in an Admiralty matter that the unsuccessful party's conduct of the litigation had been unmeritorious. He thought that it was appropriate, in that case, that an order for costs should be made on a solicitor and client basis because the proceedings were in the nature of a test case. With respect, I agree with *Kirby* P's reasoning.

In a sense, these proceedings were in the nature of a test case on the issue whether passive smoking is a hazard to the health of non-smokers. The respondent went to great lengths to demonstrate that it was not such a hazard. It is reasonable to infer that the respondent represents the interests of the tobacco industry in Australia. It was apparent from the conduct of the litigation that it expended a vast sum of money in mounting its defence. The appellant had no alternative but to incur very considerable costs if it wished to meet the challenge to its case and rebut the respondent's evidence. Its costs must run into several hundred thousand dollars. Whilst much of them will be recoverable under an order for costs on a party and party basis, the costs which will be irrecoverable are likely to be considerable.

I think some general support for the making of a special order for costs in this case can be found in the contempt cases. It seems to me that in such cases one of the reasons for making special orders for costs is that contempt proceedings serve the public interest by ensuring that the court's orders are obeyed. It is inappropriate in such cases that a person acting in the public interest should be left to meet part of his costs. Likewise, in the present case, the proceedings instituted by the applicant served the public interest, and in a very important respect.

There may well be cases where proceedings are successfully prosecuted in the public interest but in which it would be inappropriate to make orders for costs on an indemnity basis. Each case must be determined on its own facts and merits. However, in all the circumstances of the present case, I think it is appropriate that the respondent should pay the applicant's costs on an indemnity basis, and I so order.

Section Three Additional Source Material

[¶40-874] **Australian Federation of Consumer Organisations Inc. v. Tobacco Institute of Australia Ltd.**
Federal Court of Australia.
Judgment delivered 7 June 1988.

Trade practices — Misleading or deceptive conduct in the nature of a "public wrong" — Whether a compromise of a claim for injunctive relief by the Trade Practices Commission barred "any other person" from proceeding for such relief — Consumer body seeking injunctive relief — Allegedly misleading advertisement as to the effects of "passive" smoking — Complex representation with different parts grounding the respective complaints — Application for summary dismissal of the application for injunctive relief — Trade Practices Act 1974, sec. 52; 80.

On 1 July 1986 the respondent published in daily newspapers an advertisement which included statements first, that there was "little evidence and nothing which prove[d] scientifically that cigarette smoking causes disease in non-smokers" ("statement 1") and secondly, that the London Times had reported findings of the Institute of Cancer Research in Surrey "that 'passive smoking' for life-long non-smokers carrie[d] no significant increase in the risk of" various diseases, which conclusions were "based on a wealth of statistical detail from a study involving 12,000 people" ("statement 2"). The advertisement also referred to certain American research, an international conference and the World Health Organisation.

The applicant complained about the advertisement to the Trade Practices Commission ("the Commission"). The Commission sought from the respondent, inter alia, a corrective advertisement, particularly as it saw the July advertisement as misleading in so far as it indicated that certain reputable organisations had found that a "passive smoker" (that is, a non-smoker exposed to cigarette smoke) is not at risk from a health point of view. Its concern was therefore with statement 2 rather than statement 1.

Following correspondence between the Commission and the respondent, the Commission, in December 1986, confirmed that the publication by the respondent of a certain corrective advertisement to appear with the form of the original advertisement would "be accepted by the

Commission as a sufficient correction of the concerns the Commission had in relation to the 1 July advertisement'' and that it would ''take no action against the Tobacco Institute in respect of that advertisement''.

In the corrective advertisement agreed upon, which did not contain any correction of statement 1, the respondent expressly declined to accept what was described as a ''suggestion'' that the July advertisement was misleading in its reference to the study reported by ''The Times'' in that the study was based on a much lesser number than 12,000.

The respondent published the corrective advertisement.

Thereafter the applicant approached the respondent seeking undertakings that it would not in future publish statements containing assertions similar to those contained in statements 1 and 2. Those undertakings were not forthcoming, although the respondent did state in March 1987 that it had ''no present plans to publish'' the representations of which the applicant complained.

The applicant then commenced proceedings claiming contraventions by the respondent of sec. 52 of the Trade Practices Act 1974 (''the Act'') arising particularly out of both statements 1 and 2 in the July advertisement. The statement of claim asserted that the corrective advertisement published did ''nothing to correct the misleading and deceptive conduct alleged''. Injunctive relief was sought.

The respondent, by notice of motion, sought to have the proceedings struck out on the basis that the application was an abuse of process as the Commission had already pursued the alleged wrong as guardian of the public interest protected by the Act. The respondent contended that ''any other person'' within sec. 80 of the Act was barred from seeking injunctive relief under sec. 80 by a compromise by the Commission of such a claim for relief. Moreover, it was argued, sec. 52 of the Act prescribed a norm of conduct, departure from which might result in both private wrongs and a public wrong, but that the nature of the wrong was always single, at least so far as a public wrong was concerned.

Held: **notice of motion dismissed.**

1. The fact that the applicant made complaint to the Commission did not render the Commission its agent either to bring proceedings against the respondent or to compromise the matter. The applicant merely called upon the Commission to exercise the discretion conferred on it by the Act.

2. The right of ''any other person'' to seek injunctive relief under sec. 80 is a right independent of the right simultaneously given to the Commission by that section. Even if the Commission had barred itself by agreement from exercising its sec. 80 right, that would not also bar the applicant as ''any other person'' from exercising its right under that section, a fortiori where the conduct complained of was a complex representation of which only part lay at the heart of the course of action chosen by the Commission.

3. In any event this was not a case where the Court should exercise its discretion to grant a stay. That discretion is to be exercised with great caution and was inappropriate particularly where what was sought by an applicant was an injunction grounded upon fear of further allegedly misleading conduct. Assurances by another, even the Trade Practices Commission, that it will not sue in respect of particular conduct cannot make that conduct legal if that conduct would be in breach of the Act. Further, the respondent had declined to give the applicant undertakings in respect of either statement. Yet in the corrective advertisement it had already treated statement 2 as requiring clarification.

[*Headnote by the CCH TRADE PRACTICES EDITORS*]

D.M.J. Bennett Q.C. with N.F. Francey (instructed by Slater & Gordon) for the applicant.

B.S.J. O'Keefe Q.C. with P.F. Esler (instructed by Clayton Utz) for the respondent.

Before: Burchett J.

Burchett J.: On 1 July 1986, the respondent published in *The Australian Financial Review, The Australian* and *The Sydney Morning Herald*, an advertisement which bore the heading "A message from those who do ... to those who don't". The advertisement included the statement:

> "There is little evidence and nothing which proves scientifically that cigarette smoke causes disease in non-smokers."

The advertisement added:

> "The London Times reported findings from the Institute of Cancer Research in Surrey, England, published in this month's edition of the 'British Journal of Cancer', that 'passive smoking' for life-long non-smokers carries no significant increase in the risk of lung cancer, bronchitis or heart disease (all allegedly associated with smoking). The Institute's conclusions are based on a wealth of statistical detail from a study involving 12,000 people."

The advertisement also referred to certain American research, and to an international conference held in 1984 in Vienna.

There was a prompt reaction from the applicant. It complained, in the same month, to the Trade Practices Commission. As a result of the applicant's complaint, a member of the Commission had discussions with the chief executive of the respondent, and on 8 August 1986, the then chairman of the Commission wrote to the respondent expressing concern as to whether the advertisement contravened the *Trade Practices Act*. He stated the view:

> "that the overall impression intended to be conveyed by your advertisement is that *according to reputable persons and organisations* the exposure of non-smokers to cigarette smoke in the air exhaled by smokers, does not place them at risk from a health point of view. This would not appear to accord with the facts." (Emphasis added.)

He referred to sec. 52 of the *Trade Practices Act*, and to the fact that the Institute of Cancer Research of Surrey, England, and the World Health Organisation (which was also referred to in the advertisement as having co-operated in the Vienna conference) had each disputed the accuracy of the reference to its role made by the advertisement. The chairman sought a response to these matters. Consistently with the words I have emphasised in the passage quoted from this letter, and perhaps significantly in view of the attitude later taken towards what required correction in the advertisement, he added:

> "I should say the Commission is not concerned to engage itself in the subject of whether or not passive smoking exposes non-smokers to health risks."

The respondent provided some material to the Commission for its consideration. On 18 September 1986, the chairman wrote again to the chief executive of the respondent, referring to that material. He stated:

> "The Commission has concluded that the advertisement contains a number of statements which are misleading or are likely to mislead and that the advertisement creates an impression which overall is misleading as to the substance of currently available evidence regarding health risks associated with passive smoking."

The Commission sought an undertaking that the respondent would not publish the advertisement in the future, and that it would forthwith publish a corrective advertisement, a draft of which the Commission enclosed with its letter. Failing the giving of these undertakings, the Commission threatened to take proceedings with a view to obtaining orders to the same effect.

There followed correspondence between the Commission and the respondent, in the course of which the Commission advised that a number of claims about the advertisement had been made to it by various bodies and individuals, some of which it had not taken up. Several complaints about the advertisement were referred to the respondent, and the Commission repeated its request for a corrective advertisement. It made clear, however, the fact that its concern about the overall impression of the advertisement did not relate to the direct assertion that there is little evidence cigarette smoke causes disease in non-smokers, but related to the effect of certain matters of detail allegedly misstated. On 7 October 1986, the respondent discussed at length the three complaints, which were matters of detail, that it took to be pressed, and declined to give any undertaking. The Commission responded on 14 October 1986, advising that it would institute legal proceedings in the Federal Court of Australia in order to seek injunctions which would involve corrective advertising. It specifically asserted that the reference in the advertisement to "a wealth of statistical detail from a study involving 12,000 people" was misleading, since the study "was based on a much lesser number than 12,000". On 20 October, the solicitors for the respondent wrote back denying that the publication was misleading or likely to mislead in any respect, but adding:

> "However, if it will serve to avoid useless and expensive litigation the Tobacco Institute will undertake to your Commission that it will not publish the 1 July, 1986 advertisement in the future.
>
> We enclose a copy of an advertisement which the Tobacco Institute is now arranging to publish in the same newspapers and with similar prominence as the 1 July, 1986 advertisement.
>
> Having regard to the undertaking now given and the action being taken by the Tobacco Institute, we would urge your Commission to reconsider its decision to institute legal proceedings against the Tobacco Institute in connection with the 1 July, 1986 publication. In all the present circumstances the enormous costs which would be involved in such proceedings are simply not justified."

There followed further discussion, and a letter from the Commission dated 25 November 1986, enclosing a redrafted corrective advertisement, and stating:

> "If the Tobacco Institute is willing to publish this advertisement in the same newspapers as the 1 July advertisement and with equal prominence, the Commission will accept publication as a sufficient reason for it to take no action against the Tobacco Institute in respect of the 1 July advertisement. I confirm that it will agree to the matter being resolved on that basis.
>
> The Commission also accepts the Tobacco Institute's undertaking that it will not publish the 1 July advertisement in the future."

There were yet further discussions about the form of the corrective advertisement, culminating in a letter, dated 11 December 1986, from the Commission to the respondent's solicitors. That letter included the statement:

> "I confirm that publication of the advertisement now agreed between us and in the manner above-mentioned will be accepted by the Commission as a sufficient correction of the concerns the Commission had in relation to the 1 July advertisement, and that the Commission will take no action against the Tobacco Institute in respect of that advertisement."

The respondent's solicitors wrote back referring to the Commission's letter, and stating:

> "We confirm our client's agreement to and acceptance of the settlement of this matter on the basis set out in that letter."

The agreed corrective advertisement did thereafter appear. It should be noted that, by this advertisement, the respondent expressly declined to accept what was described in it as a "suggestion" that the previous advertisement was misleading, in its reference to the study reported by *The Times*, "in that the study was based on a much lesser number than 12,000". The corrective advertisement contained no correction at all of the assertion that there is little evidence and nothing which proves scientifically that cigarette smoke causes disease in non-smokers.

The corrective advertisements came to the notice of the applicant. It took the view, which it expressed in a letter to the respondent dated 12 January 1987, that "the subsequent advertisement does not remedy the misleading impression conveyed in the first advertisement" in respect of the study alleged to have involved 12,000 people. It requested a written undertaking that the respondent would not refer to the researchers' paper in future advertisements in the same or similar terms, and threatened legal action failing receipt of such an undertaking. On 22 January 1987 the respondent's solicitors wrote back:

"The Tobacco Institute will not provide AFCO with the undertaking requested in your letter."

A further letter was sent by the solicitors for the applicant to the solicitors for the respondent on 3 March 1987, which referred to the claim in the original advertisement that "there is little evidence and nothing which proves scientifically that cigarette smoke causes disease in non-smokers". The letter sought advice as to whether an undertaking would be given not, in future advertising or other promotional material, to make that representation or any similar assertion. The respondent's solicitors replied on 16 March 1987, making it clear that their client would not provide the undertaking sought, but adding:

"However we are instructed to inform you that our client has no present plans to publish the representation to which you refer in any future advertisement."

The solicitors stated they were instructed to accept service of any process.

It was in this state of affairs that the present proceedings were commenced by a statement of claim filed 11 June 1987.

The statement of claim referred specifically to the two representations which I reproduced at the commencement of these reasons (though it quoted one of them inaccurately), and asserted that the publication of these representations amounted to engaging in conduct that was misleading or deceptive or likely to mislead or deceive, in contravention of sec. 52 of the *Trade Practices Act 1974*. The statement of claim alleged that the study represented as involving 12,000 people involved, for relevant practical purposes, and according to common understanding, only 700 people. It also controverted the general proposition in the advertisement about the strength of the evidence that cigarette smoke causes disease in non-smokers.

The statement of claim proceeds to allege the applicant's complaint to the Trade Practices Commission, and that on 7 January 1987 it was advised the Commission had accepted the corrective advertisement as a sufficient correction. The statement of claim asserts that the second advertisement "did nothing to correct the misleading and deceptive conduct" alleged. The relief sought is an injunction restraining the respondent from engaging in conduct that is misleading or deceptive or is likely to mislead in the respects particularly identified in the statement of claim.

In its statement of defence the respondent denies that it has engaged in misleading or deceptive conduct, and puts in issue the question whether its conduct took place in the course of trade or commerce. It also sets up in defence that the Trade Practices Commission alleged the advertisement was misleading and deceptive, and that an agreement was made with the Trade Practices Commission that no proceedings would be taken by it against the respondent upon the respondent giving the undertaking which it gave and publishing the corrective advertisement which it published. The defence proceeds to allege that by reason of those matters:

"(a) These proceedings are barred and are not maintainable against the Respondent;

(b) Alternatively, the Respondent claims the benefit of the said matters as a basis for the Court refusing the relief claimed by the Applicant."

The defence to which I have referred was filed on 15 July 1987, but on 18 August 1987 the respondent took out a notice of motion seeking the following relief:

"1. The Statement of Claim of the Applicant be struck out.

2. Such further or other orders as the Court deems fit.

3. The Applicant to pay the Respondent's costs of this Motion."

At the hearing of the motion, it was made clear what was really sought was a stay of the application on the basis that, in the circumstances, its issue was an abuse of process, and that in fairness and convenience it ought not to be permitted to proceed. It was conceded no argument was available that the applicant was barred by *res judicata* or issue estoppel. The elements of the argument which was put are the following. In the first place, it was pointed out that the applicant sought to have its complaint pursued by the Trade Practices Commission, which, it was said, was the body specially set up under the *Trade Practices Act* as the guardian of the public interest protected by that Act. Then it was said that sec. 52 prescribes a norm of conduct, departure from which may result in both private wrongs and a public wrong; but the nature of the wrong is always single, at least so far as a public wrong is concerned. In this case, the wrong alleged is the act of misleading or deceiving constituted by publication of the advertisement.

Senior counsel for the Tobacco Institute (as I shall call it) then said that sec. 80 of the *Trade Practices Act* is designed to remove procedural problems, not to change the legal nature of the alleged wrong. But, he continued, the Trade Practices Commission is not confined to taking proceedings under sec. 80. It may uphold the public interest, and remedy a wrong perpetrated against that interest by reaching a resolution such as was reached in the present case. Senior counsel then said that once this was done, there would be an inherent jurisdiction in the court to control later proceedings which, he said, would savour of abuse of process, being in the circumstances not fair and convenient. The principle is based on public policy, as expressed by the maxims "nemo debet bis vexari, si constat curiae quod sit pro una et eadem causa", and "interest reipublicae ut sit finis litium". The argument asserted that the principle was not restricted to a second curial proceeding, but could be applied in a case where an administrative act was inconsistently followed by a later proceeding.

Just because of the special functions of the Trade Practices Commission under the Act, it is impossible to regard the fact that the applicant made complaint to the Commission about the advertisement as indicating that it constituted the Commission in any sense its agent to bring proceedings against the respondent. The Commission had discretions of its own to exercise. What the applicant did was to call upon it to exercise them. Nothing in the evidence suggests that the Commission ever advised the applicant what it was proposing to do at any time prior to taking the decision to accept the respondent's undertakings. It acted quite independently. If it had referred the proposed corrective advertisement to the applicant, prior to reaching agreement about the matter, there seems little doubt the applicant would have protested that such a "correction" was more like a repetition of the original wrong. And if there was no actual authority to compromise the complaint in this way, it is hard to see how the making of the complaint to the Commission could in itself confer any implied or ostensible authority.

Yet unless, when the Commission compromised the matter, it did so on behalf of the applicant, there is difficulty in accepting the proposition that the applicant is in some way bound by what occurred, so as to make its institution of proceedings an abuse of process. Section 80(1) of the Act relevantly provides:

> "Subject to sub-sections (1A) and (1B) [subsections which are irrelevant to the present situation], where, on the application of the Minister, the Commission or any other person, the Court is satisfied that a person has engaged, or is proposing to engage, in conduct that constitutes or would constitute—
>
> (a) a contravention of a provision of Part IV or V;
>
> ...
>
> the Court may grant an injunction in such terms as the Court determines to be appropriate."

By this provision, an independent power is given to "any other person" to seek injunctive relief in a case of this kind. That power seems expressly designed to avoid problems of standing of the kind which proved fatal to the plaintiff in *Australian Conservation Foundation Inc. v. Commonwealth of Australia & Ors* (1980) 146 C.L.R. 493. In *R. v. the Judges of the Federal Court of Australia & Anor; Ex parte Pilkington A.C.I. (Operations) Pty. Ltd.* (1978) 142 C.L.R. 113 at p. 128, *Mason* J. said of the power to grant relief on the application of "any other person":

> "The class is expressed as widely as it can be and it would require considerations of very great strength to warrant a reading down."

In the same case, at p. 131 *Murphy* J. said:

> "There is no reason for reading the words, 'any other person', down and strong reason for giving the words their natural breadth. A qualification such as suggested would lead to frequent investigations and arguments, resulting in waste of public time and resources (as has occurred elsewhere) in determining who was and who was not aggrieved. There is no hint of such qualification of the plain words. Also,

> experience shows that enforcement agencies in environmental and consumer protection (as well as those in occupational safety and health) often become unable or unwilling to enforce the law (because of inadequate resources or because they tend to become too close to those against whom they should be enforcing the law). Section 80 expresses the policy that such tendency to non-enforcement or limited enforcement should be overcome by providing that the Court may grant an injunction restraining a contravention of Pts [*sic*] IV or V on the application of the Minister, the Trade Practices Commission or (except in relation to s. 50) any other person."

It seems quite inconsistent with the view of the Act expressed by *Murphy* J., and with the breadth of the right to take proceedings which *Mason* J. asserted, to hold that an arrangement entered into with a view to persuading the Trade Practices Commission not to take proceedings could effectively bar some other person also possessed by virtue of the statute of a right to institute similar proceedings. That would be to read a very significant qualification into the section. The claimed consequence would be even less in keeping with the policy of sec. 80 if it were to apply in a case, such as the present, where the complaint relates to a complex representation, some parts of which were the subject of proceedings threatened by the Trade Practices Commission, withheld upon the respondent's undertakings, while a further part of it is now asserted by the applicant to constitute misleading conduct in respect of which it seeks relief. Even if the principle of *Port of Melbourne Authority v. Anshun Pty. Ltd.* (1981) 147 C.L.R. 589 could prevent the Trade Practices Commission, had it proceeded upon the aspects of the advertisement of which it complained, from subsequently launching proceedings in respect of another aspect of the advertisement, of which the applicant complains, that can hardly be the situation where separate proceedings are launched by different applicants, in respect of separate conduct, in reliance upon the mandate conferred by the statute upon both the Trade Practices Commission and also any other person. Of course, in the present case there has been only one proceeding, the threatened proceeding having been averted by an agreement which, it should be noted, did not purport to affect any substantive liability incurred, but was an agreement by the Trade Practices Commission not itself to sue.

Furthermore, if the Tobacco Institute is correct in contending that "any other person" can be barred by a compromise by the Trade Practices Commission of a claim for relief, what about the converse situation? Could the Commission be barred where an "other person" had claimed first, and then compromised, perhaps for private reasons? The wide language of sec. 80 cannot easily be reconciled to such consequences.

So far as the Tobacco Institute's argument depends upon the proposition that the publication of its advertisement constituted but a single wrong to the public interest, not only is it confronted by the difficulty that more than one representation was made within the advertisement, but also the argument requires a construction of sec. 52 of the Act quite different from that which was given to similar legislation in the United Kingdom by the decision of the Court of Appeal in *R. v. Thomson Holidays Ltd.* (1974) 1 Q.B. 592. That case was concerned with a provision of the (U.K.) *Trade Descriptions Act 1968* which provided:

> "It shall be an offence for any person in the course of any trade or business ... (b) recklessly to make a statement which is false; as to any of the following matters, that is to say, ... (v) the location or amenities of any accommodation so provided."

A handbill issued by the appellant having recklessly made false statements as to a relevant matter, several prosecutions were launched in respect of the making of the statement to each of several persons who acted upon it to their detriment. The appellant's argument, as recounted by the Court at p. 596, was entirely similar to that presented to me on behalf of the Tobacco Institute. It was said:

> "The fact that a statement when made was communicated to two or more million people did not affect the act of making it. There was still only one act, even though its effect might be felt over a wide area and for a long time."

The Court rejected that argument, stating at p. 598:

"As the object of the Act of 1968 is to protect members of the public as individuals, in our judgment two prosecutions in respect of false statements in the same brochure cannot be said to be either an abuse of process or oppressive. No case was made out for staying proceedings on the indictment."

In a significant respect, the applicant's argument from this case is *a fortiori*, since the several prosecutions relied on the *one* statement in the handbills, not on different representations.

The solution to the problem posed by this case depends essentially upon the true constructions of sec. 80. If, as I think, that section gives an independent right of action to "any other person", that right cannot be lost merely because the Trade Practices Commission agrees not to sue. At least this must be true of the matter of the alleged misrepresentation about the strength of the evidence that cigarette smoke causes disease in non-smokers, which was not a subject dealt with in the corrective advertisement, and was not taken up by the Trade Practices Commission as in itself constituting a misrepresentation.

There is no doubt of the existence of a discretion to stay proceedings on the ground that they are oppressive and an abuse of the process of the court: *Barton & Anor v. The Queen & Anor* (1980) 147 C.L.R. 75 at p. 96: *Phelps v. Western Mining Corp. Ltd.* (1978) ATPR ¶40-077 at p. 17,769; (1978) 20 A.L.R. 183 at p. 187. But in *Stephenson v. Garnett* (1898) 1 Q.B. 677 at p. 682 *Chitty* L.J. warned that "the jurisdiction, which is a summary one, ought to be exercised with great caution". Similarly, in the context of criminal law, Lord *Edmund-Davies*, in *Director of Public Prosecutions v. Humphrys* (1977) A.C. 1 at p. 55, said "judges should pause long before staying proceedings which on their face are perfectly regular". In the same case, at p. 46, Lord *Salmon* said:

"a judge has not and should not appear to have any responsibility for the institution of prosecutions; nor has he any power to refuse to allow a prosecution to proceed merely because he considers that, as a matter of policy, it ought not to have been brought. It is only if the prosecution amounts to an abuse of the process of the court and is oppressive and vexatious that the judge has the power to intervene."

In so far as *Barton's case* (*ubi cit. supra*) emphasises that the granting of a stay is a matter of discretion, there is a further difficulty in acceding to the motion. The application made against the Tobacco Institute is, in substance, grounded upon the basis that the advertisement gives rise to a fear of further allegedly misleading conduct occurring. (This is so despite sec. 80(4).) The only relief sought is a restraining order. Assurances by the Trade Practices Commission that it will not sue, cannot make that conduct legal, if it would be in breach of the Act. If the court is called upon, by a party given standing by sec. 80, to enforce obedience in the future to a law passed in the public interest, and a case is made out, why should assurances given by another party (even the Commission) prevent the making of an order to protect the public? See the observations of *Mason* C.J. in *Richardson v. Forestry Commission & Anor* (1987) 73 A.L.R. 589; *Richardson v. Forestry Commission & Anor* (1988) 77 A.L.R. 237 at p. 250; *Associated Minerals Consolidated Ltd. v. Wyong Shire Council* (1975) A.C. 538 at p. 560.

In my opinion, this is not a case in which an order should be made staying the application. Although I have reached this decision for the reasons set out above, I should point out that the Tobacco Institute has expressly declined to give two assurances which the applicant sought. The first related to the reference in the advertisement to the study alleged to have involved 12,000 people. That reference the Tobacco Institute has already, in the corrective advertisement, treated as requiring clarification. It is therefore difficult to see why it cannot undertake not to refer to that matter in the same or similar terms in future advertisements. An undertaking has been given to the Commission not to republish the entire advertisement, but, strictly, that undertaking might not be thought to cover publications of the particular part only which is the subject of this objection. The more substantial matter is, presumably, the applicant's request for an undertaking not in any future advertising to represent that there is little evidence, and nothing which proves scientifically, that cigarette smoke causes disease in non-smokers. As to this, the Tobacco

Institute has refused to give the undertaking sought, but has stated it has no present plans (as at 16 March 1987) to publish that representation. There is simply no evidence whether or not there has been a change of mind since. No argument was put, or could on the existing state of the evidence have been maintained, that the issue is entirely academic.

I dismiss the respondent's motion, and order it to pay the applicant's costs.

[¶40-916] Tobacco Institute of Australia Limited v. Australian Federation of Consumer Organisations Inc.
Federal Court of Australia — Full Court.
Judgment delivered 21 October 1988.

Trade practices — Injunctive relief under sec. 80 — Whether the classes of applicants for relief are alternative or cumulative — Publishing of advertisements by Tobacco Institute as to the effects of passive smoking — Injunctive relief sought by public interest body after extra-curial settlement negotiated by Trade Practices Commission with the Institute — Whether the actions of the Commission as primary vindicator of public interest rendered any subsequent application for injunctive relief an abuse of process, liable to be stayed — Safeguards provided by the Court to prevent abuse of process — Trade Practices Act 1974, sec. 52; 80; 83.

The appellant ("the Institute") had caused to be published advertisements which in effect decried the notion that passive smoking involves health risks. Subsequently the Trade Practices Commission ("the Commission"), having received a number of complaints about the advertisements including some from the respondent ("AFCO"), compromised its proposed application for injunctive relief against the Institute by accepting a form of corrective advertisement offered by the Institute.

AFCO was dissatisfied with the form of corrective advertisement. It commenced proceedings on its own account against the Institute seeking as "any other person" within the meaning of sec. 80 of the Act injunctive relief under that section based on alleged contraventions by the Institute of sec. 52 of the Act. A motion to strike out those proceedings was dismissed. The Institute had argued on its motion that "any other person" (such as AFCO, in the present case) was barred from seeking injunctive relief under sec. 80 by virtue of the Commission's compromise ((1988) ATPR ¶40-874). The Institute sought leave to appeal against dismissal of its motion. Its two principal arguments were that:

- **at least where the alleged contravention is of sec. 52, the word "or" in the phrase in sec. 80 "on the application of the Minister, the Commission or any other person" must be read disjunctively;**

- **the Commission was the primary vindicator of the public interest such that the Court should recognise extra-curial settlements negotiated by it in respect of alleged contraventions of sec. 52 by staying, as an abuse of process of the Court, another's subsequent application for relief under sec. 80 which re-agitated the matters, the subject of the compromise.**

Held: **limited leave to appeal granted; appeal dismissed with costs.**

Application for leave to appeal

The Institute's submissions raised significant issues of principle as to the construction and operation of the Act. Further, the dismissal of the Institute's motion had a significant effect upon the disposition of the litigation. In those circumstances the Court would grant leave in respect of the two issues outlined in the Institute's two principle arguments.

Construction of sec. 80

1. The right to apply for injunctive relief under sec. 80 of the Act is not limited to the applicant within the class of persons therein described who first invokes the jurisdiction of the Court. There may be a plurality of applicants each having standing to bring applications whether concurrently or consecutively. The wide discretion of the Court to stay proceedings provides adequate safeguard against abuse of process as might arise in the case of multiple proceedings under sec. 80 against the one party.

2. Under sec. 80 of the Act the Commission was not to be seen as having any pre-eminent position such that in a case where an extra-curial settlement had been negotiated by it a Court would be obliged to stay any subsequent proceedings raising the same issues and brought by another person against the party negotiating with the Commission. In some circumstances, it might properly be submitted that to the subsequent proceedings should attach the stigma of "abuse of process". However, in this case there was no footing for any such submission.

[*Headnote by the CCH TRADE PRACTICES EDITORS*]

B.J. O'Keefe Q.C. and P. Esler (instructed by Clayton Utz) for the appellant.

D.J.M. Bennett Q.C. and N.F. Francey (instructed by Slater & Gordon) for the respondent.

Before: Lockhart, Morling and Gummow JJ.

Lockhart, Morling and Gummow JJ.: This is an application for leave to appeal against an order of *Burchett* J. dismissing a motion by the Tobacco Institute of Australia Limited ("the Institute"). The Institute had sought an order striking out the statement of claim of Australian Federation of Consumer Organisations Inc. ("AFCO"). On the hearing of the application for leave to appeal, the Court heard full argument on the footing that it it were minded to grant leave, it would be in a position to dispose of the appeal without further argument.

If the Institute's motion had been successful, the result would have been to put an end to AFCO's proceedings, and whilst technically the order dismissing the Institute's motion is interlocutory in character, it plainly is of great significance to the fate of the litigation. Further, the Institute seeks to raise before the Full Court two questions of principle concerning the operation of sec. 80 of the *Trade Practices Act 1974* ("the Act"). Subsection 80(1) of the Act provides:

"80(1) Subject to sub-sections (1A) and (1B), where, on the application of the Minister, the Commission or any other person, the Court is satisfied that a person has engaged, or is proposing to engage, in conduct that constitutes or would constitute—

(a) a contravention of a provision of Part IV or V;

(b) attempting to contravene such provision;

(c) aiding, abetting, counselling or procuring a person to contravene such a provision;

(d) inducing, or attempting to induce, whether by threats, promises or otherwise, a person to contravene such a provision;

(e) being in any way, directly or indirectly, knowingly concerned in, or party to, the contravention by a person of such a provision; or

(f) conspiring with others to contravene such a provision,

the Court may grant an injunction in such terms as the Court determines to be appropriate.''

The Institute submits that, at least where the alleged contravention is of sec. 52 of the Act, the word ''or'' in the phrase in subsec. 80(1) ''on the application of the Minister, the Commission or any other person,'' must be read disjunctively so that there may be only one application for injunctive relief under sec. 80, and that where with respect to a particular advertisement an application has been made by ''any other person'' then in the absence of fraud, sham or the like neither the Minister nor the Commission can bring an application for injunctive relief with respect to the same advertisement.

Secondly, the Institute submits that the Commission is ''the primary vindicator of the public interest'', such that the Court should recognise extra curial settlements negotiated by the Commission in respect of alleged contraventions of sec. 52, by staying as an abuse of process of the Court a subsequent application for injunctive relief under sec. 80 of the Act by ''any other person'' (such as AFCO in the present case) wishing to re-agitate matters resolved as between the Commission and the respondent by agreement between them out of Court.

These submissions raise significant issues of principle as to the construction and operation of the Act. Further, the dismissal of the Institute's motion had a significant effect upon the disposition of the litigation. In these circumstances, we grant leave in respect of the two issues we have outlined above.

The Institute also sought to agitate the question whether his Honour had taken the wrong approach to the construction of sec. 52. The Institute submitted that his Honour was in error in taking the view that the one advertisement may contain within it a plurality of misstatements and thus more than one instance of conduct that is misleading or deceptive, or likely to mislead or deceive. We see no serious question arising as to the correctness of what his Honour said in this respect and would confine the grant of leave in the manner indicated above.

We turn now to consider briefly the salient facts. On 1 July 1986, the Institute caused an advertisement to be published in several newspapers distributed throughout Australia. The advertisement was headed, ''A message from those Who Do ... to those Who Don't'' and stated amongst other things that there was little evidence, and nothing which proved scientifically, that cigarette smoke caused disease in non-smokers. In its statement of claim filed in the present proceedings on 11 June 1987, AFCO says that, contrary to the statement in the advertisement, it is not the case that there is little evidence and nothing which proves scientifically that cigarette smoke causes disease in non-smokers. In particular, AFCO disputes the treatment in the advertisement of the findings of a particular body, the Institute of Cancer Research in Surrey in the United Kingdom.

The present proceedings were instituted more than a year after AFCO had complained to the Commission of the alleged inaccuracies in the advertisement.

AFCO made its complaint in July 1986, and by letter dated 7 January 1987, the Commission wrote informing AFCO that the Institute had undertaken to the Commission to run a ''follow-up'' advertisement and the text of this advertisement was accepted by the Commission as sufficient correction of the first advertisement. The result was that the Commission considered the matter closed. However, it would appear that AFCO was not the only complainant to the Commission. In its letter of 30 September 1986, the Commission informed the Institute that there had been a number of claims about the advertisement put to the Commission ''by various bodies and individuals''. On 11 December 1986, the Chairman of the Commission wrote to the solicitors for the Institute stating, inter alia:

> ''Finally and again on the Commission's behalf, I confirm that publication of the advertisement now agreed between us and in the manner above-mentioned will be accepted by the Commission as a sufficient correction of the concerns the Commission had in relation to the 1 July advertisement, and that the Commission will take no action against the Tobacco Institute in respect of that advertisement.''

The ''follow-up'' advertisement by the Institute was published during January 1987 in the same newspapers in which the original advertisement had appeared. AFCO was dissatisfied with the terms of this advertisement and asserts that it did not correct what it says was the misleading and deceptive conduct in the publication of the first advertisement. AFCO then sought from the Institute undertakings as to the content of future advertisements, which undertakings were refused. It is on that footing that AFCO seeks, in the present proceedings, injunctive relief against the Institute. No other principal relief is sought. Hence, the importance in the proceedings of sec. 80 of the Act.

Before *Burchett* J., the Institute expressly disclaimed any reliance upon the doctrines of *res judicata*, or issue estoppel (including that species of estoppel identified in *Port of Melbourne Authority v. Anshun Pty. Ltd.* (1981) 147 C.L.R. 589 and *Chamberlain v. Deputy Commissioner of Taxation* (1988) 62 A.L.J.R. 324). The Institute was clearly right to do so. Not only was there no correspondence of parties (or their privies) but there were no prior curial proceedings; rather, an agreement was reached between the Commission and the Institute containing an undertaking to the Commission by the Institute.

We turn to the first submission for the Institute, that the word "or" in sec. 80 must be read disjunctively so that there can be only one application under sec. 80 in respect of a particular contravention of sec. 52 of the Act.

The Institute sought to draw support for this submission from sec. 83 of the Act. This provides:

> "83 In a proceeding against a person under section 82 or in an application under sub-section 87(lA) for an order against a person, a finding of any fact by a court made in proceedings under section 77, 80, 80A or 81, or for an offence against section 79, in which that person has been found to have contravened, or to have been involved in a contravention of, a provision of Part IV or V is *prima facie* evidence of that fact and the finding may be proved by production of a document under the seal of the court from which the finding appears."

The Institute pointed out that sec. 83 does not give the applicant in an application under sec. 80 the benefit of any previous factual findings, for example in proceedings brought under sec. 82 of the Act by a different applicant, but against the same respondent, to recover the amount of loss or damage to that applicant suffered by conduct of the respondent in contravention of sec. 52. The Institute contended that this indicates that the Parliament did not contemplate a multiplicity of applications under sec. 80, but merely one application "to vindicate the public interest". However, the form taken by sec. 83 is equally consistent with the view that in the ordinary course an application for injunctive relief, particularly interlocutory injunctive relief, under sec. 80 is likely to precede rather than succeed the disposition of proceedings under sec. 82 or subsec. 87(1A). An example is provided by the course of litigation described in *Jones & Ors v. Sterling* (1982) 63 F.L.R. 216. There, after the Commission had obtained injunctive relief in respect of contravention of sec. 52 of the Act, various persons who had dealt with the respondent then brought proceedings seeking relief under sec. 82 and 87 of the Act.

The immediate difficulty with the submission of the Institute lies in the collocation of words in sec. 80, "on the application of the Minister, the Commission or any other person". This certainly suggests, as the Institute agreed, that on the one application there may be more than one applicant, provided each applicant satisfies the description that it is "the Minister, the Commission or any other person". However, the Institute denied there might be a plurality of applications for injunctive relief in respect of the conduct allegedly in contravention of sec. 52.

The Institute did not contend that in a technical sense the Court would lack jurisdiction with respect to the second or later application; it put the matter as one going to the proper exercise of power, rather than to the existence of jurisdiction: see *Jackson v. Sterling Industries Ltd.* (1987) ATPR ¶40-792 at pp. 48,639, 48,647; (1987) 162 C.L.R. 612 at pp. 616, 630. At bottom, the submission of the Institute was that the consequence of contravention of sec. 52 of the Act was the creation of an analogue of a "cause of action" as understood at common law, which merged in a final judgment disposing of the proceedings between the parties. Involved in this concept is the notion that the "cause of action" under the Act is one existing between specified parties and none other, and having as its substance obligations and rights existing between those parties.

The Institute sought to bolster its submission by emphasising the significant role of the Commission in the operation of the Act with respect to those matters of public interest to which the legislation is directed. Reference was made to the role of the Commission under sec. 28, 77, subsec. 80(6), 87A, Pt VII, subsec. 163(4), 167 and 171. These provisions showed, it was submitted, that the Commission occupied a special position both in curial and extra curial proceedings.

Nevertheless, in our view, whilst undoubtedly this is so, that circumstance did not assist the Institute in the interpretation of sec. 80 for which it contends. It would mean, for example, that if an applicant who is neither the Minister nor the Commission, sought injunctive relief and was unsuccessful for any one of the myriad reasons which may be present in such litigation, the effect of the failure of that application was to foreclose the making of any later application by the Commission, no matter how important an issue as to the public interest might be raised by the facts of the particular case. Further, AFCO submits that the present litigation illustrates the converse proposition. The proceedings in this Court were precipitated by what AFCO submits were inadequate efforts made by the Commission to obtain a settlement out of court with the Institute which adequately protects the public against what AFCO contends is apprehended further conduct in contravention of sec. 52.

Undoubtedly, contravention of sec. 52 may have an impact not only upon the public interest but upon private rights, and what the Parliament has done in sec. 80 is to provide the means for the vindication of the public interest at the private expense of the litigant who vindicates his private rights concurrently with the public interest; likewise, observance of the legislation may be secured at the instance of persons with an interest in the subject matter, not necessarily confined to their private legal rights: *The Queen v. The Judges of the Federal Court of Australia; Ex parte Pilkington ACI (Operations) Pty. Ltd.* (1978) ATPR ¶40-093 at pp. 17,912, 17,917, 17,918-17,919; (1978) 142 C.L.R. 113 at pp. 120-121, 128-129, 131.

Section 52 is found in Pt V of the Act. Subsection 52(1) provides:

> "A corporation shall not, in trade or commerce, engage in conduct that is misleading or deceptive or is likely to mislead or deceive."

The term "corporation" is defined in sec. 4. By force of sec. 6, sec. 52 is given a number of further and distinct operations based not upon the identification of a corporation as the actor involved, but upon engagement by persons, whether or not corporations, in such activities as trade and commerce among the States and with other countries and the use of postal, telegraphic or telephonic services.

Section 52 does not purport to create liability, nor does it vest in any party any cause of action in the ordinary sense of that term; rather, sec. 52 establishes a norm of conduct, and failure, by the corporations and individuals to whom it is addressed in its various operations, to observe that norm has consequences provided for elsewhere in the Act: *Brown v. Jam Factory Pty. Ltd.* (1981) ATPR ¶40-213 at p. 42,928; (1981) 53 F.L.R. 340 at p. 348. The consequences are provided for in a range of remedies found principally (but not exclusively — see sec. 163A) in Pt VI of the Act. The remedies include a declaration (sec. 163A), injunction (sec. 80), disclosure of information and publication of corrective advertisements (sec. 80A), recovery of the amount of loss or damage and prevention or reduction of loss or damage (sec. 82, 87), prohibition of payment or transfer of moneys or other property (sec. 87A).

The class of persons against whom these remedies lie is not limited to those who have engaged in conduct which contravenes, or is likely to contravene, sec. 52 in any one or more of its operations. Thus, for example, an injunction may be granted pursuant to sec. 80 against those who aid, abet, counsel or procure a person to contravene a provision of Pt IV or V of the Act (para. 80(1)(c)), and the amount of loss or damage to which sec. 82 refers may be recovered against any person "involved in the contravention", an expression defined in sec. 75B.

Further, between the particular remedies, there is variation as to the identity of those with standing to seek them from the Court. Section 82 is directed solely to those persons who have suffered loss or damage. Sections 80A and 87A confer standing only on the Minister or the Commission. Proceedings for declaration may be instituted by "a person" and the involvement of the Minister and the Commission are especially provided for (sec. 163A). As we have indicated, by sec. 80 standing to seek injunctive relief is conferred upon "the Minister, the Commission, or any other person".

In the judgment of the High Court in *Hooper v. Hooper* (1955) 91 C.L.R. 529 at p. 535, it was said that a substantive statutory right or duty might be created by more than one method of drafting, but the best method, according to accepted canons, was to keep substantive and adjectival matters distinct, by creating the right or duty and then providing the remedy. This counsel of perfection would not so easily have been followed with the legislation we are now considering. Here the content of the obligation created by the legislature and the identity of those by whom and to whom the obligation is owed shifts between the various operations of the legislation and according to the particular remedy available for contravention. Also, the remedies are distinguished *inter se* by the bestowal of *locus standi* among members of particular designated classes of applicant.

What follows from the conjunction between sec. 52 and remedial provisions such as sec. 80 is not simply the imposition of a duty upon particular individuals in respect of specified conduct, coupled with a right to enforce that duty, which right is vested in those individuals to whom the duty is owed; see Finnis, *Natural Law and Natural Rights*, pp. 199-205. The legislation has as a primary objective the protection of perceived public interests. Hence the complex interrelation between sec. 52 and the provisions of Pt VI of the Act, as we have sought to indicate.

Speaking of sec. 80 in its original form, *Bowen* C.J. said (in *World Series Cricket Pty. Ltd. v. Parish* (1977) ATPR ¶40-040 at p. 17,426; (1977) 16 A.L.R. 181 at p. 186):

> "An applicant for an injunction under sec. 80 need not show that a proprietary interest of his is affected, or that he has suffered special damage, or indeed, that he personally has suffered any damage at all. Even where the application is brought by a rival competitor seeking redress of damage to his business caused by the allegedly unfair and illegal practices of the respondent, the application, though it vindicates or protects the private interests of the competitor, at the same time secures the public interest of consumer protection."

At the same time, in *The Queen v. The Judges of the Federal Court of Australia; Ex parte Pilkington ACI (Operations) Pty. Ltd.* (*supra*), *Mason* J. said at ATPR p. 17,917; C.L.R. p. 128:

> "There is, in my view, no incongruity in making the provisions of Pt V of the Act, notwithstanding they have been enacted for the protection of consumers, enforceable at the instance of a competitor who is not a consumer. The enforcement, at least by injunction, by such a person of the Pt V provisions enhances the protection which they give to consumers. Indeed, it constitutes the most effective sanction for that protection because the consumer who is misled or deceived in consequence of an unfair practice is unlikely to be a suitor for an injunction against the contravening corporation; he is more likely to seek damages."

Again, in *Phelps v. Western Mining Corporation Ltd.* (1978) ATPR ¶40-077; (1978) 33 F.L.R. 327, *Deane* J., speaking of the phrase "any other person", as it appeared in sec. 80 in its then form, said at ATPR p. 17,770; F.L.R. p. 333:

> "The context in which the phrase appears ... does not, upon analysis, suggest, let alone justify, the conclusion that the Legislature intended that the phrase be modified by the engrafting of speculative qualifications such as 'who is a consumer' or 'who is a competitor' or 'who has an interest of a type which would give him standing to institute common law civil proceedings if the conduct complained of were tortious'."

What was said in these cases is true of sec. 80 in its present form, as regards claims for contravention of sec. 52. Of course, sec. 80 is to be read in conjunction with sec. 86 of the Act as conferring jurisdiction upon the Court with respect to "matters": *Philip Morris Inc. & Anor v. Adam P. Brown Male Fashions Pty. Ltd.* (1981) ATPR ¶40-197 at p. 42,699; (1981) 148 C.L.R. 457 at p. 506. The course of litigation under sec. 80 has concerned disputes and controversies between parties as to the conduct sought to be enjoined. The question has not arisen as to whether the concept of "matter" and the constitutional aspects of *locus standi* in federal law mean that the Parliament cannot legislate so as to provide that a mere belief or concern, without more, is sufficient *locus standi* in federal jurisdiction: *Australian Conservation Foundation Inc. v. The Commonwealth of Australia* (1980) 146 C.L.R. 493 at p. 551. No such question arises in the present litigation. The substantial interest of the applicant in issues of the kind involved here recently has been demonstrated in *United States Tobacco Company v. The Minister for Consumer Affairs & Ors* (1988) ATPR ¶40-909.

When sec. 52 and 80 are understood against this background, the conclusion, in our view, becomes irresistible that the right to apply for injunctive relief is not limited to the first applicant within the class of persons described in sec. 80 who invokes the jurisdiction of the Court. There may be a plurality of applicants, each having standing to bring applications whether concurrently or consecutively.

In *Cooney v. Ku-ring-gai Municipal Council* (1963) 114 C.L.R. 582 at p. 605, *Menzies* J. said, "The wide discretion of the Court is an adequate safeguard against abuse of a salutary procedure". Counsel for the Institute invited us to consider the position of a respondent subjected to a succession of applications for injunctive relief, brought by a series of applicants, each asserting standing under sec. 80. The answer to such fears lies in the power of the Court to stay proceedings which are oppressive, vexatious or an abuse of process: cf. *Phelps v. Western Mining Corporation Ltd* (*supra*) at ATPR pp. 17,768-17,769; F.L.R. pp. 331-332; *Jackson v. Sterling Industries Ltd.* (1987) ATPR ¶40-792 at pp. 48,643, 48,652; (1987) 162 C.L.R. 612 at pp. 623, 638.

That brings us to the second issue in respect of which we grant leave. It was submitted by the Institute that the Commission is to be regarded as "the primary vindicator of the public interest", and that the Court should give recognition to this and to extra curial settlements negotiated by the Commission, by staying subsequent proceedings brought by another applicant who wishes to agitate the same issues, but before the Court.

It follows from what we have said that, giving full weight to the significance of the role of the Commission under various provisions of the Act, it by no means follows that as regards standing to seek interlocutory relief under sec. 80, the Parliament regarded the Commission as having any pre-eminent position in the manner suggested by the Institute. Rather, the framework of the legislation which we have described and the authorities to which we have referred indicate the special concerns protected by widening the class of applicants in the manner that has been done in sec. 80.

There may be cases in which the stigma of "abuse of process" may be attached to proceedings brought by a third party seeking injunctive relief in respect of conduct by a respondent which has been the subject of an agreement reached between the respondent and the Commission. Each case would very much depend upon its own facts. What we can say is that, on the facts of this case, there is no footing for any such submission.

We only need refer to two passages in the judgment of *Burchett* J. [(1988) ATPR ¶40-874] to emphasise what we have said:

> "[I]n the present case there has been only one proceeding, the threatened proceeding having been averted by an agreement which, it should be noted, did not purport to affect any substantive liability incurred, but was an agreement by the Trade Practices Commission not itself to sue. [at p. 49,454]
>
> ...
>
> The application made against the Tobacco Institute is, in substance, grounded upon the basis that the advertisement gives rise to a fear of further allegedly misleading conduct occurring. (This is so despite sec. 80(4).) The only relief sought is a restraining order. Assurances by the Trade Practices Commission that it will not sue, cannot make that conduct legal, if it would be in breach of the Act. If the Court is called upon, by a party given standing by sec. 80, to enforce obedience in the future to a law passed in the public interest, and a case is made out, why should assurances given by another party (even the Commission) prevent the making of an order to protect the public?" [at p. 49,455]

For these reasons, we grant the application for leave to appeal, on the limited footing indicated, but dismiss the appeal with costs.

[¶40-909] United States Tobacco Co. v. Minister for Consumer Affairs & Ors.
Federal Court of Australia — Full Court.
Judgment delivered 15 September 1988.

Trade practices — Unsafe goods (sec. 65C(5)) — Smokeless tobacco products — Rights and standing of a participant in a sec. 65J "supplier's" conference — Participant a "public interest" body — Application by tobacco supplier for orders of review of Minister's decision to publish a notice inviting the holding of the conference — Application by public interest body to be joined as a party — Whether a "person interested" in the decision under review — Consumer body's interest as an authorised participant in the conference — Trade Practices Act 1974, sec. 65C(5); 65J(4), (5), (7); 65P — Administrative Decisions (Judicial Review) Act 1977, sec. 12.

Early in 1988 the first respondent ("the Minister") indicated by Gazette notice that he proposed to publish a notice under sec. 65C(5) of the Trade Practices Act 1974 ("the Act") that certain smokeless tobacco products were "unsafe goods". The Minister also, by notice under sec. 65J(1), invited intending suppliers to signify whether they wished the Trade Practices Commission to hold a conference in relation to the proposed sec. 65C(5) notice.

An intending supplier ("US Tobacco"), while asserting that the Commission lacked power to declare the goods to be unsafe goods and therefore to hold a sec. 65J conference, requested that such a conference be held. Pursuant to sec. 65J(5)(c) and 65J(7) of the Act any person even though not a notifying supplier was entitled, inter alia, to be present and to present its case if that presence was "considered by the Commission to be appropriate". Under such provisions the Australian Federation of Consumer Organisations ("AFCO") was given permission to attend the conference. Fifteen months earlier AFCO had written to the Attorney-General advising that the National Health and Medical Research Council had recommended that governments take steps to restrict the promotion of smokeless tobacco products and that such products be prohibited imports.

On 10 February 1988 US Tobacco instituted proceedings under the Administrative Decisions (Judicial Review) Act 1977 ("the ADJR Act") seeking, inter alia, an order of review with respect to the Minister's decision to publish the notice under sec. 65J(1). US Tobacco also sought an interlocutory injunction restraining the holding of the sec. 65J conference pending hearing of the judicial review proceedings. AFCO sought to oppose the grant of such an injunction and sought to be joined in the proceedings as a party or as an intervenor. The primary Judge held that AFCO did not have sufficient interest to be a party to the proceedings or an intervenor but gave it leave to appear as an *amicus curiae* at and prior to the hearing ((1988) ATPR ¶40-870).

US Tobacco appealed against the leave granted to AFCO to participate as an amicus. AFCO cross-appealed against the refusal to join it in the proceedings as a party.

***Held:* appeal and cross-appeal allowed; order that AFCO be a party to the proceedings and not an *amicus curiae*.**

Joinder under sec. 12 of the ADJR Act

1. Section 12 of the ADJR Act providing for joinder of "a person interested in a decision" is concomitant to sec. 5 and 6 of that Act, subject to the qualification that membership of the class defined in sec. 12(1) confers no right to joinder but rather a right to the exercise of the Court's discretionary judgment whether to make the applicant under sec. 12 a party.

The word "interest" in sec. 12 requires an involvement with a case greater than the concern of a person who is a mere intermeddler or busybody. It does not require however that the necessary interest be a legal, proprietary, financial or other tangible interest.

2. AFCO had a sufficient interest to be joined as a party to the proceedings. It had an obvious interest in the outcome of the claim for relief which differed from the interests of other citizens.

The fact that AFCO wrote to the Attorney-General seeking a ban on the importation of the subject product was not of itself a matter to found a sufficient interest in the Minister's subsequent decision. However, AFCO had acquired a special position because it had been admitted to the conference, thereby acquiring the right to attend it, to put forward material and views as it saw fit, to challenge those put forward by suppliers, to insist upon the conference being conducted fairly and to insist both that the Commission make a decision following upon the holding of the conference and that the Minister in his further deliberations have regard to any recommendation of the Commission.

Because the validity of the conference depended upon the validity of the Minister's decision under sec. 65J(1), AFCO had an interest in that decision as well as in the conference. In any event relief was sought against the conference itself.

Moreover it would be a breach of the rules of natural justice if AFCO, a participant in the sec. 65J conference, was not given an opportunity to say that the conference which was alleged by US Tobacco to be unlawful and void was indeed lawfully called under that section.

3. The submission that AFCO ought not to be admitted to the proceedings because it did not represent the interests of consumers of smokeless tobacco went to the question whether it should have been admitted to the conference rather than to whether it ought to be a party in the court proceedings.

Right to participate in proceedings as an amicus curiae

As AFCO should be a party it was not strictly necessary for the Court to consider whether AFCO could have been permitted to intervene in the proceedings as an *amicus curiae*. This was not a case where there was a role for an *amicus curiae*.

Observations were made by the Court on whether there was a possible role for an amicus in "judicial review" proceedings and the need in any event to strictly limit and clearly define that role: an *amicus curiae* would not be entitled to inspect documents discovered by the parties.

[*Headnote by the CCH TRADE PRACTICES EDITORS*]

R.V. Gyles Q.C. and B. Walker (instructed by Baker & McKenzie) for the appellant.

N.F. Francey (18 August 1988) and S.W. Gibb (1 September 1988) (instructed by the Australian Government Solicitor) for the first and second respondents.

P. Cashman (instructed by Slater & Gordon) for the cross-appellants.

Before: Davies, Wilcox and Gummow JJ.

Davies, Wilcox and Gummow JJ.:

Introduction

The appellant, United States Tobacco Company ("US Tobacco") seeks leave to appeal from an order of a single Judge of the Court granting leave to the Australian Federation of Consumer Organizations Incorporated ("AFCO") to join in the proceedings, including interlocutory proceedings, as an *amicus curiae*. AFCO itself has sought leave to cross-appeal from the decision of the primary Judge that it did not have a sufficient interest in the proceedings to be joined as a party in the proceedings or to intervene in the proceedings. Counsel for the Minister for Consumer Affairs ("the Minister") and for the Trade Practices Commission ("the Commission") adopted a basically neutral stance on both issues. For convenience, the Court has heard the parties both on the application for leave to appeal and also on the substantive appeal should leave be granted. As the order made by the learned primary Judge granting leave to AFCO to take part in the proceedings as *amicus curiae* had novel aspects and as the matter of AFCO's standing in the proceedings is a matter of importance both to US Tobacco and to AFCO, this is an appropriate case in which leave should be granted to institute both the appeal and the cross-appeal.

The principal proceedings were brought by US Tobacco under the *Administrative Decisions (Judicial Review) Act 1977* ("the *ADJR Act*") for orders of review with respect to decisions and actions taken under the *Trade Practices Act 1974* (Cth) ("the *Trade Practices Act*"). Section 65C(5) of the *Trade Practices Act 1974* provides:

> "65C(5) Subject to section 65J, where it appears to the Minister that goods of a particular kind will or may cause injury to any person, the Minister may, by notice in writing published in the *Gazette*, declare the goods to be unsafe goods."

Section 65J(1) of the *Trade Practices Act* provides:

> "65J(1) Subject to section 65L, where the Minister proposes to publish a notice under sub-section 65C(5) or (7) or 65F(1) in relation to goods of a particular kind, the Minister shall prepare —
>
> (a) a draft of the notice proposed to be published; and
>
> (b) a summary of the reasons for the proposed publication of the notice,
>
> and shall, by notice in writing published in the *Gazette*, invite any person (in this section referred to as a 'supplier') who supplied or proposes to supply goods of that kind to notify the Commission, within the period (in this section referred to as the 'relevant period') of 10 days commencing on the day specified in the last-mentioned notice, being not earlier than the day on which that notice is published in the *Gazette*, whether the supplier wishes the Commission to hold a conference in relation to the proposed publication of the first-mentioned notice."

Pursuant to these provisions the Minister published in the *Gazette* of 14 January 1988 a notice that he proposed to publish a notice under sec. 65C(5) in relation to certain smokeless tobacco products (snuff, chewing tobacco and the like) and inviting persons who supplied or proposed to supply goods of that kind to notify the Commission whether the supplier wished the Commission to hold a conference in relation to the proposed publication of the notice.

Following that preliminary notice in the *Gazette*, US Tobacco, without prejudice to its contention that the Minister and the Commission lacked power to declare the goods to be unsafe goods and therefore to hold a sec. 65J conference, requested that a conference be held. With respect to a conference sec. 65J provides:

> "65J(4) If a supplier notifies the Commission in writing within the relevant period or within such longer period as the Commission allows that the supplier wishes the Commission to hold a conference in relation to the proposed publication of a notice under sub-section 65C(5) or (7) or 65F(1), the Commission shall appoint a day (being not later than 14 days after the end of that period), time and place for the holding of the conference, and give notice of the day, time and place so appointed to the Minister and to each supplier who so notified the Commission.
>
> 65J(5) At a conference under this section —

(a) the Commission shall be represented by a member or members nominated by the Chairman;

(b) each supplier who notified the Commission in accordance with sub-section (4) is entitled to be present or to be represented;

(c) any other person whose presence at the conference is considered by the Commission to be appropriate is entitled to be present or to be represented;

(d) the Minister or a person or persons nominated in writing by the Minister is or are entitled to be present; and

(e) the procedure to be followed shall be as determined by the Commission.

65J(7) The Commission shall, as far as is practicable, ensure that each person who, in accordance with sub-section (5), is entitled to be present or who is representing such a person at a conference is given a reasonable opportunity at the conference to present his or her case and, in particular, to inspect any documents which the Commission proposes to consider for the purpose of making a recommendation after the conclusion of the conference, other than any document that contains particulars of a secret formula or process, and to make submissions in relation to those documents.''

On 18 February 1988, the Commission convened the first meeting of the conference. Shortly thereafter, the Commission directed that AFCO be entitled to attend the conference as a body whose presence at the conference was considered by the Commission to be appropriate. We shall deal later in more detail with the interest in smokeless tobacco products which led the Commission to consider it appropriate that AFCO should attend the conference. The conference has already sat for many days. It is presently adjourned but will resume in mid-November and will conclude later that month.

After the conclusion of the conference, the Commission must make a recommendation to the Minister. Section 65K provides:

``As soon as is practicable after the conclusion of a conference in relation to the proposed publication of a notice under sub-section 65C(5) or (7) or 65F(1), the Commission shall —

(a) by notice in writing given to the Minister, recommend that —

(i) the Minister publish the first-mentioned notice in the same terms as the draft notice referred to in sub-section 65J(1);

(ii) the Minister publish the first-mentioned notice with such modifications as are specified by the Commission; or

(iii) the Minister not publish the first-mentioned notice; and

(b) cause a copy of the notice in writing given to the Minister to be given to each supplier who was present or represented at the conference.''

The Minister must have regard to that recommendation and, if he acts otherwise than in accordance with it, he is bound to give notice in the *Gazette* of the reasons for his decision. Section 65P provides:

``Where the Commission, under section 65K or 65N, makes a recommendation to the Minister in relation to the proposed publication of a notice under sub-section 65C(5) or (7) or 65F(1) or in relation to a notice that has been published under sub-section 65C(5) —

(a) the Minister shall have regard to the recommendation; and

(b) where the Minister decides to act otherwise than in accordance with the recommendation, the Minister shall, by notice in writing published in the *Gazette*, set out the reasons for the Minister's decision.''

Thus, the request by US Tobacco for the holding of a conference has led to the position that AFCO is entitled to attend the conference, which has been convened, to put forward thereat evidence and views of its own and to challenge the material and views put during the conference on behalf of US Tobacco. The conference will lead to a decision in the form of a recommendation by the Commission to the Minister to which the Minister must have regard before coming to a final view.

On 10 February 1988, US Tobacco instituted proceedings under the *ADJR Act 1977*. An amended application and an amended statement of claim seek an order of review with respect to the decision of the Minister to publish the notice under sec. 65J(1) of the *Trade Practices Act*, an order restraining the Minister and the Commission from proceeding thereon particularly with any step towards making a declaration under sec. 65C of the *Trade Practices Act*, and declarations that the *Trade Practices Act* does not apply so as to permit the Minister to publish a notice under sec. 65C(5) in relation to the subject smokeless tobacco products or, in the alternative, that sec. 65C is invalid to the extent that it purports to authorise the making of a declaration under sec. 65C(5) with respect to the subject smokeless tobacco products.

The amended statement of claim alleges that smokeless tobacco products are not goods of a kind which "will or may cause injury to any person" and that, if that not be correct, sec. 65C(5) is beyond the legislative power of the Federal Parliament. The amended statement of claim also alleges that the Minister took into account irrelevant considerations, namely the furtherance of a campaign against smoking tobacco, a policy decision already taken to ban the import and sale of smokeless tobacco for reasons other than reasons connected with sec. 65C(5) of the *Trade Practices Act*, and political considerations, being the likely political reaction to the banning of smokeless tobacco products manufactured in the United States of America. It is also alleged that the Minister acted to achieve collateral purposes, namely to give effect to a policy decision already taken to ban the import and sale of smokeless tobacco, and to do so for the purpose of general health regulation as opposed to product safety control. The amended statement of claim alleges that the Minister exercised his power in an arbitrary and unreasonably discriminatory manner in dealing with only some tobacco products.

US Tobacco sought an interlocutory injunction restraining the holding of the sec. 65J conference until after the hearing and determination of the judicial review proceedings. AFCO sought to oppose the grant of the interlocutory injunction and sought to be joined in the proceedings as a party or as an intervenor. The primary Judge permitted AFCO to be heard with respect to the grant of the interlocutory injunction and he refused to grant the same. Subsequently, he heard the parties further on the question of AFCO's standing in the proceedings and, in the course of the discussion before him, mentioned the possibility that AFCO might be joined as an *amicus curiae*. On 14 July 1988, his Honour held that AFCO had not a sufficient interest to be a party to the proceedings or an intervener but held that AFCO might take part in the proceedings as an *amicus curiae*. His reasons for judgment said:

> "I therefore give leave to AFCO to appear as an *amicus curiae* at and prior to the hearing of this matter."

At the time of giving judgment his Honour gave directions which did not refer specifically to this order but included the following:

> "3. Parties including the *amicus curiae* are to inspect documents on or before August 25 1988.
>
> ...
>
> 5. All parties including the *amicus curiae* have liberty to apply on three days' notice in writing."

The appeal is against the leave granted to AFCO to participate in the proceedings as an *amicus curiae*. The cross-appeal is directed to the refusal of the application that AFCO be joined in the proceedings as a party.

AFCO, which to a large extent is funded by a grant received from the Federal Government, is a federation of many consumer organizations. It is incorporated under the *Associations Incorporation Ordinance* (A.C.T.). Its constitution includes the following objects and powers:

> "(a) to represent the views of the Federation on matters affecting consumers;
>
> (b) to provide a forum for the discussion of matters that are of common interest to consumer organizations;
>
> (c) to focus attention on consumer problems and consumer affairs;
>
> ...
>
> (k) to carry out or have carried out tests, investigations and studies on matters affecting consumers;
>
> (l) to prepare or have prepared and publish information, opinions and reports on matters affecting consumer organizations or consumers;".

As its annual report for the year ending 30 June 1987 shows, AFCO has taken a keen interest in consumer product safety standards, in food regulation and food irradiation, in the use of therapeutic drugs, tobacco and alcohol and in the use of pesticides.

On 3 September 1986, AFCO wrote to the Attorney-General advising that the National Health and Medical Research Council had recommended that governments take steps to restrict severely the promotion of smokeless tobacco and that these products be prohibited imports. The letter continued:

> "While the NH & MRC recommendation speaks for itself, AFCO would wish to make the point that the hazardousness of these products has been very clearly demonstrated overseas. The statistics are persuasive and the appalling thing is that very young adults and even children number high amongst the victims. Various mouth and nasal passage cancers result from the use of these products, many of which prove fatal. The products are as yet little used in Australia unlike, unhappily, parts of the USA and the UK. Thus banning now is entirely feasible and the right government response.
>
> I have discussed the need for a *Trade Practices Act* ban with your colleague Dr Blewett and I have no doubt that he would support such action by you and that his Department would readily provide you with the necessary details and any further information you require.
>
> I am sending a copy of this letter to Dr Blewett for his information."

Subsequently the Minister formed a preliminary view that smokeless tobacco products were unsafe. He published in the *Gazette* the notice to which we have referred.

AFCO then wrote to the Chairman of the Commission:

> "AFCO has taken a particular interest in this matter and it was in fact following AFCO's suggestion that the National Health and Medical Research Council recommended a ban under the *Trade Practices Act*. Accordingly, I would hereby like to register AFCO's request to participate in a conference on the matter should one be requested by any party."

It was presumably on the basis of that letter that the Commission admitted AFCO to the conference called under sec. 65J.

The primary Judge gave careful consideration to AFCO's standing from the point of view of the general law as exemplified in decisions such as *Australian Conservation Foundation Inc. v. Commonwealth* (1980) 146 C.L.R. 493 and *Onus & Anor v. Alcoa of Australia Limited* (1981) 149 C.L.R. 27. He considered the effect of O. 6, r. 8(1)(b) of the Federal Court Rules, the implied jurisdiction of the Court and sec. 23 of the *Federal Court Act 1976*. His Honour also considered sec. 12 of the *ADJR Act* and it is sufficient in our opinion to direct attention to that provision.

"A PERSON INTERESTED IN A DECISION" — ADJR Act sec. 12

Section 12 provides:

> "(1) A person interested in a decision, in conduct that has been, is being, or is proposed to be, engaged in for the purpose of making a decision, or in a failure to make a decision, being a decision, conduct or failure in relation to which an application has been made to the Court under this Act, may apply to the Court to be made a party to the application.
>
> (2) The Court may, in its discretion —
>
> (a) grant the application either unconditionally or subject to such conditions as it thinks fit; or
>
> (b) refuse the application."

That provision is concomitant to sec. 5 and 6 which provide that a application under the *ADJR Act* may be brought by "a person aggrieved". Section 3(4) defines that term to include "a person whose interests are adversely affected by the decision". AFCO sought to be joined as a party, being a person having an interest to uphold the Minister's decision under sec. 65J(1) and to uphold the conference which had been called as a consequence thereof. It put the case that its interests would be adversely affected if the challenged decisions and actions were quashed or restrained. In addition to showing that it had a sufficient interest to justify its joinder, AFCO had to persuade the Court in its discretion to join it as a party. The joinder may be ordered on such conditions and subject to such restrictions as the Court thinks fit.

The *ADJR Act* lays down its own criteria for standing by the medium of sec. 5 and 6 (providing for applications by "a person aggrieved") and sec. 12 (providing for applications for joinder by "a person interested in a decision"). In our view, as we have said, these provisions are to be seen as concomitant and a similar approach is to be adopted in construing them, subject to the qualification that membership of the class defined in subsec. 12(1) confers no right to joinder in a proceeding for an order for review, but rather a right to the exercise of the Court's discretionary judgment whether to make the applicant under sec. 12 a party: *Fordham & The State of Victoria v. Evans* (1987) 14 F.C.R. 474 at p. 477.

The words "interests" and "interested" are not used in sec. 3 and 5 of the *ADJR Act*, respectively, as if they were mere terms of common parlance. The term "interest" has long been an expression used in the law with respect to parties so as to require an involvement with a case greater than the concern of a person who is a mere intermeddler or busybody. Nevertheless, the criterion for standing prescribed by the Act is not a restrictive one. The broadest of technical terms has been selected. The necessary interest need not be a legal, proprietary, financial or other tangible interest. Neither need it be peculiar to the particular person. In *Tooheys Limited v. Minister for Business and Consumer Affairs* (1981) 36 A.L.R. 64, *Ellicott* J. said at p. 79:

> "The words 'a person who is aggrieved' should not, in my view, be given a narrow construction. They should not, therefore, be confined to persons who can establish that they have a legal interest at stake in the making of the decision. It is unnecessary and undesirable to discuss the full import of the phrase. I am satisfied from the broad nature of the discretions which are subject to review and from the fact that the procedures are clearly intended in part to be a substitution for the more complex prerogative writ procedures that a narrow meaning was not intended. This does not mean that any member of the public can seek an order of review. I am satisfied, however, that it at least covers a person who can show a grievance which will be suffered as a result of the decision complained of beyond that which he or she has as an ordinary member of the public. In many cases that grievance will be shown because the decision directly affects his or her existing or future legal rights. In some cases, however, the effect may be less direct. It may affect him or her in the conduct of a business or may, as I think is the case here, affect his or her rights against third parties (cf. *Robinson v. Western Australian Museum* (1977) 16 A.L.R. 623; 138 C.L.R. 283."

These remarks have been applied in subsequent decisions, including decisions of Full Courts of this Court. In *Ricegrowers Co-operative Mills Ltd. v. Bannerman & Anor* (1981) ATPR ¶40-262 at p. 43,335; (1981) 38 A.L.R. 535 at p. 540, *Bowen* C.J. and *Franki* J. said that the words "a person who is aggrieved" in sec. 5 of the Act "are not to be confined to those who can establish that they have a legal interest at stake in the making of the decision. In our view they cover a person who can show a grievance which will be suffered as a result of the decision beyond that of any ordinary member of the public". See also *Lamb v. Moss & Anor* (1983) 49 A.L.R. 533, *Ogle and Another v. Strickland & Others* (1987) 71 A.L.R. 41, and *Broadbridge & Another v. Stammers* (1987) 76 A.L.R. 339. *Ogle's case* is of particular interest. Two priests of the Anglican and Roman Catholic churches were held to have sufficient standing to challenge under the *ADJR Act* a decision of the Censorship Board to grant a licence to import the film "Je vous Salue Marie", a film alleged by the applicants to be blasphemous. At pp. 42-43, *Fisher* J. said:

> "In arriving at my conclusion, namely that this appeal should be allowed, I adopt the approach of *Stephen* J. in *Onus v. Alcoa of Australia Limited* (1981) 149 C.L.R. 27; 36 A.L.R. 425. *Stephen* J. (C.L.R. at 42; A.L.R. at 436) when speaking of the question whether the appellants had a sufficient 'special interest' to give them standing to sue said:
>
> > 'As the law now stands it seems rather to involve in each case a curial assessment of the importance of the concern which a plaintiff has with particular subject matter and of the closeness of that plaintiff's relationship to that subject matter.

> ... Courts necessarily reflect community values and beliefs, according greater weight to, and perceiving a closer proximity to a plaintiff in the case of some subject matters than others. The outcome of doing so, however rationalised, will, when no tangible proprietary or possessory rights are in question, tend to be determinative of whether or not such a special interest exists as will found standing to sue.'

In these circumstances it is not surprising that minds may differ when determining whether a 'special interest' has been established. The curial assessment which *Stephen* J. perceived as involved requires value judgments to be made, in particular when assessing matters of weight and proximity. This court is required to make for itself such assessments and judgments, even in circumstances such as the present when, as I see it, the trial Judge correctly identified the relevant principles of law. As *Gibbs* C.J. said in the *Onus case* (C.L.R. at p. 36; A.L.R. at p. 431): 'The rule is obviously a flexible one since, as was pointed out in that case, [the *Australian Conservation Foundation case*] the question what is a sufficient interest will vary according to the nature of the subject matter of the litigation.' "

At pp. 49-50, *Lockhart* J. said:

> "The importance of not giving the expression 'a person who is aggrieved' a narrow meaning is readily perceived when regard is had to the wide range of decisions under Commonwealth enactments which are susceptible to review under the *Judicial Review Act* and to the continually expanding field of Commonwealth law. As statutes, regulations, ordinances and other laws of the Commonwealth are continually emerging from the draftsman's pen, the definition of the words 'a person who is aggrieved' must be as applicable for future, as it is for current, enactments.
>
> There are sound reasons why the expression should not be extended to include a member of the public who does not have a grievance which he or she will suffer beyond that which he or she has as an ordinary member of the public. Otherwise, anyone at all could apply for review of a decision under a Commonwealth enactment and for a statement under sec. 13 of the *Judicial Review Act* of the findings on material questions of fact and the reasons for the decision in question even though the decision may not affect the person beyond being merely emotionally or intellectually concerned or interested in the decision. The right to request a sec. 13 statement is conferred by that section upon 'any person who is aggrieved by the decision': sec. 13(1) and sec. 3(4)."

See also *Wilcox* J. at pp. 56-58. In *Australian Institute of Marine and Power Engineers v. Secretary, Department of Transport* (1986) 71 A.L.R. 73, *Gummow* J. analysed the concept "person aggrieved" in the *ADJR Act*. At p. 81, his Honour said:

> "The result is that there is a measure of broad agreement as to *locus standi* both for legal and equitable remedies in public law and in that situation it would be a strange result if the *ADJR Act* posited, by use of the concept of grievance, some narrower criterion. It also has to be borne in mind that the *ADJR Act* is ambulatory in its operation and draws within its scope a diverse and extensive collection of decision making processes, truly an unclosed class. Too rigid a criterion of *locus standi* will threaten to stultify the utility of the procedures the *ADJR Act* offers."

In an analogous field, standing for the purpose of the *Administrative Appeals Tribunal Act 1975* (Cth), *Davies* J. said in *Re Control Investment Pty. Ltd. and Ors and Australian Broadcasting Tribunal (No. 1)* (1980) 3 ALD 74 at pp. 79-80:

> "In their context in sec. 27 and 30, the words 'interests are affected' denote interests which a person has other than as a member of the general public and other than as a person merely holding a belief that a particular type of conduct should be prevented or a particular law observed. The interest affected need not be a legal interest nor need the person seeking joinder establish legal ownership of the interest. As *Brennan* J. said in *Re McHattan and Collector of Customs* (N.S.W.) (1977) 1 A.L.D. 67, at pp. 69-70:
>
> > 'The relevant "interests" do not have to be pecuniary interests or even specific legal rights: cf. *Bilbao v. Farquhar*

> (1974) 1 N.S.W.L.R. 377 at p. 380 per *Hutley* J.A. Restrictions of that kind are incompatible with the variety of decisions which are subject to review — some decisions affecting legal rights, others being unlikely to do so.
>
> Thus a decision to deport a migrant clearly affects interests of a different kind from those which may be affected by a demand for customs duty, though both kinds of decision may be reviewed in certain circumstances.'

However a person seeking joinder must be able to identify a relevant interest which is his. In other contexts, dicta in cases have used the adjectives 'real', 'genuine' and 'direct' to describe the relationship required between the decision and the interest. Sections 27(1) and 30(1) do not make use of adjectives but they do require that the applicant demonstrates genuine affection of an interest which attaches to him. The nature of the interest required in a particular case will be influenced by the subject matter and context of the decision under review. As *Brennan* J. said in *McHattan's case* at p. 70:

> 'However, a decision which affects interests of one person directly may affect the interests of others indirectly. Across the pool of sundry interest, the ripples of affection may widely extend. The problem which is inherent in the language of the statute is the determination of the point beyond which the affection of interests by a decision should be regarded as too remote for the purposes of sec. 27(1). The character of the decision is relevant, for if the interests relied on are of such a kind that a decision of the given character could not affect them directly, there must be some evidence to show that the interests are in truth affected.' "

It is not necessary to determine whether or not, aside from its involvement in the sec. 65J conference, AFCO would have had a sufficient interest to justify its joinder in the present proceedings.

The fact that on 3 September 1986 AFCO wrote to the Attorney-General seeking a ban on the importation of smokeless tobacco would not of itself be a matter to found a sufficient interest in the Minister's subsequent decision. It is not shown that AFCO was the moving force behind the action taken under the *Trade Practices Act*. Its letter of 3 September 1986 makes clear that the National Health and Medical Research Council had recommended that the promotion of smokeless tobacco be restricted and that the importation of these products be prohibited.

However, the Minister's decision and the action of calling the conference, which are the decisions under challenge, are decisions which have benefited AFCO in a special way. AFCO is now entitled to and is exercising its entitlement to attend the conference called under sec. 65J and is there entitled to put forward such material and views as it sees fit to support its contention that smokeless tobacco products are unsafe and should be the subject of an order under sec. 65C(5). AFCO is also entitled to challenge the material and views put by US Tobacco at the conference. As a participant in the conference, AFCO would be entitled to insist that it be conducted in a manner that was fair to the participants. As a participant, it would be entitled to insist that the Commission made a decision by way of a recommendation to the Minister following upon the holding of the conference. And as a participant in the conference it would be entitled to insist that the Minister in his further deliberations had regard to any recommendation of the Commission, as sec. 65P requires. Mr R.V. Gyles Q.C., with whom Mr B. Walker of counsel appeared for US Tobacco, submitted that AFCO did not acquire a sufficient interest by its attendance at the conference for, he submitted, the issues all related to the validity of the Minister's decision as published in the *Gazette*. However, events have moved on and AFCO has acquired a special position because it has been admitted to the conference. The validity of the conference depends upon the validity of the Minister's decision under sec. 65J(1). Thus AFCO has an interest in that decision as well as in the conference itself. That interest is different in kind from the interest of members of the public. Moreover, relief is sought against the conference itself.

Having regard to all the circumstances we have mentioned and as the present proceedings seek orders of review relating to the conference and any step thereafter, we are satisfied that AFCO has a sufficient interest to be joined as a party in the proceedings. Indeed, it would be a breach of the rules of natural justice if AFCO, a participant in the conference, was not given an opportunity by the Court to say that the conference, which is alleged by US Tobacco to be unlawful and void, was indeed lawfully called under the provisions of sec. 65J and that the conference has the force and effect which is given to it by sec. 65J. In *Cameron v. Cole* (1944) 68 C.L.R. 571, *Rich* J. said at p. 589:

> "It is a fundamental principle of natural justice, applicable to all courts whether superior or inferior, that a person against whom a claim or charge is made must be given a reasonable opportunity of appearing and presenting his case."

After listing four factors put by AFCO to support its special interest, the primary Judge said:

> "In response to these four factors, the applicant put the view that AFCO should not be considered in any different or particular way than the other persons or bodies who made submissions to the Minister. The evidence disclosed that these included the Australian Rough Riders Association Incorporated, the Embassy of the United States of America, the Australian Bushmen's Campdraft and Rodeo Association Ltd., Curry's Merry Muster Rodeo Association, the Society of Snuff Grinders, Blenders & Purveyors of the United Kingdom, Wests Softball Club of Bundaberg (Qld) and some 43 other organizations and individuals. *Not much therefore turns on this status of AFCO as supporting the present motion. For similar reasons, the same may be said of AFCO's reliance on its attendance at and participation in the conference.* In any event, my inclination would be to treat each application on its own merits without reference to the characteristics of non applicants for joinder. These are factors to take into consideration, but by themselves they are not decisive." (The emphasis is ours.)

However, AFCO was not simply one of the many organizations that had made submissions to the Minister. AFCO is an authorised participant in the conference and, in our view, is entitled to be heard with respect to any application by way of judicial review seeking to quash the decision under sec. 65J(1) giving rise to it. Its interests are affected by the proceedings. It has an interest in the decision in respect of which orders of review were sought. Probably this aspect of the matter was not emphasised in the hearing before his Honour for his Honour had permitted AFCO to appear and to oppose the making of an interlocutory injunction restraining the holding of the conference. Therefore, the conference was still proceeding. And the question of its validity turns solely upon the validity of the Minister's decision under sec. 65J(1).

No separate challenge is made with respect to the conference. Nevertheless, the proceedings under the *ADJR Act* do challenge the validity of the conference. All the reasons which persuaded his Honour that AFCO had a sufficient interest to be heard on the question of the application for an interlocutory injunction appear applicable to the final relief which is sought in the proceedings. AFCO has an interest in the proceedings for it is an authorised participant. Its interest is not merely that of a concerned consumer body or a concerned member of the public. By reason of its admission to the conference it has a special advantage and, in our view, is entitled to be heard in proceedings which seek an order that the conference and the advantage which AFCO holds is null and void. AFCO has, to adopt the language of *Bowen* C.J., *Beaumont* and *Gummow* JJ. in *Broadbridge v. Stammers (supra* at p. 341), "an obvious interest in the outcome of the claim for relief which differ(s) from the interests of other citizens". In *Sinclair v. Mining Warden at Maryborough and Anor* (1975) 132 C.L.R. 473, *National Trust of Australia (Vic.) v. Australian Temperance & General Mutual Life Assurance Society Ltd.* (1976) 1 V.R. 592 and *Australian Conservation Foundation v. Environment Protection Appeal Board & Anor* (1983) V.R. 385, a person lacking a special interest was held to acquire such interest by taking advantage of a statutory right to lodge an objection and by pursuing that objection.

An appellate court is loath to interfere in a matter of practice and procedure. See e.g. *Adam P. Brown Male Fashions Pty. Ltd. v. Philip Morris Inc. & Anor* (1981) 148 C.L.R. 170 at pp. 176-177, *Squire v. Rogers* (1979) 39 F.L.R. 106 at pp. 113-114, *Mudginberri Station Pty. Ltd. v. Australasian Meat Industry*

Employees' Union (1986) ATPR (Digest) ¶46-011; (1986) 12 F.C.R. 10 at pp. 12-13 and *Ahern v. Deputy Commissioner of Taxation (Qld)* (1987) 76 A.L.R. 137 at pp. 146-147. However, when the matter goes to the ability of a party or other body to put its case to the court, an appellate court will more readily interfere. See *Ahern v. Deputy Commissioner of Taxation (Qld)*, cited above. When the decision under appeal defeats the rights of a party altogether or is unjust to one or other of the parties, the Court has the power, and the duty, to interfere. See *Maxwell v. Keun* (1928) 1 K.B. 645 at p. 653 and *Bloch v. Bloch* (1981) 55 A.L.J.R. 701 at p. 703.

In this present appeal, for the reasons we have given, we are satisfied that AFCO has a sufficient interest to be joined as a party in the proceedings.

Mr Gyles submitted that the application for joinder was rejected by the primary Judge not on the ground of interest but on the ground of discretion. He pointed out that the primary Judge had referred to remarks by *Jenkinson* J. in *Fordham & The State of Victoria v. Evans*, cited above, dealing with discretion. However, reading the reasons as a whole it is clear that the primary Judge found that AFCO did not have a sufficient interest to be joined as a party. Had he considered he had a discretion to do so, he would presumably have exercised the discretion in favour of AFCO, for he gave leave to AFCO to participate in the proceedings as an *amicus curiae*.

A submission was put by Mr Gyles that AFCO ought not to be admitted to the proceedings because it did not represent the interests of consumers and in particular it did not represent consumers of smokeless tobacco; rather it was seeking to prevent the importation, sale and consumption of smokeless tobacco products. We see that as a submission which goes to the question whether AFCO should have been admitted as a party to the conference rather than whether it ought to be a party in proceedings in this Court. In any event, we think that the submission understates the function of consumer organizations. It is a function of AFCO and many other consumer organizations to make public the harm which may result to users and consumers of products the use or consumption of which may cause harm. AFCO does not purport to have a specific role as a representative of consumers of smokeless tobacco. One of its roles is to expose the harm which it alleges the consumption of smokeless tobacco may cause to consumers thereof. In that role it is appropriate that it should be a party to the current proceedings for as such it is fitted to put a point of view contrary to that which will be put on behalf of US Tobacco.

Mr Gyles further submitted that if AFCO were joined as a party in the proceedings the joinder should be subject to conditions. He submitted:

> "1. The evidence before (the primary Judge) and concessions in the argument before the Full Court demonstrate that AFCO's only claim to be heard is that it has a particular point of view, which the Trade Practices Commission has permitted it to present in the sec. 65J conference, and that this point of view is very likely to be AFCO's only contribution to the Court proceedings. Terms to be imposed in the exercise of the Court's discretion under sec. 12 or in relation to *amicus curiae* procedure should therefore reflect the fact that AFCO's interest, if any, is or derives from this merely intellectual or political engagement in the controversy between U.S. Tobacco and the Minister.
>
> 2. AFCO should not be entitled to adduce evidence or cross examine witnesses or object to any questions or tenders. In the unlikely circumstance that AFCO at some stage has unforeseen and vital information to present which was not hitherto known to it or to the other parties, then AFCO may be permitted to make an application to the trial judge and show cause to justify any particular intervention of this kind, the trial judge taking into account the general condition imposed against AFCO. This is justified by (the primary Judge's) finding that there was nothing known about any contribution of this kind available from AFCO and from Mr Cashman's concession in argument before this Court to the effect that any such contribution was unlikely.
>
> 3. As a corollary of 1, AFCO should have no discovery rights.
>
> 4. In no circumstances should AFCO be entitled to any costs from U.S. Tobacco.
>
> 5. AFCO should be liable to an order for costs against it, in favour of the other

parties, in the event that the trial judge decides that the hearing has been rendered more expensive by reason of AFCO's presence."

However, in our opinion such conditions should not be imposed.

If evidence is to be submitted at the trial bearing upon the constitutional issue and upon the issue as to whether the smokeless tobacco products "will or may cause injury to any person", AFCO should be entitled to adduce such evidence and to challenge evidence to the contrary adduced by US Tobacco. We do not indicate that evidence of that type should be received; but if it is, AFCO should be entitled to participate therein.

Our orders will set aside all references to the *amicus curiae*, and therefore also the present entitlement of AFCO to participate in discovery. If AFCO is to participate in discovery, it will only be by reason of an order of the primary Judge made hereafter. His Honour will not make an order for discovery in favour of AFCO unless the issues are such that discovery is desirable. If discovery is ordered in favour of AFCO, it will no doubt be on the basis of mutual discovery. This is a matter for the primary Judge, not for the Full Court. We do not suggest that there is any issue in respect of which mutual discovery would be desirable.

Likewise, costs will be a matter for the trial Judge. If AFCO unnecessarily adds to the costs of the proceedings, any order as to costs may take that into account. No prospective order as to costs is required.

Amicus curiae

In view of our conclusions as to joinder, it is strictly unnecessary to turn to the orders made by the trial Judge giving AFCO leave to participate in the proceedings as an *amicus curiae*. However, full and careful submissions have been put to the Court and it may be appropriate to make some comments thereon.

As a court exercises a judicial, not an administrative function, its task is to determine disputes that are brought before it by parties who appear before it, adduce evidence and make submissions. Nevertheless, a court has an inherent or implied power, exercised occasionally, to ensure that it is properly informed of matters which it ought to take into account in reaching its decision. Particularly is this so in judgments which may affect the community generally or persons other than the parties who are before it. A judge hearing a civil proceeding may, in his discretion, call a witness of his own motion, though the power to do so is only rarely exercised. In *Titheradge v. The King* (1917) 24 C.L.R. 107 at p. 116, *Barton* J. said:

> "No one, then, will doubt that there are instances, not numerous, in which in furtherance of justice and in exceptional circumstances presiding Judges have rightly taken it upon themselves to actually examine a witness, and, of course, it happens every day that a Judge, in order to understand what a witness has said, asks him a question. But that is a very different matter from the assumption by the Court of the conduct of the case. A trial is a proceeding inter partes, whether the Crown is a party or not, and the conduct of the evidence, subject to questions of admissibility, is in principle the concern of the parties. Where departures from the rigid observance of this principle have occurred, it has, I think, been upon necessity, as, for instance, in the case where, the parties having definitely closed their evidence, the jury wish a person present to be called for their better information. But the right, where it exists, of a Judge to take the conduct of the examination of persons not called by either party must be used with extreme caution. In a civil case there must either be the consent of the parties or an acquiescence on their part from which the strong inference is consent. I have already pointed out that the sections of the *Evidence Act* cited at the Bar are framed, save in a sole particular, upon the assumption that the parties themselves will lead the evidence. That is the normal and proper practice, and any deviation from it must be safe-guarded by every precaution."

Further, if it considers it in the interests of justice to do so, the court may hear an *amicus curiae* or friend of the court. The institution of *amicus curiae* and the procedures relating thereto are applicable in this Court as a consequence both of its status as a superior court of record and a court of law and equity (*Federal Court of Australia Act 1976*, subsec. 5(2)) and of its powers to make appropriate orders in relation to matters in which it has jurisdiction (*Federal Court of Australia Act 1976*, sec. 23): see also *Parsons & Ors v. Martin & Ors* (1984) 5 F.C.R. 235 at pp. 240-241.

It is necessary to distinguish the position of an *amicus curiae* from that of an intervener. Although intervention has since been put on a statutory basis and provided for in various rules of court, it appears that intervention first was allowed in jurisdictions derived from ecclesiastical or civil law, such as matrimonial causes, probate and admiralty: *Corporate Affairs Commission v. Bradley* (1974) 1 N.S.W.L.R. 391 at pp. 397-398. An intervener, whether pursuant to sec. 12 of the *ADJR Act*, O. 6 r. 8(1) of the Federal Court Rules, sec. 78A of the *Judiciary Act 1903* or otherwise, becomes a party to the proceedings with the benefits and burdens of that status. In *Corporate Affairs Commission v. Bradley* (*supra* at p. 396), *Hutley* J.A. said:

> "A person accepted as an intervener becomes a party to the proceedings with all the privileges of a party. Thus he can appeal, tender evidence and participate fully in all aspects of the argument. His position is quite different from that of an *amicus curiae*.
>
> Interveners have been allowed to appeal. Thus the Attorney-General of the Commonwealth appealed to the Privy Council in *Attorney-General of the Commonwealth of Australia v. The Queen* (the *Boilermakers' case*) ((1957) 95 C.L.R. 529, (1957) A.C. 288), though he was only an intervener in *R. v. Kirby; Ex parte Boilermakers' Society of Australia* ((1956) 94 C.L.R. 254) in the High Court."

His Honour went on to describe the position of an *amicus curiae* as then understood in Australian law in the following terms (*supra* at pp. 398-399):

> "An *amicus curiae* has been permitted to argue a case: *Morelle Ltd. v. Wakeling* (1955) 2 Q.B. 379. The Attorney-General appeared as *amicus curiae* to argue among other things that a previous decision of the court had been given *per incuriam*. This is a case where the Crown sought to be made a party, which application was refused. There is no definition in this case of the role of an *amicus curiae*, but Jowitt's *Dictionary of English Law* at p. 114 defines *amicus curiae* as follows:
>
> 'A friend of the Court, that is to say a person, whether a member of the Bar not engaged in the case or any other bystander, who calls the attention of the Court to some decision, whether reported or unreported, or some point of law which would appear to have been overlooked.'
>
> A similar definition appears in Black's *Law Dictionary*, 4th ed., an American publication, and a detailed statement of the position of an *amicus curiae* is set out in the judgment of the appellate court of Indiana in *Re Perry* (148 N.E. Rep. 163 at 165 (1925)), where the court said:
>
> 'Courts undoubtedly have the right to allow an attorney, or other person, to appear as a friend of the court in a case, to act as an advisor of the court, and to make suggestions as to matters appearing upon the record, or in matters of practice. An *amicus curiae* has no rights in the matter. He can file no pleadings or motions of any kind. He can reserve no exception to any ruling of the court, and of course cannot prosecute an appeal. It has been held in this state that an *amicus curiae* may, on leave, file briefs, argue the case, and introduce evidence.'
>
> The last sentence is not consistent with the law of this State, and there is no provision for an *amicus curiae* making any contribution to the record."

More recently, in *Commonwealth v. Tasmania* (1983) 158 C.L.R. 1, counsel for the Tasmanian Wilderness Society appeared as *amicus* and seems to have fulfilled the traditional role. Other cases are referred to in the Report of the Law Reform Commission on Standing In Public Interest Litigation (A.L.R.C. 27) para. 284-290.

Counsel appearing as *amicus curiae* have been heard where the interests of an infant or other disadvantaged person might not otherwise have been protected. Counsel for the Attorney-General appearing as *amicus curiae* have often been heard to make submissions in the public interest. But there is no prescription of the circumstances in which it may or may not be proper for a court to hear an *amicus*.

As *Sangster* J. pointed out in *Johnson v. Sammon* (1974) 7 S.A.S.R. 431 at p. 433, the function of an *amicus* has not been defined by English authority. In his article "The Amicus Curiae Brief: From Friendship to Advocacy" 72 Yale L.J. 694 at p. 696, Professor Krislov put the point succinctly when he said, "In short, through lack of precise rules, the English courts developed a highly adaptable instrument for dealing with many of the problems that arise in adversary proceedings." No strict rules have been developed, no doubt because no person has the right to address the Court as an *amicus*, and it is for the Court to accept the assistance of the *amicus* if it seems proper to the Court to do so. In particular, in the present state of the Anglo-Australian authorities (and the same would appear to be so in the United States) no clear line appears to differentiate that which can never be included as part of the role of an *amicus curiae* from what in a given case, and as a permissible exercise of discretion, the Court may permit or require of an *amicus*.

The general principle is that the parties are entitled to carry on their litigation free from the interference of persons who are strangers to the litigation. But there is an overriding right of the Court to see that justice is done. An *amicus* may be heard if good cause is shown for doing so and if the Court thinks it proper. Nothing in these reasons should be understood to delimit or restrict the availability of or effectiveness of this valuable tool.

In the United States, a much greater use has been made of the *amicus curiae* procedure, a reflection both of its Constitution and of the relatively greater amount of public interest litigation. The history and use of the procedure in the United States are discussed in the article by Professor Krislov, cited above. See also *Amici Curiae* (1920-21) 34 Harv. L. Rev. 773 and the article by Loretta Re: *The Amicus Curiae Brief: Access to the Courts for Public Interest Associations* (1984) 14 M.U.L.R. 522. We have set out earlier in these reasons the description of the general role of an *amicus* in the United States given in *Re Perry* (1925) 148 N.E. 163 at p. 165. But despite the width of that statement, the development of the *amicus* procedure in the United States has occurred mainly in public interest litigation, particularly in the Supreme Court and other appellate courts.

At trial level, courts in the United States have shown reluctance to permit strangers to the litigation to intermeddle. In *Strasser v. Doorley* (1970) 432 F. 2d 567, *Aldrich* C.J. delivering the opinion of the United States Court of Appeals, First Circuit, had this to say at p. 569:

> "We recognize that the acceptance of *amicus* briefs is within the sound discretion of the court, and that by the nature of things an *amicus* is not normally impartial. Furthermore, if an *amicus* causes the district court to make an error of law — an *amicus* who argues facts should rarely be welcomed — the error can be corrected on appeal. Nonetheless, we believe a district court lacking joint consent of the parties should go slow in accepting, and even slower in inviting, an *amicus* brief unless, as a party, although short of a right to intervene, the *amicus* has a special interest that justifies his having a say, or unless the court feels that existing counsel may need supplementing assistance."

In *Leigh v. Engle* (1982) 535 F. Supp. 418 *Leighton* J., in refusing leave to a Secretary of Labor to take part in the proceedings before him, said at pp. 420-422:

> "Historically, then, an *amicus curiae* is an impartial individual who suggests the interpretation and status of the law, gives information concerning it, and whose function is to advise in order that justice may be done, rather than to advocate a point of view so that a cause may be won by one party or another . . . Indeed, if the proffer comes from an individual with a partisan, rather than impartial view, the motion for leave to file an *amicus* brief is to be denied, in keeping with the principle that an *amicus* must be a friend of the court and not a friend of a party to the cause . . . The privilege of being heard *amicus* rests in the discretion of the court which may grant or refuse leave according as it deems the proffered information timely, useful, or otherwise . . .
>
> It is true that in the appellate levels of the federal judiciary 'the institution of the *amicus curiae* brief has moved from neutrality to partisanship, from friendship to advocacy.' Krislov, 'The Amicus Curiae Brief: From Friendship to Advocacy', 72 Yale L.J. 694, at p. 704 (1963). For

example, the Supreme Court of the United States makes no pretense of disinterestedness on the part of "its friends". The *amicus* is treated as a potential litigant in future cases, as an ally of one of the parties, or as the representative of an interest not otherwise represented.' Krislov, *supra* at p. 704; see *Universal Oil Products Co. v. Root Refining Co.*, 328 U.S. 575 (1946). In the courts of appeals, Rule 29 of the Federal Rules of Appellate Procedure, while requiring written consent of all parties or leave of court before a brief *amicus curiae* can be filed, provides that 'consent or leave shall not be required when the brief is presented by the United States or an officer or agency thereof ... ' This shift in traditional *amicus curiae* practice may be useful in a reviewing court where, usually, only issues of law are resolved; it is not proper in a trial court."

In *Mines v. Olin Corporation* (1 June 1988, unreported), *McNamara* J., delivering the opinion of the Appellate Court of Illinois, First District, Third Division, said:

"We acknowledge, as stated in the Leigh case, that to a certain degree, *amicus* practice has moved from friendship to partisanship. 'The *amicus* is treated as a potential litigant in future cases, as an ally of one of the parties, or as the representative of an interest not otherwise represented.' (*Leigh v. Engle* citing Krislov, 'The Amicus Curiae Brief: From Friendship to Advocacy,' 72 Yale L.J. 694 (1963).) Notably, the Leigh court explained that although this shift in traditional *amicus curiae* practice may be useful in a reviewing court where, usually, only issues of law are resolved, it is not proper in a trial court. 535 F. Supp. 417, at p. 422."

As is indicated by the passage we have quoted from *Leigh v. Engle (supra)*, the position of the *amicus* in federal appellate jurisdiction in the United States is regulated by r. 29 of the *Federal Rules of Appellate Procedure*. This provides:

"A brief of an *amicus curiae* may be filed only if accompanied by written consent of all parties, or by leave of the court granted on motion or at the request of the court, except that consent or leave shall not be required when the brief is presented by the United States or an officer or agency thereof, or by a State, Territory or Commonwealth ... A motion of an *amicus curiae* to participate in the oral argument will be granted only for extraordinary reasons."

In his article "Public Interest Participation in the Courts" (1987) 66 *Canadian Bar Review* 490, P.L. Bryden analyses the Canadian practice with respect to "public interest intervention" in litigation. It would not be useful for the purposes of this appeal to analyse particular decisions in that country.

In the present case, the primary Judge expressed these views as to why AFCO should be permitted to take part in the proceedings as an *amicus curiae*.

"On the other hand, it is clear that AFCO has the respect of the Minister, the Commission and significant sections of the community as a specialised body with expertise and capacity to assist in the due administration of consumer protection laws in Australia. Some of these laws, and some of the factual situations which attract their operation, are complex and concern considerable numbers and particular sectors of the public in particular, as well as the society as a whole. The smokeless tobacco products under discussion in this case are not widely known and understood. Speaking for myself, I know nothing at all about them except as evidenced in the pleadings and affidavits in these proceedings. AFCO may therefore be of considerable assistance to me in the resolution of the issues to be determined here. Its independence of commercial or government interests provides an additional dimension to the role which AFCO might be able to play if allowed to intervene as an *amicus curiae*.

...

It is difficult for me to predict at this early stage of the proceedings to what extent, if at all, any public interest issues will be raised in this case. But to the extent that some such public interest issues are or may become part of the proceedings, it seems to me appropriate that AFCO be permitted to participate as an *amicus curiae*. If no wider issues arise, AFCO may have no or few interests to advance or concerns to protect, and its role may be negligible. As the matter proceeds through the interlocutory stages, this situation should become clearer. It will then be possible to hear argument on and define the appropriate extent and form of the intervention for this case.

I see no reason, by way of either principle or authority, why this role should not embrace a consideration by the Court in due course of AFCO's presentation of evidence omitted or overlooked by the parties, which is relevant to one or more of the issues before the Court, so as to assist the Court in its resolution of those issues, and to protect AFCO's own and its constituents' interests in the process. If contrary to my earlier expressed anticipation, AFCO has or wishes to proffer any such evidence, and the other parties have declined its offer that they present the material, AFCO may apply at a directions hearing or other appropriate stage to present the evidence."

His Honour then gave leave to AFCO to appear as an *amicus curiae* at and prior to the hearing of the matter.

It will be seen that AFCO, a public interest group; was permitted to appear in its own name as *amicus* at trial level. Yet, his Honour did not identify precisely what part AFCO was to play in the proceedings as an *amicus*. His Honour was in doubt that AFCO would have any evidence to tender but left that matter open for future debate. His Honour assumed that costs would not be payable for or against the *amicus*, but in the separate directions which I have mentioned ordered that AFCO as *amicus curiae* be entitled to inspect documents discovered by the parties. This was an unusual order, for there was no obligation as to discovery placed upon AFCO. The order went well beyond the limited role usually conferred upon an *amicus*.

As AFCO should be a party, it is not necessary to consider these matters further other than to observe that in proceedings under the *ADJR Act* the width of the standing provisions is so extensive and the discretion conferred upon the Court by sec. 12 is so wide that it will be a rare case in which a person admitted as an *amicus* will be admitted to fulfil a role which is other than a strictly limited, clearly defined role. It may be that even in proceedings under the *ADJR Act* there may be a role for an *amicus curiae*, for example where the interests of a disadvantaged person are otherwise insufficiently protected or where the Court would otherwise be without submissions on what appears to be an important question of law which arises in the proceedings. But that is not the present or the usual case.

Orders

As AFCO should be a party to the proceedings, not an *amicus*, the appeal and the cross-appeal should be allowed. In our opinion, the Court should set aside the orders of the trial Judge in so far as they refer to an *amicus* and in lieu thereof the Court should order that AFCO be joined as a party in the proceedings.

The costs of AFCO of the appeal and of the cross-appeal should be paid by US Tobacco, including costs of applications for leave to appeal.

This is the advertisement published by the Tobacco Institute of Australia Ltd on 1 July 1986 and referred to in the proceedings.

(Advertisement)

A message from those who do... to those who don't

Some non-smokers are annoyed by cigarette smoke. This is a reality that's been with us for a long time.

Lately, however, many non-smokers have been led to believe that cigarette smoke in the air can actually cause disease.

And yet there is little evidence and nothing which proves scientifically that cigarette smoke causes disease in non-smokers.

The London Times reported findings from the Institute of Cancer Research in Surrey, England, published in this month's edition of the 'British Journal of Cancer,' that 'passive smoking' for life-long non-smokers carries no significant increase in the risk of lung cancer, bronchitis or heart disease (all allegedly associated with smoking).

The Institute's conclusions are based on a wealth of statistical detail from a study involving 12,000 people.

In a study by a Vice-President of the American Cancer Society in 1981 which involved 175,000 people, it was reported that 'passive smoking' had "very little, if any" effect on lung cancer rates among non-smokers.

In the follow-up study published in 1985, no statistically significant increase in risk was reported.

Researchers at the Harvard School of Public Health found that a non-smoker would have to spend 100 hours straight in the smokiest bar to "absorb" the equivalent of a single filter tip cigarette.

Major reviews on 'passive smoking' over the last few years have concluded that 'passive smoking' cannot be shown to be a health risk. The weight of evidence is summed up in the remarks at the conclusion of the 1984 Vienna Health Conference which was held in co-operation with the World Health Organisation: "should law makers wish to take legislative measures with regard to passive smoking, they will, for the present, not be able to base their efforts on a demonstrated health hazard from passive smoking."

Often our own concerns about health can take an unproven claim and magnify it out of all proportion; so what begins as a misconception turns into a frightening myth.

Alright, cigarette smoke may be annoying to some non-smokers, but how shall we deal with these problems? Confrontation? Segregation? Legislation?

No.

We think annoyance is neither a governmental nor a medical problem. It's a people problem. Smokers can help by being more considerate and responsible. Non-smokers can help by being more tolerant. And both groups can help by showing more respect for each others rights and feelings.

Don't let intolerant minority pressure groups use you to create divisions between Australians.

Authorised by John Dollisson, Tobacco Institute, Gold Fields House, Sydney.

This is the advertisement published by the Tobacco Institute of Australia Ltd on 7 January 1987 and referred to in the proceedings.

Advertisement

A follow-up to — "A message from those who do... to those who don't"

A notice under the heading referred to above appeared in this newspaper in July 1986.

The notice was directed to the controversy about "passive smoking" and health hazard, and it referred in particular to conclusions expressed in a study reported by the London Times on 20 June 1986. It contained a statement that the conclusions "are based on a wealth of statistical detail from a study involving 12,000 people".

It has been suggested that this statement was misleading, in that the study was based on a much lesser number than 12,000. The Tobacco Institute of Australia does not accept that suggestion, but wishes to make available the following information so that readers may judge the matter for themselves.

1. Overall 12,693 interviews were conducted including 3,832 interviews of married cases and controls where the passive smoking questionnaire was completed.
2. Using data obtained from the interviews, the researchers identified subjects who were married and who reported that they had never smoked. They also identified appropriate controls.
3. Several statistical analyses were conducted and the final conclusions expressed in the study were as follows:
   "Our analyses showed no significant effect of passive smoking on lifelong non-smokers as regards risk of chronic bronchitis, ischaemic heart disease or stroke. In all the analyses relating the various indices of passive smoke exposure to these diseases, no significant differences were seen and slight decreases in risk were as common as slight increases."
   "While more data would be desirable for these diseases, lung cancer continues to be the major smoking associated disease for which passive smoking comes under suspicion. Since all the difficulties of carrying out good research have clearly still not yet been overcome, further research is certainly needed. Our findings appear consistent with the general view, based on all the available evidence, that any effect of passive smoking on risk of lung cancer or other smoking-associated diseases is at most quite small, if it exists at all. The marked increases in risk noted in some studies are more likely to be a result of bias in the study design than of a true effect of passive smoking."

The notice also referred to two studies by Dr Garfinkel, a Vice-President of the American Cancer Society. It has been claimed that the reference to those studies was misleading in that it suggested that the second (1985) study was the "follow-up" to the first (1981) and that the findings of the two were linked. The second study was referred to as the follow-up to the first.

The second study was separate and dealt with different people. It was conducted by the same researcher along with two others. The elevated risk of lung cancer that the second study found in women exposed to the smoke of others was reported as not being statistically significant.

The notice has been criticised for describing remarks made at the conclusion of the 1984 Vienna Health Conference as summing up the "weight of evidence" of the Conference.

The reference to the "weight of evidence" was not intended to convey that the concluding remarks expressed the **only** views put forward at the Conference – rather that they summed up the view of a substantial majority. During the proceedings various views were expressed on matters related to the issue of "passive smoking".

The concluding remarks referred to in the notice were contained in a press release by two of the organisers of the Conference (Professor H. Valentin, Bavarian Academy of Occupational and Social Medicine, and Professor E. Wynder of the American Health Foundation) as follows:

"A drawback in all epidemiological studies up to now consists in the fact that they have been conducted without sufficient quantification of the contamination from passive smoking. Further epidemiological investigations, in which the problem of registering the amount of passive contamination will have to be dealt with more, are urgently needed. New attempts at doing so have been indicated. Since, due to the annoyance connected with passive smoking and the possible hazard to high-risk groups, it also further constitutes a controversial social problem, international co-operation among the various scientific disciplines is the order of the day. Should lawmakers wish to take legislative measures with regard to passive smoking, they will, for the present, not be able to base their efforts on a demonstrated health hazard from passive smoking."

Authorised by John Dollisson, Tobacco Institute of Australia.
Gold Fields House, 1 Alfred St., Sydney Cove, 2000

Table of Cases

Table of Statutes